Turn of an Age

Turn of an Age
Zeitenwende

The Spiritual Roots of Jungian Psychology
In Hermeticism, Gnosticism and Alchemy

Alfred Ribi

Translated by Mark Kyburz

Edited with a Foreword by Lance S. Owens

GNOSIS ARCHIVE BOOKS
LOS ANGELES & SALT LAKE CITY

First English Edition © 2019 Recollections, LLC

Foreword © 2019 Lance S. Owens

Published by Gnosis Archive Books (gnosis.org/gab)
In cooperation with Recollections, LLC.

recollections
LLC

ISBN-13 978-0578565507
ISBN-10 0578565501

This work was originally published as:

Alfred Ribi, *Zeitenwende: Die geistigen Wurzeln unserer Zeit in Hellenismus, Hermetik, Gnosis und Alchemie* (Bern: Peter Lang, 2001) ISBN 978-3906766737

Biographical note: Alfred Ribi was born in 1931. He studied medicine in Zurich, followed by specialization in Psychiatry and Psychotherapy FMH. In 1963, he began analysis with Marie-Louise von Franz—a close associate of C.G. Jung—and subsequently worked for many years as a colleague with Dr. von Franz. He is a diplomat of the C.G. Jung Institute, Zurich, where he has served as Director of Studies, a teaching and control analyst, and a lecturer and examiner of the Institute. He is past President of both the Foundation for Jungian Psychology and of the Psychological Club in Zurich. Since 1968, Dr. Ribi has been in private practice in Meilen and Erlenbach.

Cover image: Mosaic of Hermes Trismegistus, Cathedral of Siena.

Contents

Translator's Note iii

Foreword by Lance S. Owens v

Preface 3

1. Hellenism: The Spiritual Melting Pot 17
2. The Hostility toward Nature and Escapism 29
3. Monotheism or Dualism? 37
4. The Problem of Matter 43
5. Liberation from the Power of Fate 67
6. Is the Creator Aware of Creation? 89
7. Gnosticism and the Christian Message 105
8. The Lost Soul and Its Redemption 141
9. The Fall of the Soul into Matter 161
10. The Role of the Redeemer 189
11. The Path of the Gnostic 261

Conclusion 343

Bibliography 353

Translator's Note

While every effort has been made to locate published translations of the many German and French sources cited by Dr. Ribi, in some cases this has not been possible. Such instances are marked "trans.," to indicate that the translation of a given passage is my own. Biblical citations are from the *New Revised Standard Edition*. Unless otherwise stated, all emphases within quotations appear in the original text. Gnostic writings cited herein are available online in the Nag Hammadi Library collection at *The Gnostic Archive* (gnosis.org). I owe special thanks to Dr. Lance Owens, who edited both this volume and the first volume (*The Search for Roots: C.G. Jung and the Tradition of Gnosis*) of this two-part work, for providing me with invaluable assistance and encouragement. My sincere thanks go to Nancy Swift Furlotti for funding this adventure.

Mark Kyburz, Zürich, July 2016

Abbreviations

CH: Brian P. Copenhaver, ed. *Hermetica: The Greek Corpus Hermeticum and the Latin Asclepius in a new English translation with notes and introduction* (Cambridge/New York: Cambridge University Press, 1992).

CW: *Collected Works of C.G. Jung* (Princeton University Press, Princeton, 1966-1992).

Letters: *C.G. Jung Letters*, eds. Gerhard Adler and Aniela Jaffé, trans. by R.F.C. Hull, 2 vols. (Princeton NJ: Princeton University Press, 1973).

MDR: C.G. Jung, *Memories, Dreams, Reflections*, ed. Aniela Jaffé, trans. by Richard and Clara Winston (New York: Vintage Books, 1989).

NHC: *The Nag Hammadi Codices*; texts from Nag Hammadi are cited by codex number and line. Several editions and translations of these texts are referenced, as listed in the bibliography. All of the Nag Hammadi texts cited are also available in: Marvin Meyer, ed., *The Nag Hammadi Scriptures: The International Edition* (HarperCollins, 2007), cited as NHS. For a complete index of the texts by codex number and line, see p. 799 of that volume.

Foreword

Lance S. Owens

This is the second volume of Alfred Ribi's two-volume opus magnum exploring the spiritual roots of Jungian psychology in Gnostic, Hermetic, and Alchemical tradition. Both volumes initially appeared in German language editions, published in 1999 and 2001. The first volume, *The Search for Roots: C.G. Jung and the Tradition of Gnosis,* was translated and issued in a new English edition in 2013. That publication stimulated a wider awareness of the historical significance of Alfred Ribi's scholarship. In response, and with Dr. Ribi's assistance, efforts were thereafter undertaken to prepare an English translation of this second volume, originally titled *Zeitenwende*. Nancy Swift Furlotti and Recollections LLC generously agreed to give the project major financial support, and Mark Kyburz was enlisted to translate the German edition.

    Translating this book was, however, a daunting task. Dr. Ribi initially addressed this volume to a readership familiar with Gnostic and Hermetic studies. He accordingly embraced a more academic exposition than was employed in the introductory volume, *The Search for Roots*. Various quotations and footnotes were presented in their original languages, including Latin and Greek. Several of the scholarly works he cited are currently in very limited circulation and practically impossible to find. In addition, many of the texts Ribi quoted have no available English translation; this required the translator to render original translations of quotations in multiple languages. Mark Kyburz capably met all these many challenges in his exacting translation of the German edition of *Zeitenwende*. The work as published here incorporates some editorial emendations to the text, and revises or updates several citations.

In this book Alfred Ribi reaches back across two millennia, gathering and engaging an extraordinary collection of writings. With authority and fluency, Ribi spins together the antique texts of Hellenism, Gnosticism, Hermeticism, and Alchemy, and illustrates how these all conjure and nurture the visionary work of Jung. Into this tapestry Ribi weaves personal insights gained over half a century of experience as an analytical psychologist. He illuminates how the dreams and visions of modern individuals intertwine with the legacy that Jung indicated to be the spiritual foundation of his psychology. This was a complex task and the result is a complex and multifaceted book. It will richly reward those who diligently engage it.

The Spiritual Roots of Jungian Psychology

In November of 1960, seven months before his death, C.G. Jung suffered what he called "the lowest ebb of feeling I ever experienced." He explained the sentiment in a letter to Eugene Rolfe:

> I had to understand that I was unable to make the people see what I am after. I am practically alone. There are a few who understand this and that, but almost nobody sees the whole.... I have failed in my foremost task: to open people's eyes to the fact that man has a soul and there is a buried treasure in the field and that our religion and philosophy are in a lamentable state.[1]

Looking back over the last half-century, it appears Jung had reason to lament. He has not been wholly understood. But the cause lay not just in the sprawling scope and complex tenor of his writings. In retrospect, it is evident Jung had not revealed the whole. During his life, Jung cautiously and consciously elected not to publicly share the

---

[1] Eugene Rolfe, *Encounter with Jung* (Boston: Sigo Press, 1989), p. 158.

experiential key to his vast opus. He knew it, too, would not—at least, not then—be understood.

The missing key was, we now see, his long-sequestered Red Book, the work Jung formally titled *Liber Novus*, the "New Book." Begun when he was thirty-eight years old and based on experiences carefully recorded in his journals between 1913 and 1916, *Liber Novus* contained Jung's account of a life-altering journey into the depths of vision.

Nearly a century after its composition, the publication in 2009 of *The Red Book: Liber Novus* instigated a broad reassessment of Jung's place in cultural history. Among many revelations, the visionary events recorded there expose the experiential foundation of Jung's complex association with the Western tradition of Gnosis.

In 1951 Jung asserted, "For the Gnostics—and this is their real secret—the psyche existed as a source of knowledge."[2] The human experience of psyche as a source of knowledge was the root matter of a perennial praxis Jung identified with Gnosis. Hermetic tradition and the traditions proximate to alchemy were, in Jung's view, historical manifestations of this perennial praxis. They interlinked historically with his psychology, forming a golden chain leading back to the Gnosis born at the turn of time two thousand years ago. In this volume, Dr. Ribi provides extensive textual evidence to support Dr. Jung's assertion.

Zeitenwende is the original German title of this book. The word literally means "a turn in time." It implies the moment of change, such as the moment when the ocean tides turn, or the turn of the season and year at Christmas. Historically it denotes the turn that marked the beginning of the Christian age. Jung suggested we are now approaching another *Zeitenwende*. To understand what awaits the coming epoch, we must comprehend what happened at that last great turn of an age two millennia ago. Alfred Ribi here dedicates himself to that task.

---

[2] *Aion*, CW 9ii, §174.

Ribi and Jung

Alfred Ribi is a formidable scholar, known to all those who have studied at the C.G. Jung Institute in Zurich over the last half century. His many books have, however, appeared heretofore in German language editions, and he has not received due recognition from English readers. Since the historical importance of this volume and the preceding volume, *The Search for Roots: C.G. Jung and the Tradition of Gnosis*, are uniquely interwoven with the author's personal background, let me introduce Dr. Alfred Ribi and tell a bit about how these two volumes came to be written.

Jung traced the historical lineage of his psychology back to the Gnostic communities that existed two thousand years ago at the beginning of the Christian age. That ancestry was important to Jung; he asserted, "The uninterrupted intellectual chain back to Gnosticism, gave substance to my psychology" (MDR, p. 201). Alfred Ribi took Jung's assertion seriously; he stands apart in the analytical community for the erudition and intellectual rigor he has applied to investigation of Jung's association with the Gnosis, and to the "uninterrupted intellectual chain" that reached back through alchemy and Hermetic tradition to that ancient root source. Allowing that Jung was correct, Ribi recognized that there was a natural and fraternal dialogue awaiting exploration between the burgeoning fields of Gnostic and Hermetic studies and Jungian psychology.

Dr. Ribi entered the C.G. Jung Institute in 1964 after having completed his medical training and a few years of scientific research. Marie-Louise von Franz, for many years Jung's closest associate, became Ribi's analyst. Jung had died three years before Ribi arrived at the Institute, but memory of him was still a vital presence. Like many others of his generation in Zurich, Ribi was introduced to Jung not only through his writings, but also by the insights, private perspectives and personal recollections of people who knew Jung well. For decades thereafter Ribi enjoyed collegial relationships with Dr. von Franz and others still active in Zurich who had worked closely with Jung.

During his association with the C.G. Jung Institute over the past fifty years, Dr. Ribi has worked continuously as an analyst, teacher, and examiner of the Institute; he also served as the Institute's Director of Studies. He is an eminent past president of both the Foundation for Jungian Psychology and the Psychological Club of Zurich. After a half-century of engagement, it is safe to say that Ribi knew Jung and the Jungian tradition from the ground up. But even more noteworthy, he recognized Jung's deeper spiritual roots, and he vigilantly sought them out.

A natural scholar with a keen talent for textual research, Ribi committed himself not only to his work as an analyst and a teacher, but also to the study of the historical and spiritual foundations of Jung's psychology. Jung's indispensable assistant during the twenty years he labored with the alchemical tradition, Dr. Marie-Louise von Franz, assisted Ribi in his early investigation of alchemical texts. In addition to studying all that Jung wrote about alchemy, he went further: he acquired and read the original sixteenth and seventeenth century documents Jung had studied, ultimately accumulating a library of original alchemical works equal to Jung's own. His studies branched out into a close reading of the Hermetic texts that nurtured alchemy, and thence back to the origins of alchemy in ancient Hellenistic traditions.

Dr. von Franz eventually provided Dr. Ribi with the rare opportunity to closely study Jung's private alchemical notebooks, composed between 1935 and 1953. Methodically working page by page through these notes and indexes, Ribi observed the method underlying the development of Jung's hermeneutics of alchemy. He further discovered that throughout these notes, Jung continued to admix excerpts from Gnostic literature he was still reading—a revealing fact not previously known.

Ribi was searching for the roots of Jung's psychology, and they apparently ran back two thousand years to the Gnostics, Jung's purported "first psychologists." It was time, Ribi saw, to extend the historical understanding of analytical psychology into the textual tradition of the Gnosis, and to do so while also linking the historical lineages of alchemy and Hermeticism.

This was a natural continuation of Jung's prior effort. But Ribi now had available what Jung did not: an extensive collection of Gnostic texts recently discovered at Nag Hammadi, Egypt. Although Jung had studied Gnostic materials for many decades, prior to the Nag Hammadi discovery only a limited number of classical Gnostic writings were available, and much existed only in recensions composed by ancient opponents of the tradition. Jung had stated as much, and therefore correctly judged that he lacked adequate primary material to solidly link his own observations and experiences with the Gnostics in the first centuries. With the addition of the Nag Hammadi materials, the situation had changed, and Ribi saw the effort was now both possible and necessary.

Toward a New Hermeneutics of Gnosis

When I asked Dr. Ribi at what point during the course of his work he first perceived the importance of the Gnostic tradition to Jung, he responded without hesitation: "At the beginning." I then questioned whether others around him in the Jungian community over the years had shared his interests or perceptions. He replied, "No. Only Quispel understood; he was the only one I could talk with."

Gilles Quispel (1916-2006) was a Dutch scholar who in 1952— with financial assistance facilitated by Jung—acquired the first "codex" (as these ancient books are termed) from the cache of Coptic Gnostic texts that had very recently been uncovered at Nag Hammadi, Egypt. This manuscript became known as the Jung Codex, or Codex I. It was formally presented to Dr. Jung and the C.G. Jung Institute in 1953 and remained with the Institute until being repatriated to Egypt in 1975. This was the first portion of the large collection of Nag Hammadi manuscripts to reach academic hands, and Gilles Quispel was one of the first scholars to fully recognize the immense importance of the discovery for Gnostic studies. Quispel would spend the rest of his long career laboring over the Nag Hammadi materials.

With the friendship and assistance of Gilles Quispel—by then a renowned scholar of Gnosticism—Ribi met other specialists studying and translating the ancient library of Gnostic writings recovered at Nag Hammadi. Before final publication of the entire Nag Hammadi collection in 1977, Ribi read every translation published in German, French and English academic editions and monographs.[3] In this current volume, Ribi cites many of these early works.

Over the years, Ribi worked methodically through each of the some fifty Gnostic texts recovered at Nag Hammadi, analyzing the translations in various languages, noting key words, concepts and recurring themes: essentially, following the same techniques Jung used in his study of alchemy. Ribi indexed the terminological interrelationships and the visionary formations appearing in the texts. In the process he compiled thousands of pages of intricate notes, all transcribed in a beautiful calligraphic hand. These notes are now bound in several volumes as a witness to his work.

Ribi's study expanded beyond the Nag Hammadi texts to Gnostic material that Jung had read, and to a careful examination of the usages Jung made of this material. Eventually, Ribi established that Jung had understood the core of Gnostic tradition very well, despite his lacking the supplementary material from Nag Hammadi. While the Nag Hammadi scriptures vastly broaden the textual evidence

---

[3] Dr. Ribi's library contains a comprehensive collection of commentaries, manuscript facsimiles, and translations of the Nag Hammadi Gnostic texts; it may comprise one of the most extensive archives of Nag Hammadi related publications in private collection.

concerning the classical Gnostic experience, the writings Jung had available to him provided an adequate foundation for his conclusions. For the most part, the newly available texts garnered support for Jung's reading.

Throughout this labor, Dr. Ribi engaged in dialogue with specialists working in the then still developing field of Gnostic studies. At the same time, he was intensely occupied in the parallel study of Hermetic and alchemical materials, much as Jung had been. Ribi's interest was not only in the scholarly work of those immersed in these specialized fields, but in sharing with these scholars psychological perspectives on the experience underlying Gnosis. The wider field of Gnostic studies needed awareness of the psychological nature of the tradition, and in Ribi's judgment, Jung's hermeneutics served that need.

The efforts of Alfred Ribi, Gilles Quispel, and others with like interests had their effect. In 2005, Dr. Marvin Meyer, the general editor and primary translator of the definitive 2007 international edition of *Nag Hammadi Scriptures,* proclaimed that in Gnostic writings, "The story ... is as much a story about psychology as it is about mythology and metaphysics."[4]

Gnostic writings are a story about psychology. Coming from Marvin Meyer, the leading academic author in this field, and stated in an introduction addressed to the general reader, this is a transformational affirmation about the root of Gnostic tradition. If these ancient manuscripts reveal a story about psychology, then where in the modern world do we find a hermeneutics for, or an analog of their ancient psychology? In the first volume of this two-volume work, Dr. Ribi offered an initial answer. In this second volume, *Turn of an Age*, he extends that study to include the chain of tradition Jung identified as reaching back across the millennia to a primal Gnostic source.

---

[4] Marvin W. Meyer, *The Gnostic Gospels of Jesus* (San Francisco: HarperSanFrancisco, 2005), p. xxiv.

The Problematic Heresy

In preceding decades, Jung's connection with Gnostic tradition naturally received comment, and occasionally it generated controversy. Plentiful evidence regarding his sympathetic interest in Gnosticism appeared throughout his published writings. More evidence came in comments he made in private conversations. And then, there was a little book he had printed, titled the *Septem Sermones ad Mortuos* (*Seven Sermons to the Dead*), which at an early date robustly signaled the Gnostic foundation of Jung's vision.

Jung privately printed the *Septem Sermones ad Mortuos* in 1916, not long after their transcription in his journal. In 1917 Jung added these Sermons—along with an amplifying Gnostic commentary spoken by his spirit guide Philemon—to the final manuscript section of *Liber Novus*, where they stand as a summary revelation of his experience.

In the mid-1930s Jung began his intense study of the alchemical tradition; over the next twenty years alchemy's symbolic language was a central theme in his many publications. In alchemy Jung believed that he had found crucial evidence for an enduring Western cultural transmission of Gnostic vision spanning two millennia, reaching from the beginnings of the Christian age forward to his own experiences of psychic reality. Readers of Jung often overlooked the fact that this study of alchemy was wed historically with his Gnostic studies—at least in Jung's appraisal. Thus, in his writings on alchemy, one finds abundant references to Gnostic texts presented with parallel commentaries. Near the end of his life Jung affirmed to Aniela Jaffé, "The main interest of my work is not concerned with the treatment of neurosis, but rather with the approach to the numinous."[5] For Jung, this was the primal experience of Gnosis.

---

[5] Aniela Jaffé, *Was C.G. Jung a Mystic? And Other Essays* (Einsiedeln: Daimon Verlag, 1989), p. 16.

Following Jung's death in 1961, the analytical community, along with a growing number of C.G. Jung Institutes dedicated to clinical training, became the primary custodians and propagators of Jung's work. For these communities, the persistent and troubling issue was whether Jung's psychology would be viewed as a spiritual discipline with historical roots in Hermeticism and Gnosticism, or as a clinically validated form of psychological therapy. There was obviously no professional profit in nominating Jung as a Gnostic prophet. Of course, many Jungian therapists continue to affirm the essentially spiritual aspects of their work, and they quote Jung in support. But culturally and professionally, it remains problematic to associate a school of clinical psychology with a widely anathematized heresy intimately entangled in the origins of Christianity. For many Jungian analysts, empathetic links between Jung and Gnostic tradition remain inimical to the scientific respectability of their profession. As Barbara Stephens stated in 2001, the issue of therapy as a spiritual praxis is the paradigmatic ground for "Holy Wars" within a fragmenting Jungian analytical tradition.[6]

In *Turn of an Age: The Spiritual Roots of Jungian Psychology in Hermeticism, Gnosticism and Alchemy*, Alfred Ribi presents ample evidence that Jung did indeed stand himself and his work in an historical and spiritual lineage. That ancient rhizome nurtured Jung's labor. The remembrance and rejuvenation of that tradition was Jung's task at this turn in time. In *Liber Novus*, Carl Gustav Jung received a vocation. He declared it thus:

> To give birth to the ancient in a new time is creation. This is the creation of the new, and that redeems me. Salvation is the resolution of the task. The task is to give birth to the old in a new time.[7]

---

[6] *Journal of Analytical Psychology*, 2001, 46, p. 457.

[7] *The Red Book: Liber Novus*, p. 311.

Turn of an Age

The Spiritual Roots of Jungian Psychology
In Hermeticism, Gnosticism and Alchemy

Preface

Since the reader of this book cannot be expected to approach its difficult subject wholly unprepared, this preface outlines the journey ahead.

At a critical stage in the middle of his life, as he observed in his memoirs, C.G. Jung realized that he needed to ask himself a fundamental question:

> In what myth does man live nowadays? In the Christian myth, the answer might be "Do *you* live in it?" I asked myself. To be honest, the answer was no. For me, it is not what I live by. "Then do we no longer have any myth?" "No, evidently we no longer have any myth." "But then what is your myth—the myth in which you do live?" At this point the dialogue with myself became uncomfortable, and I stopped thinking. I had reached a dead end. (MDR, p. 171)

Today, many people share Jung's experience, but they are unable to formulate it clearly. For them, the Christian myth is dead. It is no longer a "fountain of living waters" (Jeremiah 17:13). It no longer fructifies, enthuses, and guides them. Instead, it has become a dead letter, a lifeless image, and an obstructive law. Although we are infused by this myth, we still seek to shake it off like leg irons stifling our freedom of movement.

We must, however, acknowledge that we cannot simply free ourselves from what has shaped our Western civilization so decisively. From infancy, we are influenced in one way or another by Christian ideas and images, even if we were not brought up in the spirit of the established church. Even those who have turned their backs on the Christian faith have far from eluded the Christian myth, even if they have become atheists. That myth clings to us, ubiquitously, because it is part of our roots.

Modern Christianity is neither the original Christianity, nor does it offer an exclusive interpretation of primordial experience. On the contrary, present-day theology must be seen as an "artificial product," which tries to force primordial experience into a consciously formulated and generally comprehensible form. Primordial experience is a product of nature. Like all nature, this experience can be ambiguous, frightening, ambivalent, repulsive, cruel, and confusing. Theology is an artificial product inasmuch as it divests primordial experience of its terrifying aspect and casts it into a form acceptable to human beings. By formulating primordial experience into dogmas, theology not only invades the innermost realm of that experience, but alters it. Primordial experience is the numinous event that seizes and deeply shakes the whole person. It is precisely theology that deprives such experience of its essential emotional value. While not everyone considers such primal experience of the numinous to be salubrious, more and more people are yearning for contact with that source.

Hermeticism, Gnosticism, and alchemy all approached this experiential source, at times along different but often converging paths. At the moment of its historical emergence, Christianity was not an isolated phenomenon; it was related to similar spiritual phenomena arising during the Hellenistic period. This wider historical perspective does not, however, detract anything from its uniqueness.

Contrary to the thrust of historical-critical research, an understanding of primordial experience has nothing to do with the reconstruction of the historical life of Christ. Instead, it values the original state of being possessed by the ideas and images emerging from the unconscious. These are so powerful that, recognized or unrecognized, they guide human life. Secretly, each life is shaped by ideas and images that we have not conceived ourselves, but that nonetheless guide us from within our psychic background. Such ideas and images determine what we consider worthwhile and salutary, just as they define both what we avoid, and what we seek. Together with the outer circumstances of our life, these inner facts shape its course. The combination of these factors constitutes a person's myth.

Mostly, this myth is unconscious; it consists of rational and irrational parts. It is largely independent of conscious volition and instead determined much more by the unconscious factors of a particular time. An individual's myth depends also on the collective situation of an age, all the more so to the degree one is unconscious of it. When one is unconscious of the collective situation, the individual lives in a *participation mystique* with the other persons of that age, and less as an isolated or independent entity.

In the ancient world, few people were autonomous individuals, and as such, distinct from the collective. In that period, social affiliation was vital for survival. The individual was therefore unforeseeably entangled with the collective, and life was determined to an inconceivably greater degree by the collective myth. Individuality and becoming oneself are entirely modern phenomena.

Nonetheless, there have always existed exceptional persons whose life and work acted on the collective myth, rather than vice versa. Among these figures were the Jewish prophets—with whom we can count Jesus. They also included the ancient philosophers, who brought forth new insights and thus—though presumably without intention—altered the collective myth or the general view of life. Our modern concept of a "view of life" or "world-image" approaches what is meant by myth, provided it is not seen as something entirely conscious. It consists of highly diverse elements, whose origin often remains unrecognized. It is the system of values in which an individual lives, and which of course evolves and changes over a lifetime.

On the one hand, a worldview stems from the *a priori* myth in which a person lives and on the other hand, from that person's life experience. Thus, the individual worldview is the myth that has become partly conscious. It is a system of reception, "the lens through which we see the world." It is the outcome of a process of becoming conscious that is inalienably connected to life. The more conscious we become, the more our worldview, our notion of reality, changes. In varying degrees, each new insight affects and modifies our notion of the world. This change is partly rational and partly determined by the myth active in the background. The fact that the same worldview affects people differently needs to be attributed to events occurring in the individual psychic background. Therefore, it matters in which myth one lives, because this shapes our adjustment to our inner life and our outer experiences.

A personal worldview is the image that we create of our experienced reality. How far this coincides with objective reality is another matter. Somewhat naively, our image of the world is thought to *be* reality. This is subjectively correct, since that image acts upon us and determines our reactions to objective reality. But the myth in our psychic background determines to an unforeseeable extent our "illusions" about reality. Archaic humans were determined to a considerable extent by their experiences of this inner fact. Outer reality mattered far less to them than it apparently does to modern people. Thus, they formulated a magical and preternatural worldview; this, in short, is how ancient myths came into being.

Seen from our present times, such archaic myths may seem simple-minded, because for us they are apparently lifeless. However, myth still exists as a part of primordial nature within us. To the extent that a myth is alive in us, its effect should not be sneered at. Myth is a combination of our innate interior worldviews and our experience of outer reality. Where we stand in life, how firmly rooted we are, and how successfully we have adapted to life, depends largely on our living myth.

One might say, "We are living in a myth." But in fact, unreflected persons are much likelier to be lived *by their myth*. This goes well so long as one's instincts are adjusted to outer reality. When outer reality changes, individuals are forced to revise their view of the world. This happens countless times in the course of life. A worldview is not static; if it were, conflicts between our evolving inner and outer reality would be bound to occur.

Thus, the worldview in which we live must to a reasonable extent correspond not only to the outer but also to the inner fact—the myth within us. The inner myth serves as a guiding principle of sorts. It is a kind of "categorical imperative," which directs our life from behind the scenes. Although we do not choose this principle, we cannot simply neglect it either. It impacts our conscience and value system. This interior mythical worldview is a partially formulated system of adaptation to reality.

But what happens if a culture and people lose their myth, or if their myth has withered? In light of my previous remarks, it stands to reason that in such a case the individual and the culture both lack a vital organ, one-half of the nature that directs life. Consciousness will then seek to offset and adapt to the shortcoming. However, a life merely guided by outer facts lacks depth and meaningfulness. As required by circumstances, it will adjust to the requirements of the outer reality, but this will ultimately amount to nothing more than a directionless path. Such a life will wholly lack any orientation toward "eternal values," because without a myth, these do not exist for consciousness.

Consciousness is an outstandingly useful instrument for adjusting swiftly to changing realities, in particular in daily life. Life, however, does not consist merely in a series of outwardly experienced instances and eventualities. A life so lived is experienced to be hollow and meaningless. Since time immemorial, humans have sought to escape from the external chaos of the world by searching out an inner thread that guides them through disorder and grants them consistency amid fleetingness. The human being is unable to endure a life consisting solely of meaninglessness and instantaneousness. As the last shoot on the tree of evolution, we are only able to live if we feel embedded in a totality, and connected to our primordial rhizome. Consciousness that has lost living contact with its primal source is unable to convey the sense of a life worth living. Such a constrained and incomplete consciousness refers solely to the brief duration of the present; without a myth it has no history.

A myth provides answers to those questions about life to which consciousness has none, questions that lack rational, scientifically factual answers: "Where do we come from?"—"Why are we here?"—"Where are we going?" And yet answering these questions is vitally important. The answers we embrace provide life with depth and meaning.

I come to this study as a physician and analytical psychologist. Over the course of decades I have been privileged to hear the visions, myths, and dreams of many modern people. Throughout this work, mixed in with references to ancient texts, I will share some of these experiences.

At the beginning of his analysis, a man in his early thirties had the following dream:

> An unknown woman invites me to come on a journey with her. We travel to the sea, which lies before us utterly transparently, the seabed clearly visible, the entire scene bathed in bright sunshine. My father goes into the water first, followed by the unknown woman, and then myself. An anchor is lying on the seabed surrounded by many stones and plants. When we enter the water, suddenly it is no longer bathed in sunshine, but in the shade, although the light is still bright. Instead the anchor shines phosphorescently from the bottom of the sea. I keep swimming, because I dread the depths and have a briefcase full of books with

me that shouldn't get wet because I need them for the onward journey. I swim past the unknown woman and turn toward her. We know each other, because she smiles at me benevolently. She exudes such self-assurance that I feel like a little boy beside her.

The analysand embarks on the quest of his life. His father leads the way, just as in reality. The actual guide, however, is the unknown woman, who belongs to both the father and the dreamer. As long as they have not entered the sea, the water remains clear, transparent.

So-called initial dreams, which anticipate long-term developments, often occur at the beginning of analysis. No sooner does one "enter," however, than matters become opaque and one loses one's orientation. These dreams are about seemingly banal, everyday matters. We feel lost, without any bearings, cast out into a jungle. Now, however, an anchor shines luminously from the background of the soul. This symbol denotes that inner illumination that emanates from the bottom of the soul and that "anchors" the dreamer in the unconscious. Medieval natural philosophers called this the *lumen naturae*, which comes from the depths, not from above, and gives the dreamer certainty and orientation.

This dream reveals that from its background the psyche exerts an attraction on consciousness. This attraction consists in the numinosity of its images. Conscious thoughts as it were have no bearing. Only their relation to the ground of the soul gives these thoughts meaning. It is therefore crucial that consciousness remains connected with its origin, because only then does individual life, and that of an entire culture, become meaningful. Only then, moreover, is the great history of humankind spread out. And only then, finally, does the brief life of the individual become eternal. After all, the reflective person must account for the fact that their life is no more than a fleeting instance, and that what they create in that life is nothing but futile. If we failed to see ourselves as particles of a larger, boundless whole, we would surely despair.

No philosophy, however sophisticated, can help us to elude this despair about our existence, about our "being thrown into the world," unless it originates in the depths of our own soul. Philosophy, in the ancient world, was not a rational elaboration, but a doctrine of life, intended to provide guidance on how to live one's life correctly. It was not a system that dictated how life should be lived, but one that was lived by its adherents. Today, many beautiful and correct thoughts are rather non-committal. They resemble a work of art whose sight affords us pleasure, but little else. It does not occur to us that such thoughts have value only if they are perceived as involving an obligation. This was different in antiquity, when no mass media produced an overabundance of words and images. The "word" still possessed weight and meaning, because it was not a serially produced commodity. The word still concealed an entire world, because it was not the result of hackneyed daily routine. Indeed, it still had a touch of sacredness. It was numinous, because it created reality. Today, by contrast, we face the danger of the word replacing reality.

Thus, the ancient myths were charged with meaning, which seems barely conceivable today. If we smile at the ancient myths, this merely suggests that we are unaware of the treasure we have lost. To begin with, we are not conscious of this loss. We must first step back from ourselves and consider our life and civilization from an external standpoint to realize that we journey through life like a rudderless boat on the high seas.

Birth and death are the beginning and the end, but in-between these poles coincidence prevails. We seem to be guided by "free will," and yet we fail to notice just how unfree this will is in reality. It is manipulated to a significant extent by the collective *zeitgeist*. This is the current status of the collective consciousness. It is a complex dimension, a result of the collective situation of the unconscious and certain fashionable trends. It eludes definition, and its actual import is recognized solely in hindsight. We live in this collective *zeitgeist*—this spirit of the time—and are identical with it, which makes it extremely difficult to either recognize or escape from. Looking at photographs from the past, we are often astonished how foreign those times are, even though we experienced them ourselves and felt at ease at the time. We are unable to perceive what exactly we are identical with, because it clings to us like a second skin.

The *zeitgeist* is by no means always positive. On the contrary, there are times in which it is very destructive. Inasmuch as we are unable to distinguish ourselves from the spirit of the time, we participate in its destructive phases unawares. Only later, "after the disaster," do we rub our eyes and ask ourselves how this could have happened to a "nation of poets and thinkers." And, for that matter, we are once again wholly unaware of living in a destructive phase, and only realize this when it is too late. We have no external vantage point from which we could observe and judge our actions. We must first run into difficulties to realize that we have been unable to follow our good intentions and have instead been swept away by the maelstrom of the spirit of a time.

Yet it is only partly true that we possess no standpoint outside ourselves. This may hold true for those who are identical with their consciousness. Nature has, however, made provisions that we need not go through life undirected; nature provides us with an inner compass. Its needle will always swing erratically if we stray too far from our unconscious guideline, i.e., the dreams accompanying our everyday life at night. They fine-tune our path through life, which strives for the optimum. General orientation also stems from the unconscious. It is the myth in which one lives, and which is at work in the background. But the myth, as I have pointed out, may wither or no longer correspond to the present. Under these circumstances, so-called "great dreams," which weave the myth further, or adjust it, may occur.

The danger that a myth no longer quite captures the whole of human reality arises when a myth is dogmatized and absolutized. The living myth must be able to transform itself to remain effective. Christian Gnosticism differs from orthodox Christianity in that it does not believe that Holy Scripture should be understood literally, but that its underlying spirit needs to be explored instead. The Gnostics, then, were never tempted to create either a theology or a dogma; they trusted their imagination as a guide to understanding sacred texts. Gnostic writings—original versions of which are now available in large number since their discovery in 1945 at Nag Hammadi—offer us new interpretations, new homilies of sorts, on the sacred writings of Christianity. From these writings we can deduce not just a primarily Gnostic religion, such as the church fathers struggled against, but mythological fantasies that express the creative unconscious and its confrontations with the unanswerable questions of our existence.

This book attempts to convey a sense of these ancient spiritual currents; it does so not to substitute the lost Gnostic myth for the subsequently received Christian myth, but to inspire the reader's own creative imagination. The Gnostics were not apostates, as branded by the church fathers, but good Christians—just like their opponents. Gnostic thinking, however, strayed from the well-trodden paths of the established church, groping toward and across "uncharted terrain, ground that must not be stepped on." In the process, they achieved surprising and sometimes even shocking results. These may be highly inspiring for modern readers—if we approach them without bias.

Exploring these spiritual currents helps to convey a historical understanding of how we reached the impasse in which we now find ourselves, and how we might free ourselves from this predicament. Thus, a profound engagement with the ancient currents of the Gnosis promises a twofold benefit for those of us who sense that modern life has lost an essential dimension.

To understand these ancient spiritual currents, we must be unprejudiced and open-minded. If approached solely with the rational function, rather than allowing ourselves to be gripped by these currents, they will elude our understanding. If equated with or confined by Christian theology, their meaning will escape us. To understand these currents, we must allow ourselves to become fully involved. To be sure, it is almost impossible for modern people to feel their way into the mindset of the ancient Gnostic. The development of our consciousness has brought us to another place, which explains why we need a modern depth-psychological interpretation to understand the ancient mindset.

If such an interpretation is correct, it will build a bridge from modern consciousness to the ancient mentality. This is true because all the stages of development that we have passed through are still alive somewhere in our psyche. They need only be touched to be awakened once again. If this happens, we will realize that what happened almost two thousand years ago is far from obsolete. On the contrary, we will experience how the soul awakens, because the soul lives not only for the few decades of our physical life, but for the millennia of human history. The awakening of our soul is the actual concern of this book: it is intended not merely as a work of scholarship, but as a means of nurturing the soul. Our times are so impoverished in this respect that the soul is bound to welcome such support.

One analysand dreamed of a famine. Many people were walking along a road. When he dug up the earth beside the road, the dreamer discovered many potatoes, enough to feed everyone. But the other people ignored the potatoes and starved.

To be sustained by the depths, we must dare to leave the well-trodden collective paths. The potatoes, or "apples of the earth," found by the dreamer are the fruits of the unconscious that could satiate the starving. But instead of digging beneath the surface of consciousness, we believe the unconscious to be dirt in which nothing of value can be gotten.

This dream plainly reveals the situation in which the consciousness of our age finds itself. Nonetheless, some individuals do come across the buried fruits of the earth that can satisfy their hunger.

In the first volume of this two-part study, entitled *The Search for Roots: C.G. Jung and the Tradition of Gnosis*, I introduced the particular stance of the Gnostics. They were seekers after deeper knowledge (*gnosis*); they did not believe they possessed a truth that would provide universal happiness. Knowing itself was the goal. Modern human beings in search of their unique, unmistakable knowing will understand the Gnostics, the heretics, the Hermetics and the alchemists. They will also understand that truth, once found, can only ever be temporary and will change over the course of life. They will therefore not be tempted to absolutize or dogmatize that truth. Ultimately, the whole process constitutes an asymptomatic approximation of *the* truth.[1] This truth is not rational, but unspeakable; it is the truth for which one had best employ God's name (John 14:6).

In this second volume, I strive to keep the promise made in the first: namely, to shed light on the spiritual climate from which Hermeticism, Gnosticism, and alchemy emerged. To do so, I have had to widen the scope of my deliberations; the entire spiritual culture of the ancient world flowed into these movements as if into a reservoir. Further, I have had to place these spiritual currents within the great stream of Hellenistic mystery religions, from which Christianity ultimately evolved.

My study thus marks an attempt to describe the spiritual climate in the centuries before and after the beginning of our Christian age, the last great turning of time. As this task could easily have exceeded my abilities, I have limited myself to two themes or motifs central to my subject: the concept of matter, and the paths of redemption. Ultimately, Christianity is one of many religions of redemption that represent

---

[1] Ribi, *Wahrheit—Was ist das? Fragen anhand gnostischer und alchemistischer Texte.*

redemption as the unique deed of its redeemer. However, in the Gnosis there are parallel themes that consider redemption to be an ongoing and enduring task faced by every individual.

If one considers the state of the world and of humanity after two thousand years of Christianity, the world does not seem particularly redeemed. Given this malaise, some people might be looking for other paths leading toward redemption, which makes it interesting to explore how other paths have been attempted. But what exactly would we like to be redeemed from? Should we not accept certain discomforts as part of our ultimate task in life, the task of gaining knowledge? This was the task of Gnosis. I am convinced that those readers who recognize the relevance of my historical account for our contemporary world will also understand how that history bears upon their own life, and their own quest for knowing.

Chapter 1

Hellenism: The Spiritual Melting Pot

At the age of 20, Alexander the Great succeeded his father on the throne of Macedonia. When he died, thirteen years later, he had conquered the entire world known at the time: his vast empire stretched from the Indus River to the Aegean Sea, from the Danube and the Black Sea coast to Nubia and the Sahara. The legend of the Gordian Knot, which nobody had unraveled and which Alexander, a pupil of Aristotle, sliced in half with a stroke of his sword, aptly describes his attitude as a conqueror of the world. His empire, which had grown so swiftly, collapsed almost immediately, because it was too vast and too diverse to be governed by any single political system. This was the beginning of the Hellenic age, which extended from the death of Alexander in 323 BCE until 30 BCE, when the last Hellenistic state, Ptolemaic Egypt, was incorporated into the aspiring Roman Empire.

Despite this turn of events, the world of Hellenistic thought effectively endured until the end of the fourth century and the final victory of Christianity. In 313, after the famous Battle of Milvian Bridge, Emperor Constantine adopted Christianity and made it the state religion of the Roman Empire. The victory was further cemented in 380, when Theodosius I enacted his imperial decree, and then in 391, when paganism was prohibited and the temples closed. Amazing political changes had occurred between the culture of classical antiquity and the rise of Christianity!

Whenever a conqueror occupied a foreign territory, the risk existed that the conquest would be subverted by the prevailing spiritual and religious culture of the land. Antiquity sought to counter this process by removing the patron god of the city, or the chief god of the temple, and enthroning the god of the conqueror in its place. Of course, such efforts confronted the psychological fact that a people's religion is the deeply ingrained unconscious expression of both its life and land. For example, in the European world Christianity adopted many pagan elements of the Germanic peoples. Alexander the Great's empire suffered a similar fate: instead of classical Greek culture spreading across the ancient world, oriental religious cults alien to its classical essence infected the empire. The Mediterranean became a spiritual *melting pot*, in which the disparate ideas of Greek philosophy blended with Near Eastern cults to form the new spiritual movement we call Hellenism.

Modern scholars exploring Hellenistic religions have often been too eager to disentangle these various elements and their origins; consequently they have often neglected the creative innovations that the intermixing currents engendered. I believe that every Hellenistic movement took from the melting pot that which appealed to it. Little attention was paid to the origin of the borrowed foreign elements, as long as they had the patina of antiquity and authenticity.

The foreign bears the magic of novelty and incomprehensibility. The ancient world attested to truth by virtue of its age. Far-away India exerted a peculiar appeal through its ancient and foreign civilization, as manifested, for instance, in the art of Gandhara. Although Egypt was less distant, its incomprehensible hieroglyphs seemed to conceal ancient secret wisdom, testimonies of immeasurable age reaching back to the vanishing point of prehistoric times. On the whole, *mystery* had become a distinctive feature of the new cults; life no longer seemed possible in a demystified world.

Classical philosophy sought to decipher the riddles of the world and to render them accessible to discerning, exploratory reasoning— not that this led to rational science in the modern sense. Nevertheless, the world-creating divine reason (*nous*) indwelling in human beings was believed to enable them to solve the riddles secretly stored within them since creation. The belief in an inherent human faculty, which today we would probably call intuition rather than reason, made people in antiquity believe they could transcend their earthly limitations. This affirmation helps us to understand many irrational speculations of ancient philosophy. Human beings have never been prepared to accept the limits of their knowledge, because beyond those confines lies the allure of numinosity.

Thus, the irrational found not merely religious but also philosophical expression. It was not what we understand by the irrational today, but rather, in modern parlance, a path toward self-realization or, in ancient terms, an approximation to God. Only by accepting this orientation can we properly understand certain Neopythagorean assertions, which today strike us as quite speculative. I shall discuss this aspect in detail later. In Hellenistic culture philosophy was a form of life counseling, a guide to good living. Thus, a philosopher became "immortal." Far from being an inflationary exaggeration, as might be assumed, "immortality" was a personal experience, like the "*corpus glorificationis*" in alchemy. Encountering timelessness, that which is exempt from change, affords human beings with certainty and a sense of redemption.

As Jung noted in his memoirs, "If we understand and feel that here in this life we already have a link with the infinite, desires and attitudes change. In the final analysis, we count for something only because of the essential we embody, and if we do not embody that life is wasted" (MDR, p. 325).

The speculations about the divine found in Hellenistic philosophy emanated from the belief that the philosopher, by leading a corresponding way of life, can attain higher levels of being, from which he gains insights into worlds that remain hidden to the ordinary person. This is how we need to understand Eunapius' account of Iamblichus, according to which the latter is said to have floated ten feet above the ground while his robe took on a beautiful golden hue. In his *Life of Proclus*, Marinus of Neapolis assures us that the philosopher's eyes had gleamed brightly and all over his face spread rays of a divine illumination. Proclus had regarded death as a unification of the soul's fire with the divine fire of the stars; and while he was dying the sun is said to have darkened.[1] Such cosmic synchronicities have been reported time and again at the death of "great personalities." Whether these accounts are true or not, they illustrate either how such persons saw themselves or how they were seen after their deaths: they had ventured into dimensions unattainable for ordinary mortals, where they gained knowledge.

By no means, however, was this privilege reserved solely for the philosophers. Thus, in Paul's Second Letter to the Corinthians, probably written around 57 CE, he proclaims:

> I know a man in Christ who fourteen years ago was caught up to the third heaven—whether in the body or out of the body I do not know, God knows. And I know that this man was caught up into Paradise—whether in the body or out of the body I do not know, God knows—and he heard things that cannot be told, which man may not utter. (12:2–4)

The command of silence—to reveal nothing about what one has heard—is typical of the Hellenistic *mysterium*. This rule is constantly repeated and depicted even much later in medieval alchemical writings. The essential aspect of this command was the *arrheton* (the unspeakable), which could not be revealed to the uninitiated. Thus, in the Eleusinian mysteries, lengthy preparations were required before the *dromenon* (the thing done, the shown) could be beheld; this was to ensure that the concrete object would not be confused with its numinous meaning. For the *mystery* lies not without, but within the

---

[1] Fauth, *Helios Megistos*, pp. 142–43.

soul. Those not mature enough for such inner knowledge will continue to cling to the outer world.

Heavenly journeys, such as Paul's, are far from rare in the literature.[2] In the apocalyptic Second Book of Enoch, Enoch passes up through seven heavens, whereupon he can see God, and then further upward to the tenth heaven and where God resides. "The doctrine of the ascension of the souls to the seven heavens—whether through initiation or *post mortem*—was immensely popular in the last centuries of antiquity," writes Mircea Eliade. "Its Oriental origin cannot be denied, but Orphism and Pythagoreanism contributed greatly to its dissemination in the Greco-Roman world."[3]

One of the prominent heavenly journeys recorded in the Nag Hammadi scriptures is that of Zostrianos (NHC VIII, 1). Zostrianos recorded his journey across the heavens and his mythical experience as "Gnosis" (knowledge) for future generations. His ascent to another world means the knowledge that he gains of that world and his deliverance from the earthly one. Similar Gnostic accounts of ascent are found in the *Paraphrase of Shem* (NHC VII, 1) and in the *Apocalypse of Paul* (NHC V, 2). Epiphanius mentions Gnostic accounts of Paul's heavenly journey, including an account of Paul's state of rapture (2 Corinthians 12:2–4), in which he was permitted to reveal parts of what were otherwise unspeakable secrets (*Panarion* 38,2,5).

Aside from the redemptive nature of knowledge of the transcendent order, these examples (and there are many others) highlight the great significance of ecstasy as a means of attaining knowledge. From the perspective of depth psychology, we would no longer speak of supernatural inspiration, but of insight into the *collective unconscious*. Jung defines the collective unconscious as:

---

[2] Bousset, *Die Himmelsreise der Seele*, p. 155f; see, for instance, the martyrdom of the prophet Isaiah, chapters 7–10.
[3] Eliade, *Die Religionen und das Heilige*, p. 142—trans.

a part of the psyche which can be negatively distinguished from a personal unconscious by the fact that it does not, like the latter, owe its existence to personal experience and consequently is made up essentially of contents which have at one time been conscious but which have disappeared from consciousness through having been forgotten or repressed, the contents of the collective unconscious have never been in consciousness, and therefore have never been individually acquired, but owe their existence exclusively to heredity. Whereas the personal unconscious consists for the most part of *complexes*, the content of the collective unconscious is made up essentially of *archetypes*. The concept of the archetype, which is an indispensable correlate of the idea of the collective unconscious, indicates the existence of definite forms in the psyche which seem to be present always and everywhere....

My thesis, then, is as follows: In addition to our immediate consciousness, which is of a thoroughly personal nature and which we believe to be the only empirical psyche (even if tacked onto the personal unconscious as an appendix), there exists a second psychic system of a collective, universal, and impersonal nature which is identical in all individuals. This collective unconscious does not develop individually but is inherited. It consists of pre-existent forms, the archetypes, which can only become conscious secondarily and which give definite form to certain psychic contents. (CW 9/I §88–90)

Many readers of Jung's works struggle with this paraphrase of the archetype when it is applied in practice, especially when symbols from entirely different periods and cultures are compared. We are much better trained to value linear temporal causation, because our historiography largely involves causally deducing the present from the past. Such thought patterns have reached the limits of their validity in the world of the collective unconscious.

Individuals with a background in the natural sciences readily understand the comparison of symbols based on the example of comparative anatomy or zoology. Comparing human arms with those of a human ape, or even the front limbs of a dog, makes immediate sense. Anatomically and embryologically, our common ancestry with the four-limb blueprint is easily verifiable, even though the front limbs of human beings have evolved other functions. Comparing the pectoral fins of fish with human arms, however, may make no sense at all to the layperson. What appears so different phenomenologically nonetheless has a common evolutionary origin. To recognize a commonality, one must first ignore outer appearance and identify those criteria that substantiate common descent.

Something similar happens with ideas and symbols. These always exist in the context of a particular stage of culture, which shapes ideas and symbols according to its needs. Outwardly, these can assume quite different functions and be placed within different contexts. And yet they originate in the same archetype. The archetype is a matrix, which imprints itself on the notions, concepts, ideas, and symbols that subsequently appear to consciousness. Writing about the archetype, Jung observes:

> The archetypes have, when they appear, a distinctly numinous character which can only be described as "spiritual," if "magical" is too strong a word. Consequently this phenomenon is of the utmost significance for the psychology of religion. In its effects it is anything but unambiguous. It can be healing or destructive, but never indifferent, provided of course that it has attained a certain degree of clarity. This aspect deserves the epithet "spiritual" above all else. It not infrequently happens that the archetype appears in the form of a *spirit* in dreams or fantasy-products, or

even comports itself like a ghost. There is a mystical aura about its numinosity, and it has a corresponding effect upon the emotions. It mobilizes philosophical and religious convictions in the very people who deemed themselves miles above any such fits of weakness. Often it drives with unexampled passion and remorseless logic towards its goal and draws the subject under its spell, from which despite the most desperate resistance he is unable, and finally no longer even willing, to break free, because the experience brings with it a depth and *fullness of meaning* that was unthinkable before. I fully appreciate the resistance that all rooted convictions are bound to put up against psychological discoveries of this kind. With more foreboding than real knowledge, most people feel afraid of the menacing power that lies fettered in each of us, only waiting for the magic word to release it from the spell.[4] (CW 8 §405)

The unconscious expresses itself in symbolic language, such as we may experience in dreams. Because this language differs so strongly from that of consciousness and everyday life, consciousness and the unconscious are seemingly stark opposites. Consciousness conveys to us the familiar image of our everyday world, whereas the unconscious imparts that of a foreign, mysterious, unfathomable reality.

Thus, the complete image of our experience consists of two opposed or complementary halves. For many people, the unconscious half is always more real than the outer world. These people are by no means simply abnormal or maladjusted, but perhaps particularly creative individuals, who draw their inspiration from inner sources. Inner spiritual currents must be considered against the background of secular consciousness, to which they provide a compensating alternative.

For the sake of unambiguousness and clarity, consciousness cannot avoid rejecting its respective opposite. The act of rejection can

---

[4] Translator's note: *Spirit* is Jung's emphasis, *fullness of meaning* Dr. Ribi's.

"awaken" the unconscious, and that activation can draw from it a redemptive or unifying symbol. At first this symbol may be experienced as anything but mediating, indeed it may appear as antinomian. This explains the assertions about Christ as the stone discarded by the masons—and who became not only the cornerstone but also "the stone of stumbling and the rock of offense" (Isaiah 8:14). Nevertheless, he is a symbol of redemption, which corrects the false one-sidedness of the conscious attitude and leads others to an optimal life. To avoid misunderstandings, I must hasten to emphasize that these assertions are not theological, but psychological, and are based on experience.

The unconscious, in particular its collective part, is nothing bygone, but has existed since time immemorial. The archetypes, the primordial soul-images, can be seen as the traces of situations recurring in the life of our ancestors. Hence, these images represent the most frequent and most intense functions of the psyche. As images of the psyche, they are partly identical with, and partly merely similar to, the mythological motifs found in all peoples and cultures. They are easily verifiable among modern human beings. These archetypes are our actual roots, the ground from which we live. If we dismiss our connection with them, they can no longer stimulate and invigorate our present life, and consequently we risk succumbing to modern fads, shallow pseudo-spirituality, or narcotizing substances (including alcohol). In this state, we become susceptible to political and social suggestiveness, which sooner or later leads us into the abyss of disaster.

Only a consciousness firmly rooted in its own history will be able to choose correctly among the ideas presented in the modern culture. Many current ideas may seem well reasoned, but whether they are right is a different matter. To make such judgments we need the age-old experience of the collective unconscious; individual life depends on this ancient rhizome. As Jung explained,

In so far as an attitude is not merely an intuitive (i.e., unconscious and spontaneous) phenomenon but also a conscious function, it is, in the main, a *view of life*. Our conception of all problematical things is enormously influenced, sometimes consciously but more often unconsciously, by certain collective ideas that condition our mentality. These collective ideas are intimately bound up with the view of life and the world of the past centuries or epochs. Whether or not we are conscious of this dependence has nothing to do with it, since we are influenced by these ideas through the very air we breathe. Collective ideas always have a religious character, and a philosophical idea becomes collective only when it expresses a primordial image. Their religious character derives from the fact that they express the realities of the collective unconscious and are thus able to release its latent energies [...] The images are balancing or compensating factors that correspond to the problems which life confronts us with in reality. This is no matter for astonishment, since these images are deposits of thousands of years of experience of the struggle for existence and for adaptation. Every great experience in life, every profound conflict, evokes the accumulated treasure of these images and brings about their inner constellation. But they become accessible to consciousness only when the individual possesses so much self-awareness and power of understanding that he also reflects on what he experiences instead of just living it blindly. In the latter event he actually lives the myth and the symbol without knowing it. (CW 6 §373)

Spiritual currents of the Hellenistic age abounded with religious symbols. Thus, it is worth considering the *entire* spiritual climate of that time. Gnosticism itself teems with a richly developed, almost perversely rampant, unconscious psychology. As Jung noted, it is however not alone in this respect:

Although in crude form, we find in Gnosticism what was lacking in the centuries that followed: a belief in the efficacy of individual revelation and individual knowledge. This belief was rooted in the proud feeling of man's affinity with the gods, subject to no human law, and so overmastering that it may even subdue the gods by the sheer power of Gnosis. (CW 6 §409)

Like Gnosticism, other ancient Hellenistic spiritual currents built on the strength of their own knowledge and revealed an abundance of unconscious psychology that may help us understand our collective roots.

Chapter 2

Escapism and Hostility Toward Nature

Later Hellenism and the earlier classical culture of Greece had fundamentally different relationships with nature. In the classical period, life was lived to the full in this world; the many beauties of nature and the pleasant aspects of life were relished. Nature abounded in the numinous. Nymphs, satyrs, dryads, nyads, panes, and other larger or smaller demons inhabited each source of water, each reed, herd, and tree. Rivers were gods to whom sacrifices were made; each city had its source. Even the winds were revered and had their cults, so that the rains would come to fructify the vegetation. Seneca expresses this classic sentiment about nature in a letter to Lucilius:

> If ever you have come upon a grove that is full of ancient trees which have grown to an unusual height, shutting out a view of the sky by a veil of pleached and intertwining branches, then the loftiness of the forest, the seclusion of the spot, and your marvel at the thick unbroken shade in the midst of the open spaces, will prove to you the presence of the deity. Or if a cave, made by the deep crumbling of the rocks, holds up a mountain on its arch, a place not built with hands but hollowed out into such spaciousness by natural causes, your soul will be deeply moved by a certain intimation of the existence of God. We worship the sources of mighty rivers; we erect altars at places where great streams burst suddenly from hidden sources; we adore springs of hot water as divine, and consecrate certain pools because of their dark waters or their immeasurable depth. (*Epistles*, p. 275)

This positive attitude toward nature changed during later Hellenism; nature began to be experienced increasingly as a threat. The *Chaldean Oracles*, which have survived from the second century, warn:

> Do not look at Nature;
> its name commands Fate. (49,12)

Synesius of Cyrene (c. 400), a noble Neoplatonic philosopher and writer of hymns, mediated between the voice of the Chaldean Oracles and the Bible.[1] He claimed that his hymns were indebted to divine inspiration. He declares:

> Into the earth the teeming serpents shall sink,
> into the earth the winged serpent, the demon of matter,
> He who clouds the soul, who loves deception...[2]

Like all symbols, the serpent is thoroughly ambivalent, both positive and negative.[3] In Synesius' hymn it is portrayed in bleak aspect, as the demon of matter. In later alchemy, by contrast, the serpent embodies matter as the ambivalent mercurial snake or as the uroboros. The latter is not simply negative, but the image of eternal, constant renewal and eternal return. As a self-devouring serpent or dragon, which eats its own tail, the uroboros impregnates itself, kills itself, and rises again out of itself. It is the outer ocean that flows around the world and becomes outer darkness.

In Christianity, this figure of the winged snake or dragon is usually related to the devil—but, paradoxically, it also appears in an image of Christ as the brazen serpent lifted up on the cross (John 3:14). What is this serpent?

---

[1] Vollenweider, *Neuplatonische und christliche Theologie bei Synesios von Kyrene*.
[2] Hymn 1,86.
[3] Egli, *Das Schlangensymbol*.

In Isaiah, Leviathan is an ephemeral and coiled serpent dwelling in the sea, which will slay the Lord with its sword (Isaiah 27:1). The scribes and Pharisees in the later Christian gospels are exposed as hypocrites, *serpents*, and *vipers* that fall victim to the judgment of hell. In the Revelation of John, a war even erupted in heaven: "And the great dragon was cast out, that old serpent, called the Devil, and Satan, which deceiveth the whole world: he was cast out into the earth" (Revelation 12:9). So while heaven is purged of evil, the inhabitants of the earth must now instead grapple with this cast-out beast.

This casting out of the serpent placates the paradoxical nature of the deity, that is, the primordial co-existence of good and evil within the divine realm. It shifts the duality's opposition from the intra-divine sphere into the dual realms of heaven and earth or of God and his Creation. Recognition of this splitting of primordial unity is plainly evident in Gnosticism, where the bright and perfect Pleroma stands opposed to a failed creation. Gifted by God with an exiled dark Serpent, the world gradually became a vale of tears (Psalms 84:6), and human beings yearn to be delivered from earthly existence. This anti-material sentiment was deeply entrenched in the Hellenistic religions of salvation.

The Gnostics wondered how a perfect God could create such an imperfect world; they concluded that only a subordinate demiurge could account for this imperfection. From this notion there occasionally sprang a somewhat ascetic and escapist tendency; it was an attitude that became widespread during the early Christian centuries. But embrace of a negative or pessimistic worldview does not mean, as is often claimed, that the Gnostics were simply pessimists. Whoever recognizes the darkness and weakness of this world, whoever does not consider the world to be the best of all possible worlds, and whoever yearns for a lost home, is not simply a blind pessimist. Such recognitions and yearnings seem to be universal human experiences.

The dragon and the serpent are typical *symbols of transformation*, because they shed their skin and thus rejuvenate themselves. For the serpent to be cast out of heaven and into earth heightens the significance of the latter—the serpent now indwelling matter was in first source and ultimate origin clearly *a part of the deity*. This polarity of divine qualities—the dark/light breach of indwelling spirit (heaven) and matter (earth)—vitalizes matter. This is the vital perception of matter to which alchemy owes its beginnings.

The relationship between humans and nature changed significantly in the Hellenistic period. In the classical age, the Greeks lived in a *participation mystique* with nature. They were embedded in nature, which was their Great Mother (for instance, Demeter). This uroboric unity broke apart in the Hellenistic period, and human beings began to face nature as something quite distinct from themselves. They lost their sense of balance and were forced to find a new source of security. This new centering focus emerged in the form of the god-man.[4] A part of the deity that had descended from heaven animated the divine essence of human beings, and amplified their earthly existence.

An Anthropos myth exists in most Hellenistic systems of redemption: in a sort of *kenosis* (self-emptying), the deity renounces its transcendence and descends to earth in (almost) human form, in a hitherto unknown guise. Up until then, the deity had communicated with the human world through prophecies or oracles, visions or dreams. It never surrendered its majesty. Now, however, it sheds part of its aloofness and, in "the form of a servant" (Philippians 2:7) enters the dark material world.

In the writings of Synesius, the serpent begotten by evil *physis* relishes the abyss, lays traps everywhere for the erring souls, deceives them, causes evil, and impedes the soul's ascent to the celestial sphere (Hymn 5,52–54). Hence, the soul laments:

---

[4] Ribi, *Anthropos*.

> I descended, away from you,
> to serve the earth as a day-laborer;
> but instead of a day-laborer I became a slave:
> matter fettered me with magical arts. (Hymn 1,571–576)

For Synesius, *physis* (nature) epitomizes all evil, as does personified *hyle* (matter). Synesius refers to matter as an impersonal power, as an ocean, or as a river: "deep-flowing matter" (Hymn 8,66), "the great surging wave" (Hymn 1,582f.), "let the corrupting waves of matter dry up" (Hymn 4,27). This image denotes the vicissitude of matter, which contrasts with a constant divine eternity. It was not Synesius who first discerned this polarity, but Plato, and subsequently Xenocrates who speaks of "ever-flowing" matter.[5]

Following Aristotle the world of growth and of the elements was characterized in increasingly negative terms (*Metaphysics* 4, 1014b 26–35; 1025a 7). From this negativity grew the notion that upon its descent into earth, the bodiless soul, which originates in the divine world, clothes itself in three garments: in an *ethereal body* (*thespésion soma*), which is formed from the celestial spheres; in an *elementary body*, which consists of the upper elements (fire and air); and in the weighty *body of the earth* (earthly shroud). On re-ascent after earthly death, these bodies are guided beyond their designated regions and absorbed by the primal sphere. This, for Synesius, was the *resurrection*.

In Neoplatonic thought, God's essence excludes the possibility of a descent to earth: the One exists above all relations and reaches the lower spheres only as what has become many, as an essence deprived of its true unity. I shall discuss these matters in greater detail in the next chapter.

When the Chaldaean Oracles say that nature "commands Fate" (49,12), this refers to its ensoulment. Whereas classical Greece could devote itself blithely to this *daimonion*, the Hellenistic world

---

[5] Plato, *Politeia* 273 d, *Timaeus* 43 a; Xenocrates, fragment 28, 4.

consciously confronted the sensuous fascination of nature. The classical Greeks believed that the gods dwelled in nature, and that numinous powers could place spells on human thoughts and pursuits. Human beings, therefore, were governed by the power of such external material impressions. Hellenism sought to throw off these fetters.

The "magical arts of nature" are the numinosity in whose face human beings can find themselves helpless. Their temptation consists not merely in the impressions they make upon the soul, but crucially in their captivating closeness, a characteristic that animated pagan spirituality. To avoid being overwhelmed by these powers, the Hellenistic world withdrew from them completely. This retreat took on, in part, categorical forms, intermediary motifs common when a previous stage of development has not been entirely overcome. It was an age in which asceticism was a path to both the philosopher's and the mystic's initiation, and from which monasticism eventually emerged.[6] This escapism was meant to enable human beings to erect their own spiritual world within themselves, a world that would stand firm against the onslaught of sensory impressions.

Around the beginning of the fifth century, St. Augustine (354-430) comments:

> Men go abroad to admire the heights of mountains, the huge waves of the sea, the broad reaches of rivers, the ocean that encircles the world, or the circuits of the stars, and pass themselves by. (*Confessions,* Book X)

Only by looking inward did human beings attain independent ideas capable of withstanding aesthetic impressions, so that thought was no longer fettered by the emotional effect of outward impressions on the senses. To begin with, human thinking prevailed against this effect

---

[6] Ribi, *Was tun mit unseren Komplexen?* See especially chapter 1, "Die Dämonen der Heiligen" [The Demons of the Saints], pp. 12ff.—trans.

and later even emerged as reflective observation. The liberation from the spell of the concrete world in later Hellenism enabled a new and independent relationship with nature. This, in turn, enabled Hellenism to build further on the foundations laid by the spirit of antiquity, and to eventually revive the relationship with nature forsaken by ascetic retreat from the world.

The subsequent outcome of this development was not only medieval alchemy, but modern natural science as well. Nevertheless, writes Jung,

> the attention lavished upon natural objects was infused with something of the old religious piety, and something of the old religious ethic communicated itself to scientific truthfulness and honesty. (CW 5 §113)

Chapter 3

Monotheism or Dualism?

If any part of human existence remains excluded from the divine, a God-human dualism becomes inevitable. In his "Late Thoughts," Jung writes:

> The myth must ultimately take monotheism seriously and put aside its dualism, which, however much repudiated officially, has persisted until now and enthroned an eternal dark antagonist alongside the omnipotent God. Room must be made within the system for the philosophical *complexio oppositorum* of Nicholas of Cusa and the moral ambivalence of Jacob Boehme; only thus can the One God be granted the wholeness and the synthesis of opposites which should be His. It is a fact that symbols, by their very nature, can so unite the opposites that these no longer diverge or clash, but mutually supplement one another and give meaningful shape to life. Once that has been experienced, the ambivalence in the image of a nature-god or Creator-god ceases to present difficulties. On the contrary, the myth of the necessary incarnation of God—the essence of the Christian message—can then be understood as man's creative confrontation with the opposites and their synthesis in the self, the wholeness of his personality.

Further:

> The unavoidable internal contradictions in the image of the Creator-god can be reconciled in the unity and wholeness of the

self as the *coniunctio oppositorum* of the alchemists or as a *unio mystica*. In the experience of the self it is no longer the opposites "God" and "man" that are reconciled, as it was before, but rather the opposites within the God-image itself. That is the meaning of divine service, of the service which man can render to God, that light may emerge from the darkness, that the Creator may become conscious of His creation, and man conscious of himself. (MDR, pp. 311–312)

The Neopythagoreans grappled intensely with this problem of opposites. They are of interest here not only because their intellectual conceptions coincided with Hellenism, but also because of their original solution to this problem. Neopythagorean teaching emerged in Alexandria, where all the necessary conditions explaining its emergence intersected: a vibrant intellectual exchange between ancient Greece and the Orient, an all-encompassing scholarly preoccupation with older Platonic and Aristotelian philosophy, an associated tendency toward eclecticism, and an important influence of skepticism. There existed a practical direction of religious-ascetic observance and a more theoretical one, which interests us here. This theory was already present in Pythagorean numerology, which could be linked quite well to Neopythagorean piety. The philosophers did not consider their addenda to their precursors' teachings as innovations in the proper sense, but as a deepening of existing teachings. As Moderatus of Gades observed:

> Since the ancient philosophers did not know how to represent the highest truths in clear words [...], they chose numbers as sensuous signs for unsensuous terms, by expressing the concept of unity and sameness, the cause of harmony and the condition of all things, by means of the number ONE, and by expressing the

concept of difference and dissimilarity, of division and change, by means of the number TWO.[1]

This turn justified the equation of Pythagorean numbers with Platonic ideas, which Marie-Louise von Franz has described as the "individuality of numbers."[2] Besides its quantitative aspect, each number, she argues, has both a quantitative aspect and that of a continuum. For this reason, "every individual numerical form or structure qualitatively represents an indivisible whole" (p. 59). Each individual number always represents the whole, whereby the number one is the basic element: the One-Continuum (1+1+1+1+...). Henri Poincaré observed: "Every whole number is detached from the others, it possesses its own individuality; each of them forms a kind of exception" (p. 60). Precisely "this aspect of number appears to contain the mysterious factor," von Franz continues, and adds that this quality "enables it to organize psyche and matter jointly." Moreover:

> The number one possesses these unique qualities to a particular degree. In contradistinction to all other number it does not multiply by itself, or reduce itself by division because it is the *divisor* of all other numbers [...] It is the only natural integer which does not follow another; that is, it has no predecessor. In this sense it does not yet "count" [...]
>
> In China, as in occidental number symbolism, one signifies the indivisible Whole, the *hen-to-pan*, the All-One. The purely mathematical fact that the number series begins with the one, but extends on to infinity, indicates that this number is also conceptually bound up with the infinite. (p. 61–62)

---

[1] This account follows Zeller's *Die Philosophie der Griechen*, vol. III, pp. 511ff.—trans.

[2] von Franz, *Number and Time*, pp. 59–62.

Returning to the Neopythagoreans, these introductory remarks help us better understand Nicomachus of Gerasa, for instance, who regarded numbers as pre-existing in the *Nous*, the world-creator, as a principle and primordial image of things. Already since Plato, two world-creating principles had been assumed: unity or the deity (= One) *on the one hand*, and duality (*aoristos dyas*) or matter *on the other*. Nicomachus describes the former as the good or as reason, the latter as a demon or as evil. For the Neopythagoreans, numbers are the link between the cause of creation and phenomena. Unity is the deity, reason, the formative power, the *Lógos spermatikòs*, the good, Apollo, the sun. Insofar as everything comes from unity, it can also be called matter, darkness, chaos, Tartarus, Styx. Due to this dual meaning, unity, the singular, is referred to as even-uneven and male-female. Duality, in contrast, is the principle of disparity, opposition, change, matter, nature, the reason for divided existence, and the God-mother (Isis, Demeter, Artemis, Aphrodite).

Here, dualism manifests itself in various oppositions: unity versus duality, form versus matter (Aristotelian), good versus evil, equality versus inequality, eternity versus change. Some Pythagoreans sought to overcome this dualism, as Numenius's fragment 52 indicates: he accuses the Pythagoreans of illogicality for assuming that indeterminate and eternal duality (*indeterminata et immense duitas*) had arisen from a single monad, which they believed forsook its nature (*recedente a natura sua*) and crossed over to the state of duality (*in duitatis habitum migrante*). Numenius mocks the paradox that the existing unity disappears and that previously nonexistent duality is born in its place. No matter how weak the logical argument, it reflects the endeavor to allow duality to emerge from unity while preserving the latter. This would mean that unity persists despite all multiplicity. This constitutes a curious piece of psychological thinking. On this subject, Jung observed:

> [...] man, world, and God form a whole, a unity unclouded by criticism. It is the world of the Father, and of man in his childhood state. [...] The world of the Father typifies an age which is characterized by a pristine oneness with the whole of Nature, no matter whether this oneness be beautiful or ugly or awe-inspiring. But once the question is asked: "Whence comes the evil, why is the world so bad and imperfect, why are there diseases and other horrors, why must man suffer?"—then reflection has already begun to judge the Father by his manifest works, and straightaway one is conscious of a doubt, which is itself the symptom of a split in the original unity. One comes to the conclusion that creation is imperfect—nay more, that the Creator has not done his job properly, that the goodness and almightiness of the Father cannot be the sole principle of the cosmos. Hence the *One* has to be supplemented by the *Other*. (CW 11 §201; emphases added)

In his Commentary on Aristotle's *Physics*, Simplicius, who refers to Porphyrus, who cites Moderatus of Gades, a first-century Neopythagorean, reports an attempt to salvage unity:

> According to the teaching of the Pythagoreans, he (Plato) places the Supreme One over all being and all substance; of the second One, which is the truly existent and intelligible, he says it is the ideas; of the third One, which is the spiritual, that it partakes in the One and the ideas; according to him, the final reality, that of the senses, has no part in the others, but it is arranged so that they appear in it; the matter residing therein is a shadow on the non-existent, which is primary quantum, and seen from this also stands even further down.[3]

---

[3] Simplicius, *On Aristotle's Physics*, p. 54.

Moderatus strives to maintain unity through the various levels of creation. From the perspective of logic, his argumentation appears very shaky, whereas psychologically, it is remarkable inasmuch as the self and unity are preserved despite diversity. Matter is said to be formless, undifferentiated, yet all-receiving, invisible, least capable of partaking in the intelligible, barely tangible, and considered inferior. It approaches what we now call the *unconscious*. The alchemists called their material "prima materia" and thus referred to the concrete nature of the unconscious. I suspect that the repudiation of the unconscious in Christianity, which rests on the notion of matter as evil, originated in Hellenism. In Gnosticism and Hermeticism, the unconscious assumed strange forms whereas for the alchemists *matter* was the substance to be transformed.

Some Neopythagorean circles believed that matter coincides with the highest god, who formed the world from this material. Hence, the idea of the *increatum* (uncreated) is very old. This, however, reinforces the basic dualism. Manichaeism is the classical Gnostic form of that dualism, which presumably goes back to the motif of the opposite brothers (Ohrmazd versus Ahriman) in the Zurvanism of ancient Iran.

Chapter 4
The Problem of Matter

Ancient Ionian natural philosophers—the "Pre-Socratic" philosophers—studied matter in their search for the primordial substance from which the totality was made. Anaximander (c. 610–c. 546 BCE) proposed a theory of the *apeiron* (the infinite) as the proper primordial ground. This strained suggestion constituted an abstraction from what confronts the senses to an over-arching principle that informs *all* phenomena (*arche*).

The next step in abstraction was taken by Xenophanes (c. 570–c. 475 BCE), who emphasized the *All-One*, which he regarded as unchanging. This, he asserted, is the deity, which is bound up with the totality of things and whose shape is spherical. Only a single deity exists, claimed Xenophanes.

Abstraction reached its peak in Parmenides (c. 500 BCE), who maintained that *being*—that which is—is ungenerated, unchanging, whole, unique, unshakable, and boundless. If it had *become*, there would be a different being, a being-before-being, a *non*-being. Being is indivisible, uniformly shaped, perfect in every respect, like a well-rounded sphere, its center equidistant from all sides.

The later Neopythagorean judgment that matter is evil rested on the assumption that whatever *changes* cannot possibly be divine. Of course, such views are alien to modern considerations, which hold matter to be inanimate. This was not so for the classical Greeks, who still projected their psychic processes outward into the world and thus animated matter. Hence, the surround of nature was populated by many creatures.

In compensation, the disciples of Parmenides described what was perceptible to the senses as unreal, as merely *seemingly* existent. They held that in "being" there was "truth," but in "becoming" there dwelt only "opinion." This perspective marked another step in abstraction away from outward sensory perceptions, and toward interior or psychological experience. It explains why Zeno (c. 490–c. 430 BCE), a disciple of Parmenides, struggled to explain multiplicity in the face of undivided being. This was also a cardinal question of subsequent Neopythagorean thought: how could the manifold arise from a unity? None of their solutions were entirely satisfactory.

A depth-psychological view—such as forwarded by C.G. Jung—provides insight into the situation. It is indeed paradoxical that unity and diversity co-exist. In psychological terms, one might say that unity corresponds to what Jung termed the *Self*; diversity corresponds to ego-consciousness, which emerges from the boundless Self.

Empedocles (c. 490–c. 430 BCE) maintained that being is at once diversity *and* unity. Empedocles' theory of the four elements (water, air, fire, earth) was embraced until the end of the Middle Ages. "These last eternally," he said. Aristotle successively declared, "they do not come into existence." Empedocles examined the unification and separation of the elements and their transformation. He called the forces at work in these events "love" (*philia*) and "strife" (*neikos*). If strife prevailed, everything collapses and dissociation occurs; if love predominated, unity (*sphairos*) ensues.

Anaxagoras (c. 510–c. 428 BCE) was a contemporary of Empedocles. He, too, believed that there is no actual "becoming" or "passing-away." Instead, he referred to coming-into-existence as *mixing-together*, and passing-away as *dissociating*. Becoming and passing-away, for Anaxagoras, are no more than qualitative changes. Nothing arises from nothing. Thus, there is no *creatio ex nihil*—the "creation from nothing" embraced by later orthodox Christian theology. Phenomena are merely the result of mixture ratios.

In Anaxagoras' conception, it is no longer a mechanical, coincidental mixture of the elements that is at work. Instead, it is the ordering mind (*nous*) that inhabits all parts of nature, and that originates the cosmos and the world-order. Anaxagoras was the first thinker to separate matter, which he considered boundless, from the arranging principle, the divine mind or *nous*. This mind is infinite and autocratic, not blended with anything else. It has the greatest power. It has generated rotational movement from a small point. It recognizes everything as it ought to become, as it was, and as it is now. It is the finest and purest of all things, and as such removed from all suffering (*apathes*). Its power derives entirely from itself (*autokrates*).

According to Anaxagoras, pure matter is "devoid of spirit" and lacks mind. This marks a first step toward dualism and the Neopythagorean concept of formless matter, which must initially be shaped by an active "spiritual" principle. Here occurs the division between mind (as a purely intellectual principle) and matter (as that which emerges). The mind is thereby assigned the dominant position.

These Pre-Socratic concepts had a powerful influence on medieval alchemy. The *Turba Philosophorum*, or "Assembly of the Philosophers," is one of the oldest alchemical texts. It is closely related to sources in Greek alchemy and was apparently compiled in a first Arabic edition around the beginning of the tenth century. It purports to record a Pythagorean Synod, wherein nine ancient Greek philosophers gathered to debate the foundations of alchemy. Even though this assembly was probably purely imaginative, the text reveals just how highly the earliest alchemists esteemed the Pre-Socratics, and in particular Pythagoras, whom they identified as the Grand Master of the Wise and of the Illuminati, and whom they likened to Hermes Trismegistus, their highest authority.

Medieval alchemy regarded the *Turba Philosophorum* as an ancient, seminal and authoritative text of the tradition. This valuation is connected to the work's supposed exposition of the Pre-Socratic struggle with the essence of matter, which in turn became the primal concern of alchemy. To the degree that they could access Pre-Socratic views—and the *Turba Philosophorum* was a purported source—the alchemists generally revered the ancient philosophers. Alchemical tradition held their names in such high regard that later writers pseudepigraphically published several treatises that attributed authorship to Pre-Socratic characters, thus bestowing the authority of antiquity upon their own expositions.

The paradox of unity and diversity that occupied prior Greek philosophers converged on Plato, where the nature of multiplicity and unity appeared in his theory of knowledge. He explained that since experience shows there are many beautiful things, men do conceive an idea of the beautiful (*Republic* 507 b). But phenomenal experience and primal idea differ. For Plato, "eternally true and essential being" denotes those ideas that stand behind the world of phenomena.

In the *Republic*, Plato presented the famous allegory of the cave, according to which people do not see things as they really are, but only as deceptive shadows. What we perceive is merely the unreal play of shadows of true being.

> So then, my dear Glaucon, I said, we must fit this image in its entirety to what we were discussing before, comparing the place that appeared through our sight to the dwelling in the prison chamber and the light of the fire there to the power of the sun. If you take the upward journey and the seeing of what is above as the upward journey of the soul to the intelligible realm, you will not mistake my intention, since you are keen to hear this. Only God knows, I suppose, if this is entirely true ... (Book VII, 517 a)

In Plato's early dialogues, *idea* was the overarching term under which many individual objects (particulars) could be subsumed. The term was later hypostatized—it was objectified, and assumed an existence of its own. "Idea" is spaceless and timeless, liberated from all confines and relativity, and exists beyond the senses. It is persistent, unalterable, and true being. For Plato, the relationship between the idea and the particulars is twofold: first, it is the *participation* of things in the idea, or vice versa the *presence* of the idea in things. Second, the idea is the primordial image, whereas particulars are its image or imitation (*eidolon*). This is important especially in the creation of the world. In the creation, ideas are visualized as matter, which is the mother of all becoming. Its material character, however, has evaporated into space. Nevertheless, there are four elements, which consist of ideal bodies. From these the world's body is formed.

Psychologically, Platonic ideas, as eternal images "stored up in a supercelestial place," correspond to the archetypes. (CW 8 §388) They are the philosophical formulation of a psychological fact. The archetypes, as the term suggests, are primordial images. They bear a resemblance to consciousness, that is, they possess a *numinosity* besides their luminosity.

The symbol of the soul-spark corresponds to that experienced in spontaneous dreams and visions.[1] For example, a middle-aged female analysand, who had fallen into hopeless and unrequited love, had the following dream:

> I am standing outside, at the top of a small staircase. To my left, a spark ignites in the earth and leaps onto the first step, where it burns as a *white* fire.

Strikingly, the spark comes from the earth, a symbol of our earthly reality. The already married dreamer, it must be noted, had not gone out seeking this love. Rather, it had happened to her. Often represented as a fire, love in this case is a white fire. This is remarkable, because

---

[1] Tardieu, *Psychaios Spinter*.

usually fire is experienced as red. It was a quiet, not excessively hot fire. It compensates for the panic into which the dreamer had fallen because of her impossible love. This love wanted to contribute to a progress of her consciousness rather than to call into question her marriage.

The Gnostic treatise *On the Origin of the World* (NHC II, 5) says:

> Out of this first blood Eros appeared. Eros is androgynous. His masculine side is Himeros, because he is fire from the light, and his feminine side is a soul of blood from the substance of Forethought. He is extremely handsome in appearance, and more attractive than all the creatures of chaos. When all the gods and their angels saw Eros, they fell in love with him. (109, 1–10)

No force fosters the process of becoming conscious as strongly as love, especially if it remains unrequited. Love activates myriad sacred projections. The analysand needs to recognize these projections cast onto the outer subject and meet them within the psyche. Hence, the symbolism of light and fire. The feminine aspect of Eros is a blood soul, which manifests itself in bodily form. This, of course, recalls Apuleius' tale of Amor and Psyche. Whoever endures such love without resigning becomes a light for others. For then it is not a projection that constitutes the relationship, but the capacity to love.

Following this digression on projection and the symbolism of the soul-spark, let us return to Plato's theory of ideas. Although frequently modified, this theory exerted a tremendous influence on the development of the mind. At the age of eighteen, Aristotle entered Plato's Academy and remained his student for twenty years. After Plato's death (348/7 BCE), Aristotle left Athens. Eventually he arrived at the Macedonian court (343/2 BCE), where he became the private tutor of the young Alexander, who would soon venture forth to conquer the world. When Alexander ascended the throne (335/4 BCE),

Aristotle returned to Athens and founded his academy, the Peripatos (336/5 BCE).

Plato and Aristotle both individually debate the problem of universals. According to Platonic doctrine (*universalia ante rem*), universals and ideas are real entities and exist independently of particulars. Aristotelian doctrine (*universalia in rem*), in contrast, is more realistic, claiming that form (*eidos*) and matter co-exist. Plato represents realism, because universals have their own existence *ante rem* (before the fact). Aristotle, however, stands for nominalism, inasmuch as he views universals as nothing but *nomina* (words) rather than as something that resides in particulars. As Jung has shown, these two positions both represent a respective typology. (CW 6 §48ff)

The problem of universals pervades Western intellectual history and has sparked a never-ending polemic. Some periods in that history of ideas tended more toward the Platonic concept, others more toward the Aristotelian. Each claimed to possess the sole and complete truth, and hence vehemently opposed the other school. Lacking a psychological perspective, neither direction could grasp that its particular typology, its subjective *a priori*, was the pivotal issue.

Beneath the surface, this argument is still ubiquitous today.[2] Platonic realism, which places the idea before the fact, prevails in Gnosticism, Hermeticism, alchemy, and for that matter, in all esoteric movements which believe that the world of appearances—the world immediately perceptible to the senses—does not represent the final truth of being. For these movements, ideas are the *primum moves*, the primary concern. The opposed nominalist perspective does not attach such importance to universals, and concentrates instead on the precise investigation of actual particulars. This typological standpoint is common to modern natural science, which therefore cannot understand the Gnostics, for whom ideas are hidden in matter. Modern

---

[2] Ribi, *Die feindlichen Brüder*.

science considers this Gnostic enterprise futile, and hence denounces the alchemists as charlatans. Nonetheless, both camps are fascinated by the secret of matter.

The nominalists cannot understand the value of the realists' standpoint, because they consider the *object* in itself worth exploring. For the realists, however, the *object* only attains its value when it is investigated by a *subject*. Such opposed human attitudes are apparently innate; each position assumes it is the singular prerequisite of understanding, and therefore cannot comprehend the diametrically opposite assumptions of the other. Only the critical examination and comprehension of one's own viewpoint relative to its opposite has a balancing and relativizing effect. As Jung emphasized, this is a practical value of a psychological and typological perspective in understanding the conflict between nominalism and realism.

Although Aristotle criticized the Platonic theory of ideas for assuming that universals exist independently of particulars (*universalia ante rem*), he did not succumb entirely to the opposite idea that universals are secondary (*universalia post rem*). Instead, he realized that subjective universals stem from an objective reality existing in particulars (*universalia in re*):

> The doctrine that all knowledge is of the universal, and hence that the principles of existing things must also be universal and not separate substances [namely, Platonic ideas], presents the greatest difficulty of all that we have discussed. (*Metaphysics*, Book XIII, 1087 a)

Given his typology, Aristotle could not accept that idea exists independently of particulars. Psychologically seen, it appears that the time was concerned with the soul (psyche) from the perspective of consciousness. People consider *true* that attitude which corresponds to their psychological temperament. A psychology of the unconscious sheds light on these age-old issues by revealing the existence of typical and perhaps innate attitudes, whose effect is such that the outer world appears to us in one way and not in another. With that realization, we reach the limits of our cognition, the point where a long-standing controversy no longer constitutes a philosophical problem, but a psychological fact.

Aristotle distinguishes between form or essence (*morphé, eidos*) and matter or substrate (*hylé*). Potential or disposition (*dynamis, potentia*) inheres in matter, whereas form is the realization or fulfillment (*enteléchia, energeia*) of that disposition.

This idea, it seems to me, manifested itself in alchemy as the *materia prima*, the unformed mass. Thus, the alchemist shapes this mass and hence takes on the role of the Creator. Movement or change (*kinesis*) marks the transition from possibility to reality. The process of becoming conscious is projected onto this physical shape: the unconscious is merely a possibility, and consciously lived life its realization. Because a depth psychological approach was impossible at the time, philosophy and alchemy both projected a great deal onto matter—and imaginatively saw the contents of the unconscious reflected back to them from matter. This explains the interest of Jungian psychology in these intellectual currents, which may be understood as proto-psychologies of the unconscious. The unconscious was being projected. Only the fact that the alchemists were utterly naive about their projections spared them from extreme inflation, particularly when they saw themselves in the role of the Creator, the worker whom Aristotle called the prime mover (*próton kinoun*).

In the ancient Stoicism, substance or matter lacks quality; the active force is reason (*nous*), which inheres in matter, or the deity, which is also conceived in material terms, even though it consists of the finest substance, fire (*pyr*). This fiery *pneuma* holds together the totality. It is the source of the coarser elements, which once again dissolve therein. Everything that is, is the primordial fire or the deity in its different states. At times, the entire world is dissolved in fire, at others a part of this fire becomes denser matter. This fire is the world-soul, the guiding principle, Zeus. Whereas Zeus is eternal, the sun, the moon, and the other gods have all become, and can all pass away again.

Later in Stoicism, the emerging coarser matter is contrasted with the shaping force, the *Logos spermatikos*. Diversity emerges from the shaping, material seeds inherent in the particular. The Stoics were the first materialists so to speak, a model for the alchemists, who projected everything into matter, to which they attribute a formative potency. The Stoics were fatalists in that they believed that everything happens out of necessity or *Heimarmene*. Not even forethought (*pronoia*) is exempt from this seminal principle. It merely designates the wise and benevolent care of God, who has arranged everything for the benefit of humankind. Everything proceeds according to stringent laws and causality, from which magic also arises.

This strict determinism could not prevail in the long term, because it left too little space for the human and for individual ethics. This brings us to the fundamental question of what it means to be human, whether in the past or today: is there such a thing as free will, or is everything determined in advance?

This question can also be phrased differently, thus giving it a surprising slant: does the Creator possess self-awareness, or not? If he were aware of himself, why did he create the world? Writing to Erich Neumann on March 10, 1959, at the age of 84, Jung observes:

> The question: *an creator sibi consciens* [is the creator self-conscious] is not a "pet idea" [of mine] but an exceedingly painful experience with well-nigh incalculable consequences, which it is not easy to argue about.... We still have no idea where the constructive factor in biological development is to be found. But we do know that warm-bloodedness and a differentiated brain were necessary for the inception of consciousness, and thus also

for the revelation of meaning.... Since a creation without the reflecting consciousness of man has no discernible meaning, the hypothesis of a latent meaning endows man with a cosmogonic significance, a true *raison d'être*. If on the other hand the latent meaning is attributed to the Creator as part of a conscious plan of creation, the question arises: Why should the Creator stage-manage this whole phenomenal world since he already knows what he can reflect himself in, and why should he reflect himself at all since he is already conscious of himself? Why should he create alongside his own omniscience a second, inferior consciousness—millions of dreary little mirrors when he knows in advance just what the image they reflect will look like?

After thinking all this over I have come to the conclusion that being "made in the likeness" applies not only to man but also to the Creator: he resembles man or is his likeness, which is to say that he is just as unconscious as man or even more unconscious, since according to the myth of the *incarnatio* he actually felt obliged to become man and offer himself to man as a sacrifice. (*Letters*, vol. 2, pp. 493ff.)

Jung asks elsewhere,

But why on earth should it be necessary for man to achieve, by hook or by crook, a higher level of consciousness? This is truly the crucial question, and I do not find the answer easy. Instead of a real answer I can only make a confession of faith: I believe that, after thousands and millions of years, someone had to realize that this wonderful world of mountains and oceans, suns and moons, galaxies and nebulae, plants and animals, *exists*. From a low hill in the Athi plains of East Africa I once watched the vast herds of wild animals grazing in soundless stillness, as they had done from time immemorial, touched only by the breath of a primeval world.

> I felt then as if I were the first man, the first creature, to know that all this *is*. The entire world round me was still in its primeval state; it did not know that it *was*. And then, in that one moment in which I came to know, the world sprang into being; without that moment it would never have been. All Nature seeks this goal and finds it fulfilled in man, but only in the most highly developed and most fully conscious man. Every advance, even the smallest, along this path of conscious realization adds that much to the world. (CW 9/I §177)

Recalling this experience in his memoirs, Jung writes:

> There the cosmic meaning of consciousness became overwhelmingly clear to me. Man, I, in an invisible act of creation put the stamp of perfection on the world by giving it objective existence. This act we usually ascribe to the Creator alone, without considering that in so doing we view life as machine calculated down to the last detail, which, among with the human psyche, runs on senselessly, obeying foreknown and predetermined rules. In such a cheerless clockwork fantasy there is no drama of man, world, and God; there is no "new day" leading to "new shores," but only the dreariness of calculated processes... Now I knew what it was, and knew even more: that man is indispensable for the completion of creation; that, in fact, he himself is the second creator of the world, who alone has given to the world its objective existence—without which, unheard, unseen, silently eating, giving birth, dying, heading nodding through hundreds of millions of years, it would have gone on in the profoundest night of non-being down to its unknown end. Human consciousness created objective existence and meaning, and man found his indispensable place in the great process of being. (MDR, pp. 240–241)

Naturally, such a psychological perspective was alien to the early Stoics. And yet the fact that their philosophy was unable to convey a satisfying meaning to the life of the time may have contributed to the emergence of the Hellenistic mystery religions. Accordingly, Middle Stoicism abandoned this prior rigorous determinism.

The positive aspect of the Stoic attitude was the attempt to overcome the existing dualism in favor of a monism—that is, a philosophical view that holds that the diversity of what exists can be explained in terms of a single reality. For Posidonius of Apameia (c. 135–c. 51 BCE), human beings occupy a central position in the cosmos as its principal aim, and as a crowning of the earthly world, due to their upright posture and their ability to cognize the totality and govern nature; this notion anticipates modern views, of course. Nevertheless, a strict opposition between body and soul prevails in human beings. The body, in Posidonius' thinking, which still adheres to the common Greek conception, shackles the soul and impedes its power of cognition. However, human beings, as a small cosmos, are connected with the larger cosmos by *syndesmos*, the concept of conjunction characteristic of Plato's *Timaeus*. Overall, Stoicism marks the most important step toward Neoplatonism and Gnosis.

This tendency intensified during late Stoicism, when philosophy became strongly tinged with religious sentiment, the conception of a personal relationship between humans and the deity, an emphasis on the human kinship with God, the commandment of human kindness, and finally, in Seneca, with seemingly Christian notions of otherworldliness. Late Stoicism belongs to the powerful intellectual current that encompasses Hellenistic mystery religions, Hermeticism, Gnosticism, alchemy, and Neoplatonism. The influence of the Romans—who emphasized the practical significance of philosophy and to whom more subtle speculations were foreign—also became increasingly apparent.

Let me briefly return to the Stoic concept of *syndesmos*. The term means "bond," "ligature," "connection." Its Latin cognates are *colligatio*, *coniunctio*, *copula*, and *vinculum*. In Plato, it takes on the meaning of a universal, metaphysical-cosmic connection. Proclus even speaks of "divine syndesmos" (*theias*). Just like Stoic *sympatheia* (the affinity of the parts with the whole), it denotes the unity of and the overall connection between things. Cicero speaks of a *continuatio coniunctioque naturae*, which parallels Stoic *philia* (love) and contrasts with strife (*neikos*).

The Stoics claimed that the entire cosmos is permeated by *pneuma*, which maintains the tension between all things, so that the individual parts are interdependent and influence one another due to their mutual affinity. This notion infused not only magic and astrology, but also ancient medicine. It also became the basis for the maxim "like cures like" (*similia similibus*). In his *History of Nature* (37,59), Pliny the Elder described in detail the effects of *discordia et concordia rerum* (the discord and harmony of things). In the Renaissance, this natural-philosophical, magical concept became powerfully effective in *magia naturalis* and in alchemy.[3] In early modernity, it formed the basis of homeopathy.

These ideas coincide with the *qualitas occulta*, or "hidden qualities within things." This designates a phenomenon that cannot be traced to a known quality of the elements and is hence considered unintelligible. It was widely believed in antiquity that certain forces are hidden in things (*quaedam occultae seminariae rationes*). This applied to all phenomena for which no explanations were known at the time, like the influence of the stars on the earthly world, magnetism, the tides, and the effects of medication. The idea came to full fruition in alchemy, where it designates the opposition to the manifest properties of a

---

[3] Ribi, "Magia naturalis."

substance. In a modern depth psychological view, these alchemical attributes appeared magical but are rooted in the unconscious.

Common to all these concepts is the idea of the *unus mundus* (unified reality). Although this concept confronts the limits of sensory experience, it nevertheless rests upon certain experiences—what Jung called *synchronicity*. Jung explains:

> Synchronistic events rest on the *simultaneous occurrence of two different psychic states*. One of them is the normal, probable state (i.e., the one that is causally explicable), and the other, the critical experience, is the one that cannot be derived causally from the first. ... An unexpected content which is directly or indirectly connected with some objective external event coincides with the ordinary psychic state. (CW 8 §855)

Before Jung developed the concept of synchronicity, such events were called *coincidences*. The new aspect of his definition is that such coincident concurrences are *meaningful*. That is to say, a sense of *meaning* is the binding element between the external or causal event on the one hand, and the internal or acausal one on the other. In everyday life, we are mostly aware only of the causal link between two events. If the sequence of cause and effect does not make immediate sense to us, we search for it by all necessary means. If no sequence can be discovered, or if the relationship between one event and another defies the laws of physics, it is termed acausal. Because we have such a tremendous need to explain matters, to accommodate our experiences into a consistent image of the world, the pious speak of "miracles," the rationalists of an "inexplicable coincidence." "Inexplicable" means nothing other than an experience that does not fit into the rationalist's causal conception of the world.

The oscillation between a strictly deterministic worldview and a conception open to coincidence began in Greek antiquity. The ancient

Greeks seem to have considered the strictly deterministic worldview unsatisfactory, because it offered no substantive answer to the meaning of life. In his study of Hellenistic beliefs, Ulrich von Wilamowitz-Moellendorf wrote:

> The decades between the battles of Issus [November 333 BCE] and Ipsos [301 BCE] were a period in which, contrary to predictions and expectations, so many incredible things, upheavals, reconstitutions, the rise of powerful persons to absolute heights, sudden overthrows and, sometimes, equally surprising resurgences occurred, that neither any God nor any law seemed to preside over human destiny, but blind coincidence [...]. Demetrius of Phalerum cites the fall of the Persian Empire and the rise of Macedonia [Alexander] as evidence, and he expected the fall of Macedonia [...]. Tyche [destiny] governed individual fortune no differently; thus, already Menander deplored her blindness and often nothing but coincidence has prevailed ever since. Yet this does not necessarily inhere in the word itself. Elsewhere, Menander leaves open the question whether *nous*, that is, deliberate [divine] intention resides therein, or whether she is driven by a *Pneuma theion*, a divine spirit, so that she finds all human *nous*, all human forethought, invalid. If a *Pneuma theion* was in her, so that she was said to be an active, hence divine power, even her justice could be recognized [...]. Only very gradually did Tyche become a ruling power, before she ultimately became a goddess in whose honor temples were erected.[4]

Tyche, the Greek tutelary deity of destiny, was associated with Moira, a person's destiny or fortune. Tyche, however, also represented

---

[4] *Glaube der Hellenen*, vol. 2, p. 295f.—trans.

or brought success. This was true of medical practice, in that a physician's expertise needed to be complemented by Tyche so that things were blessed with good fortune. Her power is indefinite and eludes human control. Under her auspices, things may go well or not; we simply do not know the outcome in advance. Sometimes, Tyche is seen as the most powerful among the Moirai (Pindar). Not even Zeus can overrule her counsel; her law presides over his. She appears as Pherepolis ("supporter of the city") and wears a mural crown to designate her patronage of the city-state. Eventually, she assumes an even more personal guise and resembles a person's daimon, the attendant spirit with which one is born.[5]

Aristotle represented the teleological view also espoused by the Stoics: all elements and all parts of the world act in unison according to a preordained plan. The gods, in Seneca's conception, are not charitable by nature and are unable to act otherwise. The totality of nature obeys its own necessity. So despite evil, the world is the best world possible, because *evil is a logical and real necessity*. How could we experience justice in the absence of injustice; and how could we recognize bravery in the absence of cowardice? Sickness, poverty, and similar plights are not real evils. They belong to the indifferent things, which do not, however, impede bliss. Within the whole, everything that nature does fulfills its purpose, even evil, without which the good would not exist.

Fate (*Heimarmene*), says Seneca, is nothing but the uninterrupted, orderly succession of causes. Jupiter is the primary cause, upon which all others depend. For Zeno, Heimarmene (the necessity inhering in all events, order, and the fate of the planetary spheres) is the power that moves matter according to the laws of nature. The world is an organism that consists of unified life and the interaction of all its parts. If, however, a single natural force pervades the world, the individual causal sequences cannot be independent, but must all

---

[5] Ribi, *Die Dämonen des Hieronymus Bosch*; see esp. chapter 10, "Der Stein: Dämon der Zeugungskraft," p. 124f.

originate in the power (Logos) of nature. Heimarmene is not "blind" destiny: instead, as Chrysippus (c. 279–c. 206 BCE) argues, it is the cosmological law of reason, the law of reason according to which all worldly things are governed by providence; it is "the law of reason according to which that which has become has become, that which is becoming becomes, and that which will be becomes;" it is "eternal, continuous, law-governed motion;" it is "the ordering of all events that is caused by nature, due to which one thing has followed another since time immemorial and occurs just as it does, in all its unswerving complexity." Thus, no such thing as causeless "coincidence" exists. What human beings designate as such, is the cause inaccessible to human reasoning.[6] (This view seems feasible in light of how many things we are now able to reasonably explain that were inaccessible to human reasoning in antiquity).

However, synchronicity, as defined by Jung, is causeless coincidence; it requires that one *exclude* any causal connection. Esoteric circles like to assume that unknown physical forces, such as earth radiation and magnetism, or unknown psychic ones, such as thought transmission (telepathy), involve causal relationships. In a depth psychological view, no such linkage exists. The former thinking remains trapped within pseudo-causality. One must free oneself from such everyday and cherished thought patterns and recognize synchronicity as a meaningful linkage in its own right, apart from but on a par with causality.

Despite their strictly causalistic notion, the Stoics also had to assume that free choice and responsibility are part of the essence of humanity, without which no moral standards would be possible. This view raises a difficult problem: how to reconcile the moral postulate of free choice and psychological experience with the assumption that,

---

[6] Pohlenz, *Stoa und Stoiker*, pp. 88–92.

under fate's influence, everything occurs according to a predetermined causal sequence?

Chrysippus proposed a plausible solution to this problem by distinguishing two types of causes: one is the decisive or primary cause (which we can call necessary); the other is the auxiliary or proximate cause. He explains his theory of causal determinism with the example of a cylindrical stone that is thrown onto a sloping surface, down which it thereupon rolls. The person throwing the stone is merely the secondary cause, the external impulse. But it is the inherent property of the stone, its roundness, that necessarily causes it to roll down the slope. Consequently, human volition has two causes: one is Heimarmene's endless chain of causes, which proceeds independently of human agency and merely provides the incentive for human action. The decisive cause, however, is a matter of our consent, which we are free to give or not. Our task is to educate our Logos to withstand external stimuli and to follow its inner essence. While we can neither influence nor alter the external course of events, our attitude toward these is crucial. Seneca therefore says: "Fate leads the willing and drags the unwilling, like a dog chained to a moving carriage" (*Ducunt volentem fata, nolentem trahunt*; *Epistles* 107, 11).

Stoic philosophy remains potent to this day. How far we are self-determined, or how far external forces determine us, still remains heavily disputed. Today, we believe that personal or social disposition or even environmental factors curtail self-determination. To be sure, human beings are able to act responsibly only if they enjoy the freedom of choice. If people are unconscious, not they will decide, but the "stars residing in our chest," to cite Wallenstein. What was once said to be "the fate of the stars" (*Heimarmene*) is now the archetypal constellation residing within the psyche. With the discovery of depth psychology, the archons (the powers governing the world, the celestial emperors) have translocated into the collective unconscious, where they still may determine fate. This highlights just how important the process of becoming conscious of such factors is to leading a responsible life.

The Gnostics, Hermeticists, and alchemists all set themselves this task, although in different ways. The alchemists engaged not only with the mind, but also with matter. To the enlightened modern person, it seems inconceivable that the alchemists' process of becoming conscious proceeded synchronically with their laboring with unknown matter. Only if one understands the principle of synchronicity does one realize that because a causal relationship is ruled out, such "meaningful coincidences" can be explained solely in terms of an acausal principle. Far more human activities occur synchronistically than is generally assumed. We are unaware of this synchronicity because no constant relationship exists between an activity and its outcome.

"Magical" effects are due to synchronicities because they proceed through the unconscious. Magic is called "the science of the jungle," because all civilizational and rationalist aids are absent. And yet magical effects are discussed as if a chain of causality existed. Primitive medicine has apparently sometimes enabled humanity to survive with the help of magic. It should therefore not be belittled. Magic played a significant role in Hellenism and should not be dismissed as mere superstition. Otherwise we would need to mock a part of modern medicine, which still allows magical (and psychological) powers into its quest for healing. Doing so would cheat ourselves out of one of medicine's key aspects, as well as draw closer to a soulless, entirely mechanistic "science of healing."

The *unforeseeability* of synchronicity as an individual observational event, and its *non-reproducibility*, explain its persistent exclusion from our concept of science. It is not that the synchronistic event is unscientific, however, but that our understanding of what constitutes science is too narrow—too tied to the concept of causality. In order to understand Hellenistic religious phenomena, one must take into account synchronistic events.

The alchemists were very conscious of the fact that they could not reckon with success, no matter how well they performed their work. Therefore, they invoked a divine assistant (*paredros*, "attendant spirit") and knew that they would succeed by the grace of God (*deo concedente*). We often lack the humility of the alchemists in reckoning with failure. If the moment is inopportune (*kairos*), the work will not succeed. Thus, as emphasized by the alchemists, the "right moment" plays a crucial role in all such events.

Jung explained, "The interconnection of meaningfully coincident factors must necessarily be thought of as acausal,"

> Here, for want of a demonstrable case, we are all too likely to fall into the temptation of positing a *transcendental* one. But a "cause" can only be a demonstrable quality. A "transcendental cause" is a contradiction in terms, because anything transcendental cannot by definition be demonstrated. (CW 8 §855–56)

Unlike our enlightened society, people in antiquity did not feel compelled to find a "natural" explanation for everything. Instead, they left this to the gods or demons. For people in antiquity, the world was an organism, a living creature, not a dead machine. It was pervaded, invigorated, and ordered by a divine logos or *nous*. No more than a small step was required to even further discover latent meaning in the Creation.

Synchronicity and the latent meaning that manifests in a synchronistic event are subjective experiences, which must be distinguished from Stoic philosophy that is at best unconscious speculation. Nevertheless, I find the unconscious knowledge of ancient society remarkable.

It is significant that mystery religions emerged during Hellenism; they contained mysteries that did not previously exist in their homelands. A strong need for the integration of the irrational arose in

Hellenism. Miracles, of course, carried great significance for archaic people. But this period was not more superstitious than others. I suspect, instead, that the mysteries offered a form of access to the unconscious. They enabled ancient people to establish a potential relationship with a mysterious, miraculous world, in which the laws of everyday life applied only to a partial extent. The power of the new mystery religions—which included Christianity, but also Gnosticism, Hermeticism, magic, and alchemy—were part of this fundamental Hellenistic current, whose power stemmed from the collective unconscious. It gave the life of its time a different meaning. Unlike their ancestors, the people were no longer determined entirely by external collective circumstances. Instead, they took on an individual dimension.

The origin of the *individual* needs to be searched for precisely here—an existence in which humans are not merely part of a collective, but individuals who each represent a totality. In the collective, the individual gained value from society as a *zoon politikon* (political animal). The individual was now assigned a value that constituted society. While mysteries were celebrated in association with others, participation elevated the individual to a divine level.

This is evident in the famous scene of Lucius's transformation in Apuleius's *Golden Ass*. Prior to his initiation, Lucius, the protagonist of the tale, is a collective person, as expressed by his appearance as an ass. Like every animal, he lives on his instincts. Only his liberation from his asinine state and his subsequent initiation make the ass-man Lucius an individual and "indivisible," whole person. The Anthropos myth, and its elevation of the individual, is the mythological expression of this shift from the collective to the individual.

The separation from the collective denotes a distinction from the mass of people and the bestowal of worth upon the individual. Not only slavery, but also the Circensian games in ancient Rome are expressions of how little the individual mattered. Individual worth was attached at most to the Roman emperors, who on their death took their place among the stars and thus became immortal.

Only those who value themselves can dissociate themselves from a totality. Participation in the mysteries, in which a hero or demi-god performs redemptive deeds, assigned value to the initiated by analogy or *participation mystique* (mystical participation). The redemption associated with this value resided in the certainty of no longer being merely at the mercy of a fickle fate, but of being accepted into a meaningful totality. Collective affiliation—belonging to an external community—yielded to a universal context. By participating in the fate of their God-man, human are accepted into a cosmic context which preserves their value as individuals.

One of the Nag Hammadi codices contains an interesting Hermetic doctrine of creation:

> God, the Father and Lord, created humanity after the gods, and he took humanity from the material realm. [Since God has given] matter [a place equal to spirit] in creation, there are passions in it, and they flow over a person's body. [...] God has perfected learning and knowledge, as we have been discussing, so that by means of learning and knowledge (Gnosis) he might restrain passions and vices, by his will. God has brought human mortality into immortality, and humanity has become good and immortal, as I have said. So God has created a twofold nature in humanity, immortal and mortal. It turned out this way because of the will of [God] that people should be better than gods, since the gods are immortal but only people are both immortal and mortal. People are related to the gods, and they know about each other with certainty. The gods know the concerns of the people and people know the concerns of the gods. Asclepius, I am talking about people who have attained learning and knowledge (*gnosis*). (*Asclepius*, NHC VI,8, 66,35–67,2; 67,23–68,16)

Those who have become conscious attain the level of the gods and even surpass them. Thus, human beings are no longer helplessly at the mercy of the influence of the gods on their lives. Becoming conscious enables people to wrest themselves free from Heimarmene's iron grip. Most spiritual currents of the Hellenistic Age engage this central topic.

Chapter 5

Liberation from the Power of Fate

The previous chapter offered a detailed account of how people in antiquity sought to disentangle themselves from the material world. I focused there mostly on the relevant Stoic and Platonic concepts, upon which the more specific Hermetic, Gnostic, and alchemistic notions are based.

Didymus of Alexandria (also known as Didymus the Blind, c. 313–398) who led the Catechetical School of Alexandria—a major center of Christian biblical exegesis and theology during late antiquity—writes in his *Commentary on Ecclesiastes*,

> Also that Egyptian whom they call Trismegistus says: the wise man cancels out fate (Heimarmene). He is not governed by necessity (*ananke*) and is not subject to the laws of the cosmos, but has reached heaven. His thinking has taken its place above, among the heavenly manifestations.

In Didymus' *Commentary on the Psalms*, especially in his commentary on Psalm 25:17 ("O bring thou me out of my distresses"), he warns against listening to those who devise birth charts and who believe that destiny holds in store certain events. Because, so he argues, if a person is devout, and possesses wisdom in divine matters, they will be released from the power of fate. In Hermetic tradition, Hermes Trismegistus similarly teaches that the wise person is not subject to fate and stands outside the cosmos. Citing John (15:19; 17:14,16), Didymus says that it is possible to be in the world, and yet no longer part of that world, if one directs one spirit upward and if one is a citizen of heaven (Philippians 3:20).

These texts reveal both the parallels and the contrasts between the Christian and Hermetic viewpoints. Zosimos, one of the earliest alchemists, born in Panopolis in Egypt (d. 300 CE), writes:

> Hermes, in his "Concerning Nature," hath called such men mindless—naught but "processions" of Fate—in that they have no notion of things incorporeal, or even of Fate herself who justly leads them, but they blaspheme her corporal schoolings, and have no notion of anything else but of her favors.[1]

Here the "mindless" are the unconscious persons who are motivated solely by their bodily needs and consequently fall under the spell of fate. The body itself is not evil, but the planetary powers exploit the body for their own purposes. As the Hermetic text "The Discourse of Hermes to Tat" explains:

> But those who missed the point of the proclamation are people of reason because they did not receive <the gift of mind> as well and do know the purpose or the agents of their coming to be. These people have sensations much like those of unreasoning animals, and, since their temperament is willful and angry, they feel no awe of things that deserve to be admired; they divert their attention to the pleasures and appetites of their bodies; and they believe that mankind came to be for such purposes. But those who participate in the gift that comes from god, O Tat, are immortal rather than mortal if one compares their deeds, for in a mind of their own they have comprehended all—things on earth, things in heaven and even what lies beyond heaven. Having raised themselves so far, they have seen the good and, having seen it,

---

[1] Mead, *Thrice-Greatest Hermes*, vol. 3, pp. 273-74, (translation modified).

they have come to regard the wasting of time here below as a calamity. They have scorned every corporeal and incorporeal thing, and they hasten toward the one and only. (CH IV, 4–5)

Zosimos was undoubtedly familiar with Hermeticism. In a letter to Théosebeia, his *soror mystica* (mystical sister), he seemingly alludes to a passage in the "Discourse of Hermes to Tat," and to the redemptive symbol of immersion in the "mixing bowl" or "cup." The "Discourse of Hermes to Tat" expounds:

> He [God] filled a great mixing bowl with it [with mind (*nous*)] and sent it below, appointing a herald whom he commanded to make the following proclamation to human hearts: "Immerse yourself in the mixing bowl if your heart has the strength, if it believes you will rise up again to the one who sent the mixing bowl below, if it recognizes the purpose of your coming to be." All those who heeded the proclamation and immersed themselves in mind participated in knowledge and became perfect people because they received mind.[2] (CH IV 4)

This proclamation coincides strikingly with Zosimos' advice to Theosebeia in his "Final Account":

> But be not thou, O lady, [thus] distracted, as, too, I bade thee in the actualizing [rites], and do not turn thyself about this way and that in seeking after God; but in thy house be still, and God shall come to thee, He who is everywhere and not in some wee spot as are daimonian things.

---

[2] Translator's note: the passages in brackets contain explanations inserted by Dr. Ribi.

And having stilled thyself in body, still thou thyself in passions too—desire, [and] pleasure, rage [and] grief, and the twelve fates of Death.

And thus set straight and upright, call thou unto thyself Divinity; and truly shall He come, He who is everywhere and [yet] nowhere.

And [then], without invoking them, perform the sacred rites unto the daimones,—not such as offer things to them and soothe and nourish them, but such as turn them from thee and destroy their power, which Mambres taught to Solomon, King of Jerusalem, and all that Solomon himself wrote down from his own wisdom.

And if thou shalt effectively perform these rites, thou shalt obtain the physical conditions of pure birth. And so continue till thou perfect thy soul completely.

And when thou knowest surely that thou art perfected in thyself, then spurn ... from thee the natural things of matter, and make for harbour in Pœmandres' arms, and having dowsed thyself within His Cup [*krater*], return again unto thy own [true] race.[3]

Finding one's own seed—an idea that frequently recurs in Gnosticism—is the step toward an individuality that no longer depends on the human collective, but whose home is the divine. Olympiodoros of Thebes (fl. c. 412–425), another Greek alchemist and poet whose observations much resemble those of Zosimos, highlights the importance of keeping the body still, as one does in Yoga exercises, and describes the following outcome:

---

[3] Emphasis added; Mead, *Thrice-Greatest Hermes*, vol. 3, pp. 283–84.

And when you have recognized yourself, you will also recognize the one who alone is really God.[4]

Commenting on the preceding passage from Zosimos, Jung writes:

> The *krater* is obviously a wonder-working vessel, a font or piscina, in which the immersion takes place and transformation into a spiritual being is effected. It was the *vas Hermetis* of later alchemy. I do not think there can be any doubt that the krater of Zosimos is closely related to the vessel of Poimandres in the Corpus Hermeticum. The Hermetic vessel, too, is a uterus of spiritual renewal or rebirth. (CW 13 §97)

If one speaks of redemption, one must always ask, what does humankind wish to be redeemed from, what does it suffer from? Here, it is clearly *agnosia* (unconsciousness). Because people in antiquity could not express their suffering psychologically, they projected it onto matter or nature, which were believed to be evil and therefore needed to be overcome. Once more, I must emphasize that the Gnostics were not pessimists, as is so often claimed. One must consider just how intensely the ancient Greeks and Romans sought to live within the world in order to comprehend Hellenism's radical renunciation of the world. In Hellenism, the *inner universe* could be discovered only through strict introversion, turning away from the outward object. This is the actual meaning of the term "spiritual rebirth."

Hermeticism, Gnosticism, and alchemy were expeditions into the realm of the unknown psyche. Contents of the collective unconscious or objective psyche that were met on the expedition would naturally also be projected into religious ceremonies and rites. Based on the Nag Hammadi scriptures, it is unclear what role rites played in the life of the

---

[4] Festugière, *La Révélation d'Hermes Trismégiste*, vol. I, pp. 280–81—trans.

Gnostics. There is mention of baptism and of anointing, but mostly in symbolic terms.[5] As recorded by Hippolytus, in Justinus' *Book of Baruch* the initiated swear to preserve the secrets. After they have done so they behold,

> "whatever things eye hath not seen, and ear hath not heard, and which have not entered into the heart of man;" and he drinks from life-giving water, which is to them, as they suppose, a bath, a fountain of life-giving, bubbling water. For there has been a separation made between water and water; and there is water, that below the firmament of the wicked creation, in which earthly and animal men are washed; and there is life-giving water, (that) above the firmament, of the Good One, in which spiritual (and) living men are washed.[6] (Hippolytus, *Refutatio omnium haeresium* V 27,2)

How did the baptism with water above the firmament take place? Was the image itself primary, or was there an associated ritual act? The imaginal nature of such texts becomes even more obvious in Hippolytus' example of a Sethian Gnostic teaching:

> But he says it is not sufficient that the Perfect Man, the Word, has entered into the womb of a virgin, and loosed the pangs which were in that darkness. Nay, more than this was requisite; for after his entrance into the foul mysteries of the womb, he was washed, and drank of the cup of life-giving bubbling water. And it was altogether needful that he should drink who was about to strip off the servile form, and assume celestial raiment. (Ibid., V 19,21)

---

[5] Sevrin, *Le dossier baptismal Séthien;* NHC II, 5; 111, 2–8.
[6] Hippolytus, *The Refutation of All Heresies*. Translated by J.H. MacMahon (Edinburgh: Clark, 1868).

Gnostics were undoubtedly familiar with numerous sacramental rites and actions, however these had a primarily spiritual value. Once again, this supports the distinction discussed in *The Search for Roots* (the first volume of this two-volume work) between the established church, with its appealed to ordinary people, and Gnosticism, with its rather demanding spiritual orientation. Gnosticism was quite rightly reproached for its elitism; it was not a mass movement.

Following the discoveries at Nag Hammadi, the reliability of early Christian polemic writings against Gnosticism has been placed in a clearer perspective. An example is the anti-Gnostic *Panarion* of Epiphanius of Salamis (c. 315–403). Although Epiphanius claimed to have frequented a Gnostic circle in Egypt, his writings are replete with all the suspicions constantly projected onto heretics. Of course, he came from a monastic background before being appointed abbot and later a bishop. It is thus unclear how far his accusations about the Gnostics are sheer speculation, and how much they reflect fact. He writes, accusing one sect of bizarre sexual rituals:

> For I happened on this sect myself, beloved, and was actually taught these things in person, out of the mouths of practicing Gnostics. Not only did women under this delusion offer me this line of talk, and divulge this sort of thing to me. With impudent boldness moreover, they tried to seduce me themselves [...] because they wanted me in my youth. (*Panarion*, 26,17,4)

Of course, Epiphanius did not write the *Panarion* ("Medical Chest") for scholarly reasons; it is composed to show believers the right path amid the maze of different views. In this sense, it is pedagogical. In the Preface, Epiphanius writes:

> I shall be telling you the names of the sects and exposing their unlawful deeds like poisons and toxic substances, matching the

antidotes with them at the same time—cures for those who are already bitten, and preventatives for those will have this experience. (Ibid., Proem I, 1,2)

He was impelled to describe these heretics in the most drastic terms to deter his beloved believers. Unlike Hippolytus a century and more earlier, Epiphanius appears less interested in understanding the Gnostic systems than condemning them. That may explain misinterpretations, even if his insights were indeed based on personal contacts. The Gnostic viewpoint is complex and by definition unorthodox; to understand it, one must fully engage it. Consider how Epiphanius responds to one Gnostic vision text:

They base their teachings on foolish visions and testimonies in what they maintain is a Gospel. For they make the following allegation: "I stood upon a lofty mount, and saw a man who was tall, and another, little of stature. And I heard as it were the sound of thunder and drew nigh to hear, and he spake with me and said, I am thou and thou art I, and wheresoever thou art, there am I; and I am sown in all things. And from wheresover thou wilt gatherest thou me, but in gathering me, thou gatherest thyself." What devil's sowing! How has he managed to divert men's minds, and distract them from the speech of the truth to things that are foolish and untenable. (26,3,1–2)

While this vision text is neither as foolish nor as untenable as Epiphanius alleges, it is not derived from his own tradition. It attests a visionary experience that is to him aberrant. The established church was vexed that no doctrine of faith would exist if believers relied on their own revelations.

Mountains are excellent places for the occurrence of curious and profound experiences. Visions received in that setting are attested to in texts accepted by Epiphanius. So why would some such accounts be considered foolish, and others significant? Visionary experience was both a crucial narrative, and a thorn in the side of the established church.

Did Moses not encounter God in the burning bush on God's mountain (Exodus 3:2)? And when God revealed himself to Moses on Mount Sinai, to give him the Ten Commandments,

> There were thunders and lightnings, and a thick cloud upon the mount [...] And Mount Sinai was altogether on a smoke, because the Lord descended upon it in fire: and the smoke thereof ascended as the smoke of a furnace, and the whole mount quaked greatly. And when the voice of the trumpet sounded long, and waxed louder and louder, Moses spake, and God answered him by a voice. (Exodus 19:16–19)

I see no reason why these Old Testament visions and experiences should be more valid or valuable than those of the later Gnostics. They are powerful manifestations, each in its own time, of the objective psyche. Both historians and Protestant theologians, however, remain ambivalent about whether visions equate to mental pathology. As a psychiatrist, I am familiar with this question. In my experience visionary experiences are not always pathological, and some are far from it.

Several of the visionary texts in the corpus of Gnostic writings are certainly not in any sense pathological products. One such account appears in the *Acts of John*. The text relates how at the time of the crucifixion, John fled up into the mountain and into a cave. In the cave he met, "My Lord standing in the midst of the cave and enlightening it." The Lord spoke, saying:

> John, unto the multitude below in Jerusalem I am being crucified and pierced with lances and reeds, and gall and vinegar is given me to drink. But unto thee I speak, and what I speak hear thou. I put it into thy mind to come up into this mountain, that thou mightest hear those things which it behoveth a disciple to learn from his teacher and a man from his God.
>
> And having thus spoken, he showed me a cross of light fixed (set up), and about the cross a great multitude, not having one form: and in it (the cross) was one form and one likeness [so the MS.; I would read: and therein was one form and one likeness: and in the cross another multitude, not having one form]. And the Lord himself I beheld above the cross, not having any shape, but only a voice. (97,5–98,4)

This passage plainly exemplifies a Gnostic standpoint. The multitudes gathered below by the cross are the *psychikoi*, for whom concrete events are the *sole* reality. John, the Gnostic visionary up on the mountain, beholds the spiritual reality concealed behind the external, visible reality. The former consists of the cross of light; two figures appearing in it.[7] The phrase "therein was one form and one likeness" refers to Genesis 1:26, which speaks of man's likeness to God. The *pneumatikoi* have been created in the "image" of God, an image embodied in humankind as the Great Man. The "small" person is the empirical person, in this case the visionary John; the "great person" is the *Anthropos*.

Similar insights appear in many text considered representative of Gnostic tradition. The *Pistis Sophia* states:

> Now, therefore, amen, I say unto you: Every man who will receive that mystery of the Ineffable and accomplish it in all its types and all its figures, he is a man in the world, but he towereth above all

---

[7] For a detailed interpretation, see CW 11 §429.

angels and will tower still more above them all ... all archangels ... all tyrants ... all lords ... all gods ... all light-givers ... all pure [ones] ... all triple-powers ... all forefathers ... all invisibles ... the great invisible forefather ... all those of the Midst ... the emanations of the Treasury of Light ... the Mixture ... the whole region of the Treasury ... he will rule with me in my kingdom ... he is king in the Light ... he is not one of the world. And amen, I say unto you: That man is I and I am that man.[8]

In the Greek *Papyrus Oxyrhynchus* fragments of the *Gospel of Thomas*, we find:

Where there are three they are without God. And where there is only one, I say, I am with him. Lift the stone and there you will find me. Split the wood and I am there. (I 24–30)

In the Manichaean "Kephalaia of the Teacher," we read:

The beginning of the greatest honoured ones [...] is the Light Mind; who is the awakener of they who sleep, the gatherer in of the ones who are scattered. (44,10–12)

In the Nag Hammadi Gnostic treatise *Thunder*, a female voice declares:

For I am the wisdom of the Greeks and the knowledge of the barbarians. I am the judgment ... I have been hated everywhere and loved everywhere. I am the one called life, and you have called me death. I am the one called law, and you have called me lawless. I am one you pursued, and I am one you seized. I am one you have scattered, and you have gathered me together. I am one before whom you have been ashamed, and you have been

---

[8] *Pistis Sophia: A Gnostic Miscellany*, pp. 191-192.

shameless to me. I, I am godless, and I have many gods. (NH VI,2)

Thunder, speaking in antinomies about herself, is Sophia—universal wisdom and the enlightener of the Gnostics. The ambivalence expressed toward her explains why she is scattered across the world and must be gathered up time and again. Hence, the Gnostics, on their ascent through the spheres of the seven archons, must solemnly declare:

> I have recognized myself and gathered myself from every quarter. I have pulled up his [the archon's] roots, and gathered my scattered members, and I know who thou art. For I am of those on high. (Epiphanius, *Panarion* 26,13,2)

In psychological perspective, gathering the "scattered members" corresponds to withdrawing the projections placed into the outer world. This act dissolves the magical attachment to the object, which, in turn, has a liberating effect on the subject. Only thus do individuals set themselves free from a *participation mystique* with their surroundings, and from the projections that generate many unfulfilled expectations and disappointments.

In perspective of other Gnostic writings, the vision text recounted above by Epiphanius was probably immensely significant for the initiate. Nonetheless, we do not know exactly how ancient Gnostics understood these accounts.

I mentioned at the outset that the *Corpus Hermeticum* is a collection of disparate Hermetic writings. We need to next examine what these several texts say about fate and redemption.

> The mind who is god ... by speaking gave birth to a second mind, a craftsman, who, as god of fire and spirit, crafted seven governors; they encompass the sensible world in circles, and their government is called fate. (CH I 9)

This statement about the seven planetary governors suggests why astrology experienced a revival during the Hellenistic age. Just as genetic analysis may do nowadays, so then did astrology offer a science that helped individuals apprehend fate. But the mind played a special role in regard to fate:

> The mind, the soul of god, truly prevails over all, over fate and law and all else. And nothing is truly impossible for mind, neither setting a human soul above fate nor, if it happens that a soul is careless, setting it beneath fate. (CH XII 9)

The mind, "the soul of god," stands above fate; this insight suggests an increasing human emancipation from fate. The Hermetics, however, made little use of this idea.

> But all things that come to pass by nature and there is no place destitute of Providence. Now Providence is the sovereign design of the God who rules over heavens; and that sovereign design has under it two subordinate powers, namely, Necessity and Destiny. Destiny is subservient to Providence. And the stars are subservient to Destiny. For the stars are the instrument of Destiny; it is in accordance with Destiny that they bring all things to pass for the world of nature and for men. (Stobeaus, *Excerpt* XII)

This excerpt from Stobaeus' *Extracts*—taken from a treatise addressed by Hermes to King Ammon—almost seems to contradict the assertion cited at the beginning of the chapter, namely, that the sage stands above fate. But, then, how many sages are there? The assertion is an encouragement to defy fate, at whose mercy we remain unless we become conscious:

> And the power which holds the whole Kosmos in its grasp is Providence; but that which puts constraint on particular things within the Kosmos is Necessity. And Destiny makes all things move with a cyclic movement, working in accord with Necessity; for it is the nature of Destiny to compel. (Stobeaus, *Excerpt* XIV)

Providence (*Pronoia*) is not, as might be suspected, God's free will, but what his wisdom has foreseen for the world. Hence, he does seem to be particularly conscious, because he, too, must submit to what he has established:

> For the human race is apt to err, because it is mortal, and is composed of evil matter; and the men most liable to slip are those who do not possess the power of seeing God; and on those men above all does Penal Justice lay her hold; and men are subject to Destiny by reason of the forces at work in their birth, but are subject to Penal Justice by reason of their errors in the conduct of life. (Stobeaus, *Excerpt* VII 3)

To evade the power of fate, which human beings bring upon themselves by their misconduct, they must behold God.

Hermes instructs Asclepius, "*Heimarmene* comes first, begetting the sources of all things, but the things that depend on her beginning them are forced into activity by Necessity" (*Asclepius* 39). Hermes continues, Fate, *heimarmene*,

> provides progeny enough for all to come with the seed she has sown, as it were, and Necessity follows, forcing them all into activity by compulsion ... But accident and chance are also mixed into everything material in the world. (40)

This leads to a curious and paradoxical deliberation about soul and body, and the synchronistic effects of accident and chance:

> Soul then, Ammon, is a substance which is self-determining in the beginning; but when it has chosen that course of life which is dependent on Destiny ... takes on as an appendage something irrational, which is similar to matter. (Stobeaus, *Excerpt* XVII 1)

> But we have the power to choose; for it is in our power to choose the better, and likewise to choose the worse ... involuntarily; for the soul, when it cleaves to evil things, draws near to corporeal nature, and for this reason the man who has chosen the worse is under the dominion of Destiny. (Stobeaus, *Excerpt* XVIII 3)

Now we confront a contradiction. If choice is determined so powerfully, and unilaterally, by something as unalterable as the body, then we can no longer speak of a freedom of choice. Nonetheless, Stobeaus declares,

> The intelligent substance in us is self-determining. The intelligent substance remains ever in the same state without change, not partaking of the nature of the things which come into being, and therefore Destiny has no hold on it. (Stobeaus, *Excerpt* XVIII 4)

Here lies a fundamental crux: human beings are exposed to two overwhelming opposites—body and mind—and are supposed to negotiate between one and the other. Were we truly free, we could determine our own fate. But since these opposites surpass our powers, we are at their mercy and essentially fettered by them. Unless we are born as uniquely enlightened sages—a rare occurrence—we must engage in a lifelong struggle to liberate ourselves from this opposition. In this struggle, we need a ray of light:

> Thus, if by way of the sun anyone has a ray shining upon him in his rational part (and the totality of those enlightened is a few), the demons' effect on him is nullified. For none—neither demons nor gods—can do anything against a single ray of god. (CH XVI 16)

"Because of this," another passage explains,

> unlike any other living thing on earth, mankind is twofold—in the body mortal but immortal in the essential man. Even though he is immortal and has authority over all things, mankind is affected by mortality because he is subject to fate; thus, although man is above the cosmic framework, he became a slave within it. (CH I 15)

Humans are composed of two opposites, "in the body mortal but immortal in the essential man." These opposites trouble us and produce a dynamics, a life-long process of spiritual growth. In psychological understanding, this process is directed toward the realization of one's essential person. Bringing forth the immortal person was a common concern of Hellenism, and is psychologically mirrored in the process of human development that Jung termed "individuation."

For insight into the Gnostic notion of Fate we are fortunate to have the *Apocryphon of John* (also known as the *Secret Revelation of John*).[9] This Gnostic treatise has survived in four manuscript versions that preserve two longer and two shorter copies of the text. The fact

---

[9] Three separate copies of the text were preserved in the Nag Hammadi collection: NHC II, 1; III; IV, 1. Another copy was discovered around 1900 in a manuscript now known as the Berlin Gnostic Codex, BG 2.

that four copies of such an ancient document are preserved perhaps attests to its ancient popularity. The *Apocryphon of John* is a complex scripture, and I can here summarize only a portion of it. Our present interest is the Gnostic understanding of the meaning of fate revealed in the text. At the beginning of the Apocryphon of John, the Savior appears to John in a vision and indicates he will instruct him, announcing:

> I am the incorruptible and the undefiled one. Now I have come to teach you what is, what was, and what is to come, that you may understand what is invisible and what is visible; and to teach you about the unshakable race of perfect humankind. So now, lift up your head that you may understand the things I shall tell you today, and that you may relate them to your spiritual friends, who are from the unshakable race of perfect humankind. (Meyer trans., *Gnostic Bible*)

The Savior explains to John that the ruling powers (*archons*) created humankind in the image of the sacred, perfect Father, who they had seen reflected in the lower waters. They called their creation *Adam*. Adam's knowledge, however, far surpassed theirs and that of their chief archon, Yaldabaoth:

> Although Adam had come into being through all of them, and they had given their power to this human, Adam was more intelligent than the creators and the first ruler. When they realized that Adam was enlightened, and could think more clearly than they, and was stripped of evil, they took and threw Adam into the lowest part of the whole material realm.

The blessed Father sent a salvific power, the Epinoia of the light, to come to the aid of Adam. *Epinoia*—a name sometimes translated as

"Conception" or "Afterthought" is the primal feminine power, the syzygy of primal *Nous*. The text explains,

> She helped the whole creature, laboring with it, restoring it to its fullness, teaching it about the descent of the seed, teaching it about the way of ascent.... Enlightened afterthought [*Epinoia*] was hidden within Adam so that the rulers might not recognize her....

The rulers brought Adam into the shadow of death so that they might produce a figure again, from earth, water, fire, and the spirit that comes from matter, that is, from the ignorance of darkness, and desire, and their own false spirit. This is the cave for remodeling the body that these criminals put on the human, the fetter of forgetfulness. Adam became a mortal being, the first to descend and the first to become estranged. The enlightened afterthought (Epinoia) within Adam, however, would rejuvenate Adam's mind.

> The chief archon thereafter placed Adam in what he called a paradise, telling him it was blissful: "But in fact," the text proclaims, "their [the archons] pleasure is bitter and their beauty is perverse. Their pleasure is a trap, their trees are a sacrilege, their fruit is deadly poison, their promise is death." (Meyer trans., NHS)

The tree of knowledge of good and evil in the garden, however, harbored the Epinoia of the light. Hence the chief archon commanded that it should not be eaten from. The *Apocryphon of John* explains it was the Savior who advised the primordial parents to eat from this tree of knowledge, or gnosis. Appearing in the guise of an eagle on the tree of knowledge, the Savior proclaimed that Adam should eat knowledge so that he would remember his state of perfection.

The Savior then reveals to John that those to whom the spirit of life had descended would be saved, because they could purge themselves of any depravity and of the temptations of evil. They are no longer seized by the passions; instead they endure everything to complete their struggle and to inherit eternal life.

When the chief archon realized that the perfect, eternal lightman had been created by the Epinoia of the light, which surpassed his wisdom, he decided to take possession of his power of thought. To do so, he created Heimarmene by binding together with all his might the ages and periods of the gods, angels, demons, and human beings. Thus, they all fell victim to the fetters of fate, which became their master. In the longer version of the Apocryphon of John, this passage reads:

> He [the chief archon] devised a plan with his authorities, who are his powers. Together they fornicated with Sophia, and through them was produced bitter fate [Heimarmene], the final, fickle bondage. Fate is like this because the powers are fickle. To the present day fate is harder and stronger than what gods, angels, demons, and all the generations have encountered. For from fate have come all iniquity and injustice and blasphemy, the bondage of forgetfulness, and ignorance, and all burdensome orders, weighty sins, and great fears. Thus all of creation has been blinded so that none might know the god that is over them all. Because of the bondage of forgetfulness, their sins have been hidden. They have been bound with dimensions, times, and seasons, and fate is master of all. (Meyer trans., NHS)

We must now ask, what are the differences between the Gnostic and Hermetic concepts of fate? For the Gnostics, Heimarmene is the cause of all evil, because fate has been created by the chief archon and his powers to bind and blind the world. Both the Gnostic and the Hermetics seek to free themselves from these bonds of fate. Typically, however, the Gnostics conceive that they bear the power of liberation within themselves, by possessing the Epinoia of the light, which frees them from the blindness and forgetfulness imposed by the archons. Hence, in contrast to the Hermetic view, they can (at least "ideally") remain largely unaffected by fate. If they belong to the chosen few upon whom knowledge has been bestowed, they must merely be mindful not to lose that gnosis.

This certainty gives the Gnostics the strength to withstand depravity and the temptations of evil in the world. This explains why the Carpocratian Gnostics conceive that they escape the works of the world-creator by virtue of a force received from the uncreated God, the highest primal source. They can thus engage in every act of life, because their soul takes no part in these actions; in all acts they scorn the works of creation (*Against Heresies* I 25,1–6). The Gnostics were thus considered arrogant for presuming, beyond doubt, that they were the elect and the singularly free humans.

Psychologically, the "ideal" Gnostic primarily identifies with what Jung describes as the *Self*. The "ideal" Gnostic's actions are unable to decenter him; his attachment with the Self ensures that he does not become embroiled in the causal chain of fate. I describe this attitude as "ideal" because it is the goal toward which the Gnostic strives, but which he may never reach. This is much like the alchemist's stone: although endowed with miraculous properties, it was never actually produced. As a goal of development, however, it retains its value, because the journey matters more than the destination.

The notion of fate captures life within a dynamics, whereas the Gnostic concept of a life free from fate is liberated from that dynamics. Gnosticism maintains that various types of people and consciousness co-exist. Contrary to ideal Gnostic descriptions, in reality the individual develops from one level to another, for better or worse. Presumably most humans aspire to that highest Gnostic pneumatic category that leads to redemption. This may be regarded as the aspiration driving the Gnostic toward his goal.

Jung wrote, "The self could be characterized as a kind of compensation for the conflict between inside and outside." He continued,

> This formulation would not be unfitting, since the self has somewhat the character of a result, of a goal attained, something that has come to pass very gradually and is experienced with much travail. So too the self is our life's goal, for it is the completest expression of that fateful combination we call individuality....
>
> Sensing the self as something irrational, as an indefinable existent, to which the ego is neither opposed nor subjected, but merely attached, and about which it revolves very much as the earth revolves around the sun—thus we come to the goal of individuation. I use the term "sensing" in order to indicate the apperceptive character of the relation between ego and self. In this relation nothing is knowable, because we can say nothing about the contents of the self. The ego is the only content of the self that we do know. The individuated ego senses itself as the object of an unknown and superordinate effect. It seems to me that our psychological inquiry must come to a stop here, for the idea of a self is itself a transcendental postulate which, although justifiable psychologically, does not allow of scientific proof. This step beyond science is an unconditional requirement of the psychological development I have sought to depict, because without this postulate I could give no adequate formulation of the psychic processes that occur empirically. At the very least, therefore, the self can claim the value of an hypothesis.... And even though we should once again be enmeshed in an image, it is nonetheless powerfully alive, and its interpretation quite exceeds

my powers. I have no doubt at all that it is an image, but one in which we are contained. (CW 7 §404–405)

This idea seems central to Gnostic thinking. The Gnostics moved away from the psychology of ego-centered consciousness, which makes their assertions often seem rather bizarre. Fate is constellated in ego-consciousness, which explains why the Gnostics rule out the possibility of swaying or influencing fate. The most pressing question for the Gnostic is how to escape the material world and the fetters of its creator. This question is fateful, because the powers of the archons—the rulers of both earthly and heavenly spheres—manifest themselves in the material world. In summary, from a psychological perspective, the Gnostics seem to consider life and worldly events from the vantage point of the Self.

Chapter 6

Is the Creator Aware of Creation?

This question already occupied us in Chapter 4, in the context of our discussion of Stoic determinism. It also plays a part in the concept of Heimarmene, specifically whether fate proceeds according to a predetermined plan.

The *Corpus Hermeticum* contains the commonplace ideas about the Creator, who is invisible and eternal. His creation is the second god, the visible one, wherein the invisible one manifests himself. Humankind is the third god (*Asclepius* 10). Of interest for our present concern is the presence of evil. According to XIV 7, the Creator has made everything, because he considers nothing to be depraved or evil. Nor has he created depravity, which emerges as the creation ages. He has therefore created change, as it were as a purification of what has become. The Hermetics liken evil to the verdigris that affects bronze solely as time passes. For God has only one single attribute: benevolence (XIV 8-9). His creation is eternal (XIV 3).

The invisible is eternal and inconceivable. In his creation, he appears and becomes imaginable, because a perfect correspondence exists between the imagination and becoming (V 1). Thought alone sees the invisible with the eyes of the mind. The All-One, the Father, has created order by number and place. Even the subordinate is part of that order and subject to a master who has not yet imposed order (V 4). He can be eternal only if he makes everything for eternity, in those things that are and those that are not. He allows being to become visible and conceals non-being within himself (V 9).

Both texts are of great interest for our present concern: in the first, neither the Creator nor the human being is responsible because

EMBLEMA XIII. *De secretis Naturæ.*

Æs Philosophorum hydropicum est, & vult lavari septies in fluvio, ut Naaman leprosus in Jordane.

EPIGRAMMA XIII.

PRætumido languens æs turget hydrope Sophorum,
    Inde salutiferas appetit illud aquas.
Utque Naman Jordane lepræ contagia movit,
    Abluitur lymphis térque quatérque suis:
Ergo præcipites in aquam tua corpora dulcem,
    Moxq́, feret morbus illa salutis opem.

Figure 1. Michael Maier, *Atalanta Fugiens*, 1618

the Creator "knew" this when he made the cosmos, just as he made change, which is able to remedy the damage. This perspective is almost alchemistic: the alchemist, after all, is meant to transform inferior metals, which often suffer from "leprositas" (leprosy), into incorruptible gold. Gerhard Dorn, the famous seventeenth-century physician and Paracelsist, observed:

> The blood of his [the alchemist's] philosophical stone liberates leprous metals and human beings from all their infectious diseases. Thus, their stone is not called ensouled for no reason.[1]

Here an obvious parallel is drawn between leprous metals and human diseases. This *leprositas* can be cured with the blood of the miraculous stone, because this panacea—the self—is alive within the human being. Dorn therefore explains elsewhere: "Those who wish to eliminate the leprosy of metals may do so."[2] This is the case because aside from the sun- and moonlike metals (*solaris et lunaris*), all other metals (*saturnina, jovialis, martialis, venerea*) are impure or leprous, because their primary substances (*principia*), sulphur and mercury, are impure, whereas the first kind originates in pure substances.[3]

Even the Messiah is regarded as *leprosus*, "because he has carried all our diseases" (Isaiah 53:4).[4] In his *Atalanta Fugiens*, Count Palatine and alchemist Michael Maier refers to the story of the leprous Captain Naaman, who was healed only after he immersed himself seven times in

---

[1] Congeries Paracelsicae Chemiae. *Theatrum Chemicum* 1659 I 515.
[2] Physica Genesis: *Theatrum Chemicum* 1659 I 359: "Poterit quicunque volet metallorum lepram tollere."
[3] Exercitationes in Turbam: De prima materia metallorum. *Artis Aurifere* 1593, I 157.
[4] Christian Schoettgen: *Horae Hebraicae et Talmudicae*, p. 11: "Quia omnes infirmitates nostras suscepit."

the Jordan (2 Kings 5:1–4).[5] [Figure 1] Describing the magnificent engraving, Maier writes:

> The copper of the philosophers suffers from edema and must be washed seven times in the river, like the leprous Naeman was in the River Jordan.

The *Filius Philosophorum* (the philosopher's son) may also be leprous if he is born from an impure womb. Thus the *Rosinus ad Sarratantam Episcopum* says:

> [...] although the sperm was pure, the son is still leprous and impure due to the corrupted womb, as happens with all imperfect metals, which are corrupted by Venus or the foetid soil.[6]

Evidently, Venus corrupts the white, fertile soil (*terra alba fructuosa*), so that it turns into foetid soil, from which only corrupted metals or a leprous son are born. The alchemists repeatedly emphasize the importance of their earth (silver and golden earth, foliated white earth). Hence, in German we say that one should not carve flutes from bad wood.

Like every other alchemical symbol, however, the leprous ore can also be interpreted positively due its green color. Thus the *Rosarium Philosophorum* cites the Arabic alchemist Senior (ibn Umail):

> You, however, sought the color green because you thought that copper is a leprous body, because it, too, is green. So let me tell

---

[5] Emblema XIII: Aes Philosophorum hydropicum est et vult lavari septies in fluvio, ut Naeman leprosus in Jordane. (See Figure 1.)

[6] *Artis Auriferae* I 318: "quamvis sperma fuerit mundum, tamen puer sit leprosus et immundus causa matricis corruptae, et sic est de omnibus Metallis imperfectis, quae corrumpuntur ex Venere, et terra foetida."

you that everything that is perfect is contained in copper, that unique greenness contained therein, because our art turns that which is green swiftly into our truest gold. We have experienced this ourselves.... O blessed green, you who engender everything.[7]

In the Hermetic *Asclepius*, "God, the father and master, made gods first and then humans, taking equal portions from the more corrupt part of matter and from the divine" (*CH* 22, I 283). Consequently, "the vices of matter" persisted. "Hence it is inevitable that the longings of desire and the other vices of mind sink into human souls." The gods, who are made from the purest part of nature, are subject to "an order of necessity framed in law." That law is "eternal." Thus because they are made from inferior matter, human beings have vices. These, however, create an inner freedom, which the gods lack.

The aging of the world, which is treated in Chapter 26 of *Asclepius*, leads to irreverence, disorder, and unreason. Human conduct is directed entirely toward indulgence, from which spreads universal depravity. The Creator rights this evil by "washing away malice in a flood" or "by consuming it in fire or ending it by spreading pestilential disease everywhere." This restores the world to its original form, which is its hour of birth. These ideas recall Augustine's evening and morning knowledge.[8] He says:

> For god's will has no beginning; it remains the same, everlasting in its present state. God's nature is deliberation; will is the supreme goodness. (26)

This sounds commonplace. But if we add Chapter 30, these assertions become meaningful:

---

[7] *Artis Auriferae* II 220.
[8] Ribi, "Morgenerkenntnis und Abenderkenntnis bei Aurelius Augustinus: Wo stehen wir heute?"

> This god, the only and the all, completely full of the fertility of both sexes and ever pregnant with his own will, always begets whatever he wishes to procreate.

This points to a *creatio continua*, a never-completed, ongoing Creation. I referred to this above as eternal (XIV 3). The Creator holds within himself non-being (CH V 9), that which he has not yet summoned into being or what he has not yet ordered (V 4).

Psychologically, consciousness, as the second creator, thus never ceases to expand. The process of becoming conscious lasts a lifetime. Jung called it *individuation*, and alchemy represents it as the *arbor philosophica* (tree of philosophy; CW 13 §304). This makes sense insofar as this spontaneous process of growth makes humans and trees become what they have long been destined to become. Just as a child grows and matures without contributing to its growth, consciousness develops spontaneously from the unconscious, and according to its own nature.

On a deeper level, Jung applied the notion of the *creatio continua* to *acts of creation taking place in time* (CW 8 §957 A 151). All synchronicity is such an act, because it cannot be deduced from the act of creation. It is without cause. In this act, the act of creation is eternally present and time suspended accordingly. Neither a before nor an afterward exists, but solely simultaneity, as is evident in dreams that anticipate events. Such dreams prefigure an event that still lies in a future unknown to consciousness. All synchronicity represents novelty, singularity, the previously nonexistent. In this sense, creation is not a unique act, but instead, as the term "*evolutio*" suggests, a never-ending series of events. However, biologists still understand evolution largely in causal rather than in synchronistic terms. This is a fascinating area, which unfortunately lies beyond our present discussion.

For the church fathers, the question whether or not the Creator was conscious of his creation is clear. Without dwelling on matters, the

Valentinian School regarded the Creator as a subordinate divinity, a *deuteros theos*, who created a failed creation due to his incompetence. For the Gnostics, the task is not to abandon oneself to this world, but instead to rescue oneself into the true world of the fathers through one's knowledge of the world. This task expresses the Gnostic sense of life. The Gnostics despise matter and commit themselves to the spirit, which promises redemption. This condemnation of the world may manifest itself in libertine rites. The *Apocryphon of John* is a typical example of Valentinian Gnosticism:

> He [the Demiurge] conjoins with ignorance, who is with him.... (NH III 16,7)
>
> Yaldabaoth [the Demiurge] was full of ignorance (NH II 63,5)
>
> He is ignorant darkness (NH II, 11,10)

Another Valentinian treatise, included in the *Gospel of Truth*, says:

> For this reason error (*plane*) became powerful; it worked on its own matter foolishly, not having known the truth. It set about with a creation, preparing with power and beauty the substitute for the truth.... For this reason despise error. ...It had no root; it fell into a fog regarding the father.... (NH I, 17,14)

In the *Gospel of the Egyptians*, it is Sakla, the blind man:

> And after the founding [of the world] Sakla said to his [angels], "I, I am a [jealous] God, and apart from me nothing has [come into being," since he] trusted in his nature. (NH III 58,23)

Irenaeus reports that "the Demiurge, desiring to imitate the infinitude, and eternity, and immensity, and freedom from all measurement by time of the Ogdoad above, but ... he was the fruit of defect". (*Against Heresies* I, 17,2)

The Creation is a defective imitation of the eternal, perfect world of the Pleroma. "The Demiurge, while ignorant of those things which were higher than himself" (I, 7,4), is unable to create a better world. The tragic story of humanity, as a conflict between the demiurge and the world of light, is the theme of the *Apocalypse of Adam* (NHC V. 5). This conflict, according to the *Tripartite Tractate* (NH I, 5), occurs because the demiurge occupies only third place:

> The demiurge is called "the image of the Father's image," the image of the Son. (NH I 110,35)

Historically, the Gnostics assign to the God of the Old Testament a subordinate role. Only their perfect, unrecognizable Father represents the revelation. Striving to recognize this Father, the Gnostics realize that this is possible only through knowledge (Gnosis) and grace:

> But the Father is perfect, knowing every space within him (NH I, 27,23). He alone is the one who knows himself as he is... since he has the ability to... see himself... to comprehend himself... (NH I, 54,40)

For the Gnostics, a sharp distinction exists between the *deus absconditus*, who stands above everything, and the Creator. This is how they answered the question of how a perfect God could produce an imperfect creation. From the perspective of depth psychology, the demiurge is the consciousness that has emerged from the ego. It never has the all-encompassing qualities of the unrecognizable Self, which can be described as the image of God in the human being.

Withdrawing the libido from the outer world awakens the Gnostic's unconscious and produces manifold images, including the image of God. The Gnostic attitude toward the world is not simply pessimistic, but introverted. Whenever possible, this attitude devalues the objects of the surrounding world, which causes the inner objects to impose themselves even more tenaciously. Presumably, this explains the often muddled, unsystematic fantasies of the Gnostics, which stood in the starkest possible contrast to the progressive systematization of theology. Valentinus and Basilides were probably the only Gnostics to establish a reasonably well-ordered system. The danger of systematization is an increasing literalism and the loss of primordial experience. Not Gnosticism, but systematic theology is exposed to this threat. *The Gospel of Truth* says:

> After all these, there came the little children also, those to whom the knowledge of the Father belongs.... There was manifested in their heart the living book of the living—the one written in the thought and the mind [of the] Father, which from before the foundation of the totality was within his incomprehensibility—that (book) which no one was able to take, since it remains for the one who will take it to be slain.... (NH I 19,27–20,6)

This book unmistakably contains the spirit and the thoughts of the unrecognizable Father. Only children, who live in the Father's world of the unconscious, can read and understand this book (Revelation 5:6–8). No theology is made from this book. Instead, it is the Book of Life, into which the Gnostics seek to be accepted (Revelation 3:5). This, however, requires the child's impartiality and spontaneity. Here, "children" should not be understood concretely, but symbolically.

To my knowledge, the only text within the Nag Hammadi collection in which the Creation is not described as unconscious is the *Teachings of Silvanus* (NH VII, 4). This treatise resembles ancient sapiential literature, meaning that it is not strictly Gnostic, and occasionally even apparently anti-Gnostic:

> Let no one ever say that God is ignorant. For it is not right to place the creator of every creature in ignorance. For even things which are in darkness are before him like (things in) the light. (NH VII 116,8)

Already in our discussion of the Creator's consciousness, a pressing question loomed in the background, namely, whether two gods exist, as Marcion of Sinope and the Gnostics seem to assume. One of these gods towers lonely above everything else. He is not responsible for the flawed creation, since he creates only perfection, because he, too, is perfect. For this reason, the creator of a flawed creation can only be a subordinate god. Already Plato maintained that as the Creator the highest god created only divine beings and things. He left the creation of mortal creatures to the "new gods." They tried to imitate the highest Creator, but failed. They are therefore responsible for everything that goes amiss in the creation (Tim. 30 A, 41 C). The Gnostics regarded the demiurge, since he is depicted in the Old Testament as a Creator (Genesis 1:1), as a subordinate god. For the Gnostics, the New Testament evidently initiated a new chapter in God's self-revelation. Thus, behind a somewhat dubious demiurge emerges a superior God, who lets his son, Christ, become human. For the Gnostics, a God who must look for Adam in Paradise (Genesis 3:9) cannot be omniscient. They interpret the fact that it is forbidden to eat from the Tree of Knowledge (Genesis 3:5) as a knowledge of the fact that the human being will subsequently be equal to the Creator, if not even superior:

> And he [= God] said, "Behold, Adam has become like one of us, knowing evil and good." Then he said, "Let us cast him out of Paradise lest he take from the tree of life and eat and live for ever." But what sort is this God? First [he] envied Adam that he should eat from the tree of knowledge. And secondly he said, "Adam, where are you?" And God does not have foreknowledge

(*prognosis*), that is, since he did not know this from the beginning. [And] afterwards he said, "Let us cast him [out] of this place, lest he eat of the tree of life and live for ever." Surely he has shown himself to be a malicious envier.[9] (NH IX 47, 7–30)

The fact that the Gnostics attribute Yahwistic features to the demiurge has led scholars to accuse them of anti-Semitism. My own view is that this need not be the case. As I said earlier, one reason for this might be the Gnostic expectation that a superior divinity nevertheless exists in the background. The transition from the Old to the New Testament signifies a tremendous collective development of the image of God (Jung, *Answer to Job*; CW 11 §560). The Gnostics were acutely aware of this, whereas the established church desperately sought to emphasize the unity of God's self-revelation. The division into the Creator God of the Old Testament and the loving Gnostic Father expresses a secular transformation of the image of God. The demiurge represents the surmounted level. This, however, is not an actual dualism. As a rule, the surmounted images of God assume demonic traits.

It is barely comprehensible how an image of a law-giving God can transform into that of a loving God. Insofar as the Jews adhered to the old image of God, the Gnostics may be polemicizing matters. This transformation seems to have caused the established church no headache. On the other hand, this transition has barely borne any fruit to this day, although the "loving God" is constantly invoked from the pulpit.

We should never forget that quite possibly a gulf exists between the conscious image of God and the image effective in the unconscious. Their writings suggest that the Gnostics struggled for a new image of God. This explains why much Gnostic thinking remained incomprehensible to the established church fathers. Origen fiercely criticizes the views of the Gnostics, most of all Marcion's:

---

[9] See also Pearson, ed. *The Testimony of Truth*, NHS XV, p. 163.

> After this, it is worthwhile to look at the phrase which has been assailed in a sophistical way by those who say that the God of the law and the God of the Gospel of Jesus Christ are not the same.[10]
>
> The heretics do not make "one loaf from two tenths" (Leviticus 24:5) for they deny that God the Creator is the Father of Christ, and they do not make the Old and New Testament "one loaf," and they do not profess one Spirit to be in each document.[11]

Today, we are able to judge this dispute from a safe historical distance. The established church prevailed, but at what cost? Christianity has never coped with the dualism between a "loving, benevolent God" and the devil. While ancient Gnosticism attempted to answer the question *"unde malum?"* (where does evil come from?), it did not dare conclude that the perfect Father, to be perfect, necessarily also contains evil; or at least they never formulated this conclusion.

The *Apocryphon of John* mentions the highest, transcendental God, whose aeon

> looks at him in his light which surrounds [him]. This is the spring of the water of life which gives to [all] the aeons and in every form. He [gazes upon] his image which he sees in the spring of the [Spirit. He] puts his desire in his light-[water], that is, spring of the [pure] light-water [which] surrounds him. (NH II, 1; III, 1; IV, 1; BG 2)

It is not clear from the text whether the aeon is the highest deity or already an emanation aware of itself. The image or consciousness that the deity gains through this reflection is *Ennoia*. Is this the Sophia that

---

[10] *Commentary on the Gospel of Matthew*, XI, 14.
[11] *Homilies on Leviticus*, XIII 4.2, p. 239.

helps the deity acquire consciousness? Discussing the Valentinians, Epiphanius says:

> They say there is a perfect Aeon, preexistent in invisible, nameless heights: Him they call Prior Principle, First Progenitor, and Depth. He is uncontainable and invisible, eternal and unbegotten, and has existed in calm and deep tranquility for boundless ages of time. And with him also is Ennoia, whom they term both Grace and Silence. (Panarion 31,10,5)

It has been fiercely debated whether absolute consciousness, that is, consciousness in and of itself, as it were a cosmic consciousness clearly separate from the human being, exists. In the Indian philosophy of religion, this notion is self-evident. We must, however, note that what the Indians call consciousness corresponds to our unconscious.

The question of the consciousness of the Creator is a projection of the question whether a consciousness of sorts dwells in the self. Near-death experiences of patients diagnosed as brain-dead have often been observed to involve a curious perception of events. Although they have entered a state of utter helplessness, such patients are able to describe circumstances and events with baffling accuracy. Helplessness in this context refers to the disabling of consciousness, which is located in the cerebral cortex. If some kind of perception exists despite the disabling of consciousness, then a "consciousness" of sorts must exist independently of the body. "If we are correct in this assumption," writes Jung,

> then we must ask ourselves whether there is some other nervous substrate in us, apart from the cerebrum, that can think and perceive, or whether the psychic processes that go on in us during loss of consciousness are synchronistic phenomena, i.e., events

which have no causal connection with organic processes. (CW 8 §955)

Because no second nervous substratum possessing the functions of consciousness is known to exist, other than the sympathetic or parasympathetic nervous system, the hypothesis of synchronicity seems more likely, since this is known to be involved whenever the unconscious has a hand in things. Because consciousness emerges from the unconscious, and because the self is at work in the individuation process as a *spiritus rector*, one must acknowledge that it possesses some kind of "consciousness." I am deliberately highlighting this term to emphasize that this is not ordinary ego consciousness, but a mysterious spirit that bestows on psychic development a certain finality and meaning. This "consciousness" might also secretly observe our activities, offering its life-furthering comments in dreams. It might be the director of our psychic development, orienting it conclusively toward achieving completion.

This compass does not constitute a rigid and predetermined approach, but rather a general orientation toward a virtual goal. This is changed plentifully by the reactions of consciousness. Thus, it is far from being a clock mechanism that goes through its motions on its way to reaching its predetermined objective. On the contrary, outer and inner influences constantly modify its actions. But like the needle of a compass, it keeps its goal firmly in its sights, persistently and regardless of the vicissitudes of life. It remains steadfastly unperturbed by a strong will or by magical procedures. It might be called an unconscious knowledge of one's destiny, one's karma.

The question of the Creator's consciousness is crucial for Gnostic philosophy. Since their demiurge is blind, the Gnostics attach the greatest importance to becoming conscious. The pneumatic who achieves gnosis is superior to the demiurge: "You will be like God" (Genesis 3:5). Thus, we can understand the Creator's envy, which is meant to prevent the primordial parents from eating from the Tree of Knowledge.

Calculating fate, the horoscope is the orientation of life determined by the archons. These are the difficulties of life caused by outer and inner circumstances. Depth psychology calls them complexes. By attaining consciousness, the Gnostics are meant to free themselves from these complexes, in order to develop into what corresponds to their destiny. Subjectively, this destiny is the supreme, unrecognizable Father-God, since our purpose does not depend on our ego, whereas vice versa our ego depends on our destiny. If our purpose can realize itself, a sense of redemption, freedom, and meaningfulness arises. This is the goal of the Gnostic.

Chapter 7
Gnosticism and the Christian Message

Many scholars of Gnosticism have the (bad) habit of speaking of "editors" or "revisions" whenever "seams" appear in Gnostic treatises. So self-evident does this seem to these scholars that they almost presume to have been present when these texts were written. They treat the Gnostic treatise as if it were a conscious elaboration or even a philosophical treatise that is expected to exhibit logical coherence and to be free of contradiction. Whenever scholars encounter internal contradictions, they claim the existence of disparate sources, which, so they argue, have been pieced together into a treatise. Scholarly fantasies have no limits, since the poor authors of these texts can no longer defend themselves against these allegations.

By contrast, nobody objects to inconsistencies occurring in the manifestations of the unconscious, as these are the order of the day. This happens because the unconscious is subject to another order than a purely logical one: namely, context. Various treatises found at Nag Hammadi exhibit features typical of the products of the unconscious. This, of course, immediately raises the question how biblical citations and ancient philosophy entered these texts. This is hardly surprising, since the unconscious draws on the entire stock of cultural knowledge. A nice, although much later, testimony in this respect is the *Aurora consurgens*, a text attributed to Thomas Aquinas. In "Did Thomas Aquinas write the 'Aurora consurgens?'" Marie-Louise von Franz provides conclusive evidence that this text was written by a cleric who knew his Bible by heart and whose biblical and alchemical references seek to express an overwhelming inner experience.[1] Studying this example offers us insights into how the unconscious uses cultural knowledge to impart itself to consciousness.

The elements from which novelty arises are well known. The work done by scholars of Gnosticism is doubtless important. I have absolute admiration for their erudition and painstaking endeavor to trace the origins of the elements assembled in a particular treatise. Works on mineralogy do not discuss Cologne Cathedral, although this magnificent building is made of stone, because the synthesis is more than the sum of its elements. Scholars of Gnosticism are not familiar enough with the unconscious. They are often theologians interested in fathoming unconscious primordial experiences in rational terms. This, I argue, explains why the particular character of the Nag Hammadi scriptures has eluded these scholars.

Typical of the products of the unconscious is their *compensatory* nature, compensatory relative to consciousness. This led Jung to regard Gnosticism as an unconscious *reception* of the emergence of Christianity:

> By this term I mean to delineate those specifically psychic reactions aroused by the impact that the figure and message of Christ had on the pagan world, most prominently those allegories and symbols such as fish, snake, lion, peacock, etc., characteristic of the first Christian centuries, but also those much more extensive amplifications due to Gnosticism, which clearly were meant to illuminate and render more comprehensible the metaphysical role of the Saviour. (CW 18/II 1827)

In his "Address at the Presentation of the Jung Codex" on November 15, 1953, he elaborated on these thoughts:

---

[1] *Mysterium coniunctionis*, GW 14/III.

> For the modern mind this accumulation of symbols, parables, and synonyms has just the opposite effect, since it only deepens the darkness and entangles the light-bringer in a network of barely intelligible analogies.
>
> Gnostic amplification, as we encounter it in Hippolytus, has a character in part hymn-like, in part dream-like, which one invariably finds where an aroused imagination is trying to clarify an as yet still unconscious content. These are, on the one hand, intellectual, philosophical—or rather, theosophical—speculations, and, on the other, analogies, synonyms, and symbols whose psychological nature is immediately convincing. The phenomenon of assimilation mainly represents the reaction of the psychic matrix, i.e., the unconscious, which becomes agitated and responds with archetypal images, thereby demonstrating to what degree the message has penetrated into the depths of the psyche and how the unconscious interprets the phenomenon of Christ. (CW 18/II §1828)

Unfortunately the translations of the Nag Hammadi scriptures were not accessible to Jung when he formulated these ideas. However, he had avidly studied all of the sizable corpus of previously extant Gnostic literature, as well as the writings of the ancient church fathers, who fiercely opposed the Gnostics.

If we ignore the doubtful biography of Christ in the synoptic gospels, then darkness surrounds the beginnings of Christianity. I have discussed the intellectual environment of Hellenism in such detail because it represents the unconscious conditions for the appearance of the God-man. The numerous parallel manifestations (Heracles, Dionysus, Osiris, etc.) bear witness to the constellation of the archetypal anthropos. This manifested itself in the archetypal figure of Christ, which assimilated several traits of its parallel manifestations and thus expanded its own dimensions. The established church associated this archetype with the historical figure of Jesus. For Gnosticism, this concretism was too unspiritual, which explains why the Gnostics mostly understood this figure in purely spiritual terms. The historical figure, however, convinced the ordinary person far more than the spiritual Christ of Gnosticism. Had the Gnostics not been possessed, we would be looking at a somewhat pallid image of the God-man compared to the lively figure apparent in the gospels. Gnosticism, however, is a spiritual church and thus convinces only those who are connected with the living spirit, the *pneumatics*.

The two currents are *complementary*: the one that found the anthropos embodied in a concrete figure (i.e., Jesus) and the one for whom he is a spiritual figure. For the former, the archetype is projected, which involves the danger that the divine remains outside, as proven by the resistance against the "Christ in you" (Romans 8:10). For the latter, the danger is that the archetype does not become real enough, except if the state of possession, that is, numinosity, comes to its aid. Probably, the established church sensed the lack of spirituality and therefore supplemented the three synoptic gospels with the Gospel of John and the Epistles of Paul. This becomes clear, among other things, in the fact that popular scriptures, like *The Shepherd of Hermas*, were not included in the canon because they fell short of spiritual standards. Why, one might ask, were the so-called "Apostolic Fathers" not included in the canon? In its confrontation with Gnosticism, the established church seems to have been infected by the latter insofar as it supplemented its too concretistic attitude by absorbing more spiritual scriptures. Or how else should one understand that Paul, who knew only a spiritual Christ, assumed such dogmatic weight?

While little is known about when and in which form the gospels emerged, just as little is known about the genesis of the Gnostic Nag Hammadi scriptures. The latter are assumed to go back to an original ancient Greek manuscript, which was translated into Coptic, as the numerous Grecisms and translation errors suggest. Only in highly exceptional cases, such as the *Gospel of Thomas* (NHC II,2), have Greek parallels been found. Possibly, most Gnostic scriptures developed parallel to canonical ones, since initially no one assumed that individual texts possessed greater authority than others.

At this juncture, I must reiterate that the confrontation with Gnosticism may account for the fact that certain scriptures were separated from the rest and canonized. The five books written by Irenaeus against the Gnostics less describe Gnostic teachings than they distinguish his own theology from Gnosticism. Since various other spiritual scriptures were accepted into the canon, this may well have been awkward. A theology, i.e., a systematization of these texts, did not emerge until the latter half of the second century. I would therefore gather that the Gnostic "ur-texts" need to be dated much earlier than hitherto assumed, even though testimonies thereof are sparse. The fact that Gnostic treatises include Christian testimonies points to their ubiquitousness. These are not citations from the existing gospels, which were fixed in writing only later anyway. Quite possibly, many Gnostic visions or revelations may have circulated by word of mouth, before one felt compelled to commit them to paper. As a non-theologian, I must leave aside the problem of Marcion's significance for the emergence of the canon, also because this issue is too controversial. In the foregoing discussion, I have referred to the Gnostic scriptures known to us from the discovery at Nag Hammadi. I have not referred to the great Gnostic theologians like Valentinus and Basilides, whose original writings have survived only in scant fragments.[2] What is certain, however, is that in the early period no testimony was credited with absolute truth; a historical-critical conception of such texts was still a very remote prospect. What mattered was the spirit in which a tradition expressed itself.

---

[2] Markschies, *Valentinus Gnosticus?*

Nowadays, we are far too obsessed with whether an event is historically verifiable. With synchronistic events, however, external facts are less important than spiritual meaning. Jung has illustrated this in *Aion* by highlighting the coincidence of fish symbolism and the astrological Age of Pisces (CW 9/II). Gnostic scriptures may therefore be seen as a spiritual reaction to the "historical" events depicted in the gospels; a reaction not in terms of a contradiction, but in an attempt to reveal the other side of the coin. Presumably, these views did not rival each other at first. Some were more attracted to one view, others more to the other. This is a matter of temperament, as I explained in the first volume, based on the controversy between *devotio* and Gnosticism (Chapter 3).

I would like to verify these hypotheses by studying a concrete example: a comparison of *Eugnostos* (NHC III,3) and the *Sophia of Jesus Christ* (NHC III,4). These scriptures follow each other directly in the same codex. *Eugnostos the Blessed*, as the first treatise is fully titled, has also survived in Codex V,1; the *Sophia of Jesus Christ* has been handed down as the third scripture in the Berlin Codex 8502,3. This suggests that both texts were popular among a wider audience. *Eugnostos* is said to be a non-Christian Gnostic scripture, whereas the *Sophia of Jesus Christ*," on account of its parallels, appears as a Christian reworking of the first text. Eugnostos means "the one who is well known." He conveys his message to "his own" in epistolary form, which establishes a certain intimacy, which seems to contrast with the text's seemingly philosophical content. At the very beginning, however, Eugnostos resists the philosophers, since his message is a revelation. Not, however, in the usual form, as in some Nag Hammadi treatises, where the revelation is mentioned explicitly and guaranteed the truth.

With these treatises, we are in the comfortable position of having not only four versions of Coptic texts, and even fifty lines of a Greek text (*Oxyrhynchos Papyrus* 1081), but also numerous editions. I refer to the following:

1. M. Krause, "Der Eugnostosbrief," *Die Gnosis*, vol. 2, p. 32 and 37ff. Edited by W. Foerster (1971).

2. M. Tardieu, *Codex de Berlin*, pp. 47–67 and 167–215, 347–402 (Paris, 1984).

3. D. M. Parrot, Nag Hammadi Codices III, 3–4 and V,1 with Papyrus Berolinesis 8502,3 and Oxyrhychus Papyrus 1081 (Leiden 1991).

4. Cathérine Barry, "La Sagesse de Jésus-Christ," *Bibliothèque copte*, vol. 20 (Québec, 1993).[3]

Of course, I can comment on these texts solely from the perspective of depth psychology.

Already the title "Sagesse" has baffled scholars of Gnosticism. They consoled themselves with the existence of an extensive sapiential literature, not only within the Old Testament (The Book of Wisdom, Proverbs, Ecclesiastes, Sirach, Job), but also elsewhere (The Odes of Solomon), as well as in the literature of the ancient Orient.[4] One such text even exists among the Nag Hammadi scriptures: the *Teachings of Silvanus* (NHC VII,4).[5] Our treatise (BG 3; III, 4) does not exhibit the features typical of sapiential literature. I have in mind rather the significant role played by the *Sophia* in Gnosticism. The "teachings" that the resurrected one imparts to his disciples and female companions do not resemble the doctrines of wisdom, but rather Gnostic revelations or intuitions of the collective unconscious. This is the function of the female Sophia as a mediator between the material world on the one hand, and the spiritual one on the other. Thus, Christ does not appear to them in his earthly form, but as an "invisible spirit"). This revelation recurs in many other Nag Hammadi scriptures after his

---

[3] In the subsequent discussion, these authors are cited using the above numerals. A complete bibliography is included at the end of this volume.

[4] Pritchard, *Ancient Near Eastern Texts*.

[5] Zandee, *The Teaching of Sylvanus*.

death and after his resurrection, i.e., in an intermediate stage. The rationale underlying this arrangement is that in his life Christ has done and spoken everything that is recorded in the gospels. Now, in this intermediate stage, he supplements his message with "esoteric" communications, which represent an addition to the secret meaning of the gospels. Whereas the "truth" of the gospels is presumed, it must nevertheless be supplemented with secret meaning. This lies not on the concrete level, but on the spiritual one. A clear, and typically Gnostic, question emerges from the text: what is the foundation of the totality, the order, the holy providence, the power of the archons, and everything that the savior has done under their rule amid the mystery of the divine order? Essentially, the Gnostics are concerned with the same questions, which ultimately lead to the pivotal issue: their redemption.

It might be objected that the savior has already redeemed humanity through his death on the cross. But I am not sure whether the early Christians entertained this idea so very clearly or whether it was perhaps formulated only later by theology. In any event, the Gnostics did not feel fully redeemed by Christ's death on the cross. They felt, instead, that they had to contribute to their own redemption, and thereby anticipated the alchemists (CW 12 §332). In actual fact, the Gnostic idea that attaining consciousness (Gnosis) is absolutely necessary for redemption, complements the Christian notion of redemption. On its own, either conception is one-sided. The Christian conception expects all salvation to come from God. Burdened by original sin, it feels utterly dependent on divine grace and condemned to passivity. Consciously proud of its human dignity, and its likeness with God, the Gnostic conception tries to shake off the yoke of an incapable Creator, banishing him to agnosia in the search for a true spiritual home through knowing (gnosis) the unrecognizable Father. Whereas the Christian attitude places the human being beneath God, the Gnostic, conscious of having tasted the Tree of Knowledge (Genesis 3:5), elevates himself to become an equal partner: "and you will be like

God, knowing...." *The Hypostasis of the Archons* (NHC II,4) recounts how in Paradise the serpent, appearing as a female spirit, presumably Sophia, instructs the primordial parents to eat from the Tree of Knowledge to overcome the archontic powers.

Gnosticism was often accused of *self-redemption*. This, however, is as incorrect as it is with the alchemists. Still, the redeemer occupies a different role among the Gnostics than among the Christians. In the above treatise, it is the female spirit within the serpent that offers the primordial parents salvific advice, without which they would have remained trapped within their ignorance. The redemptive authority helps the Gnostics attain salvific illumination. This coincides with the psychological experience in which we will struggle in vain for the liberating insight unless the divine light has mercy on us, whether in a clarifying dream, a life-saving idea, or an instinctive reaction. So instead of self-redemption, the Gnostics assume a much more active role in the redemptive event. In our treatise, Christ is the angel of light (*grand ange de la lumière*).

Only the names in this frame narrative, which is missing from *Eugnostos*, are Christian. Hence, we cannot justifiably speak of a Christian revision (1, p. 35). The Christian aspect manifests itself not primarily in citations from the gospels, but in the form of Christian ideas. Notably, both are absent from the introduction to this text.

Now follow the actual instruction and the parallel between *Eugnostos* and the *Sophia of Jesus Christ*. In the latter, instruction is introduced by the question concerning both the foundation of the totality and the savior's mission. This is the central Gnostic question. The answer given by the revelatory angel is characteristic: while all philosophers have tried to answer this question, they have all failed, because each found a different answer, whereas in fact there is only *one* truth. Some philosophers, like Epicurus, claim it is a pure spirit; others, like Philo of Alexandria in the first century,[6] maintain it is providence; yet others assert it is fate (Heimarmene).

We have already come across the trinity Pronoia, Ananke, and Heimarmene in Hermeticism. To avoid unnecessary repetition, I refer the reader to the corresponding discussion.[7] The *Tripartite Tractate* (NHC I,5) also resists Greek philosophy (109, 24–110,22) and mentions similar categories.[8] Thus, the Gnostic author distinguishes himself from both philosophy and astrology. For the Gnostics, Greek philosophy is inspired by lower powers anyway, because the Greeks worship stone and other hylic forces. Basilides calls Greek philosophy *inanis* (inane, empty) and *curiosa varietas* (exhibiting a questionable variety) (fragment 1). The testimonies of Gnostic rejection could be extended at will. Gnosticism, therefore, must be understood as a *counter-reaction to ancient philosophy*. The self-evident objection to this claim is that Gnosticism refers heavily to the ancient philosophers. Yet a knowledge of ancient philosophy gained through Neoplatonism belonged to the cultural inventory informing Gnosticism. Drawing such clear boundaries, the Gnostics sought to refer to their own—"supernatural"—source of inspiration. Today, we would simply call this the unconscious, since it is not subject to any nature. Christ, as the angel of light, is such a source of inspiration, not the earthly Jesus of the gospels: "Only he who came from the eternal light knows it and can offer instruction about the real nature of the truth" (BG 81, 17–82,2).

Considering how much Christian theology owes to ancient philosophy in its distilling of a dogmatics from the revelation enables us to gauge just how far removed it is from Gnosticism. The Gnostics had to liberate themselves from these dogmatics to attain "true knowledge." Those who are born to receive knowledge will do so because they

---

[6] De Providentia (I,33), citation 4.
[7] For a good summary, see Nock-Festugière, *Corpus Hermeticum* III LXXIX–LXXXIII.
[8] Thomassen and Painchaud, *Le Traité Tripartite*, p. 412.

descend from "the First One who was sent," "the Immortal One amid the mortals." "No one can find the truth, says Matthew, other than through you" (i.e., the angel of light) (BG 83,1–2). The only "Christianized" element in the *Sophia of Jesus Christ* is that the revelations are induced by the questions asked by the disciples. This seems to have precious little to do with orthodox Christianity.

The revealer explains that the unrecognizable Father of the totality *is who he is* because he is intangible. The reference to the transcendental principle as "Being" is not specific to Exodus 3:14, but appears in Jewish, Christian, and other Hellenistic speculations on the first principle. Human beings can recognize him only through Jesus Christ: "I am the Great Redeemer," he says of himself (BG 83,13).

The Gnostic redeemer does not nail human sins to the cross, but helps the pneumatics to attain knowledge. This is the purpose of the instructions he gives to his disciples. The unbegotten one can be described only in terms of negative theology (immortal, unbegotten, ungoverned, nameless, lacking human form, infinite, imperishable). "He is the Father of the Totality" (BG 86,5).

Hence, Philip's question is purely logical: "How does [the Unrecognizable One] manifest Himself to the Perfect [the pneumatic Gnostics]?" (BG 86,6).

The revealing spirit explains how everything became from "He who is." If we compare this to the corresponding passages in the *Septem Sermones*, interpreted in the first volume of this book, a remarkable similarity becomes evident.[9] The *Tripartite Tractate* summarizes matters:

> In order to be able to speak about exalted things, it is necessary that we begin with the Father, who is the root of the All and from whom we have obtained grace to speak about him. For he

---
[9] 1,6–2,3, pp. 152-160.

existed before anything else had come into being except him alone. (NHC 51,1–8)

It continues as follows:

> The Father is singular while being many. For he is first and he is unique, though without being solitary. How else could he be a father? For from the word "father" it follows that there is a "son." That singular one who is the only Father is in fact like a tree that has a trunk, branches, and fruit. Of him it may be said that he is a true father, incomparable and immutable, because he is truly singular and God. For no one is god for him and no one is father to him—he has not been born—and no other has brought him into being. For whoever is the father of somebody, or his maker, himself has a father and a maker in turn. It is certainly possible that he may become the father and the maker of whoever comes into being from him and is made by him; still, he is not a father in the true sense or a god, insofar as [52] someone has given [birth to him and] has brought him into being. The only Father and God in the true sense, therefore, <is> the one who has been born by no one, but who, on the contrary, has given birth to the All and has brought it into being. (NHC 51,1–30)

Strangely, Hippolytus' *Refutatio omnium haeresium* (VI 29,2 and 29,5) coincides with the above passage and demonstrates that it contains typically Gnostic thinking. Thus it is questionable whether the various schools are as distinct as is commonly assumed. Hippolytus attributes these thoughts to the Valentinians:

> As for what we can say about the things which are exalted, what is fitting is that we begin with the Father, who is the root of the

Totality, the one from whom we have received grace to speak about him.

He existed before anything other than himself came into being. The Father is a single one, like a number, for he is the first one and the one who is only himself. Yet he is not like a solitary individual. Otherwise, how could he be a father? For whenever there is a "father," the name "son" follows. But the single one, who alone is the Father, is like a *root*,[10] with tree, branches and fruit. It is said of him that he is a father in the proper sense, since he is inimitable and immutable. Because of this, he is single in the proper sense, and is a god, because no one is a god for him nor is anyone a father to him. For he is unbegotten, and there is no other who begot him, nor another who created him. For whoever is someone's father or his creator, he, too, has a father and creator. It is certainly possible for him to be father and creator of the one who came into being from him and the one whom he created, for he is not a father in the proper sense, nor a god, because he has someone who begot him and who created him. It is, then, only the Father and God in the proper sense that no one else begot. (NHC I,5; 51,1–30)

Considering these texts, we must remind ourselves that the Gnostics were not practicing philosophers, even if that is what they sound like. These texts circumscribe something indescribable, an inner Gnostic experience, something discovered afresh although it existed beforehand, yet only as a projection. Today, we call it the *self*:

As a result of the complete detachment of all affective ties to the object, there is necessarily formed in the inner self an equivalent of objective reality, or a complete identity of inside and outside,

---

[10] My emphasis, echoing the title of the first volume.

which is technically described as *tat tvam asi* (that art thou). The fusion of the self with its relations to the object[11] produces the identity of the self (*atman*) with the essence of the world (i.e., with the relations of subject to object), so that the identity of the inner with the outer *atman* is cognized. (CW 6 §189)

Elsewhere, Jung defines the self as follows:

> As an empirical concept, the self designates the whole range of psychic phenomena in man. It expresses the unity of the personality as a whole. But in so far as the total personality, on account of its unconscious component, can be only in part conscious, the concept of the self is, in part, only potentially empirical and is to that extent a *postulate*. In other words, it encompasses both the experienceable and the inexperienceable (or the not yet experienced). It has these qualities in common with very many scientific concepts that are more names than ideas. In so far as psychic totality, consisting of both conscious and unconscious contents, is a postulate, it is a *transcendental* concept, for it presupposes the existence of unconscious factors on empirical grounds and thus characterizes an entity that can be described only in part but, for the other part, remains at present unknowable and illimitable. (CW 6 §789)

The reader may be wondering how I have gone from these magnificent transcendental Gnostic statements to empirical psychology. We do not know what these Gnostic speculations beyond the human sphere could be based on, except that they make sense only if they are integrated into human life. We can compare them here with similar experiences and recognize their eminent numinous value. This helps us to understand

---

[11] See Chapter 4, "The Problem of Matter."

the exalted style of Gnostic texts. Depth psychology, as an empirical science, strives to classify phenomena in a sanguine manner. This, however, does not mean that it overlooks their emotional content. The Gnostics were literally "ensouled" by their experiences.

In the gospels, there is abundant mention of God, but seemingly without any need for closer description. Jesus bears witness to God, who is characterized by Jesus' words and deeds. The introverted Gnostics explored this question in greater depth. In this sense, the myth recounted in the *Tripartite Tractate* establishes that God's "love" consists in his relationship with his creatures. This myth also suggests that God created these creatures to avoid solitude after spending an eternity on his own. He sought an opposite, with whom he could engage in a relationship, and therefore revealed himself to humans in search of recognition. This is the human deliverance from unconsciousness, which is not willed by God, and the acceptance into the pleroma (fullness).

The next question (BG 87,8–11) comes from Thomas. In the Nag Hammadi treatises, he occupies a privileged position as the twin brother of Jesus: the corpus includes the *Gospel of Thomas* (NHC II,2) and the *Book of Thomas* (NHC II,7). In the latter, the savior tells Thomas:

> Examine yourself and understand who you are, how you exist, and how you will come to be. Since you are to be called my brother, it is not fitting for you to be ignorant of yourself. And I know that you have understood, for already you have understood that I am the knowledge of truth. So while you are walking with me, though you do lack understanding, already you have obtained knowledge and you will be called one who knows himself. For those who have not known themselves have known nothing, but those who have known themselves already have acquired knowledge about the depth of the All. So then, my

brother Thomas, you have seen what is hidden from people, what they stumble against in their ignorance. (138,8–18)

This passage reveals just how important self-knowledge is for the Gnostics. It is identical with knowing the totality, and thus the unrecognizable Father. The *Gospel of Truth* (NHC I,3) says:

But those who are to receive teaching [are] the living who are inscribed in the book of the living. It is about themselves that they receive instruction, receiving it from the Father, turning again to him. Since the perfection of the totality is in the Father, it is necessary for the totality to ascend to him. Then, if one has knowledge [gnosis], he receives what are his own and draws them to himself. For he who is ignorant is in need, and what lacks is great, since he lacks that which will make him perfect. Since the perfection of the totality is in the Father and it is necessary for the totality to ascend to him and for each one to receive what are his own, he enrolled them in advance, having prepared them to give to those who came forth from him. (21,3–25)

This passage amplifies and complements the previous ones in two ways. First, the revelation and instruction of the Gnostic serves no other purpose than self-knowledge. What once possessed cosmological or theological form is now formulated in psychological terms, because ultimately it is about individuation. This process concerns the question of "what are his own." "Perfection," in our text, therefore means completeness and not perfection, i.e., the attainment of a "totality."

According to the *Excerpts of Theodotus*, the purpose of Gnosticism is to raise the following questions:

Who were we? What have we become?

Where were we? Were we cast out?

Toward which goal are we hastening? From where have we redeemed ourselves?

What is creation? And what recreation? (72,2)

In the course of history, seemingly grotesque comments on the Gnostic revelations have been deployed to answer these questions. Martin Buber, for instance, remarked, somewhat derogatorily yet humorously, that the Gnostic "draws the map of the seventh heaven."[12] I sincerely hope my readers have gained a different impression. Logion 2 of the *Gospel of Thomas* (NHC II,2) says:

> Jesus said, "Let one who seeks not stop seeking until one finds. When one finds, one will be troubled. When one is troubled, one will marvel and will reign over all."

Logion 111b:

> Jesus said, "Whoever has found oneself, of that person the world is not worthy."

Finally, Logion 39 plainly shows how the Gnostics distinguished themselves:

> Jesus said, "The Pharisees and the scholars have taken the keys of knowledge and have hidden them. They have not entered, nor have they allowed those who want to enter to do so. As for you, be as shrewd as snakes and innocent as doves."[13]

Let us return to the text where Thomas asks, "Why did these [members of the Father] come to be, and why were they revealed?" (BG 87,9–11).

---

[12] Schilp and Friedeman, *Philosophen des 20. Jahrhunderts*, p. 273—trans.
[13] See also Luke 11:52 and Matthew 23:13.

The complicated answer given by the revealing spirit is that the "immovable race," i.e., the race that does not waver, brings forth fruit. These are the pneumatics.

The notion of the "immovable race" was unknown until the discovery of the Nag Hammadi library.[14] It occurs in five scriptures:

1. The *Apocryphon of John* (NH II, 1). Here, the revealing spirit of Christ calls on the disheartened John, and says:

> Now, therefore, lift up your face, that you may receive the things that I shall teach you today, and may tell them to your fellow spirits who are from the unwavering race of the perfect Man.

> Then he [the Lord] said to me, "The Mother-Father, who is rich in mercy, the holy Spirit in every way, the One who is merciful and who sympathizes with you (pl.), i.e., the Epinoia of the foreknowledge of light, he raised up the offspring of the perfect race and its thinking and the eternal light of man."

> It is not as Moses said, "They hid themselves in an ark" (Genesis 7:7), but they hid themselves in a place, not only Noah, but also many other people from the immovable race.

> And behold, now I shall go up to the perfect aeon. I have completed everything for you in your hearing. And I have said everything to you that you might write them down and give them secretly to your fellow spirits, for this is the mystery of the immovable race.

2. The *Gospel of the Egyptians* (NHC III, 2; IV, 2):

> The incorruptible man Adamas asked for them a son out of himself, in order that he (son) may become father of the immovable, incorruptible race....[15] (III, 51,5–9)

---

[14] Williams, *The Immovable Race*.

> She (metanoia) received her completion and her power by the will of the Father and his approval with which he approved of the great, incorruptible, immovable race of the great, mighty men of the great Seth.... (III, 59, 10–14)
>
> Then the great Seth saw the activity of the devil, and his many guises, and his schemes which will come upon his immovable, incorruptible race.... (III, 61, 16–19)

3. In the introduction to *The Three Steles of Seth* (NHC VII, 5), it says:

> The revelation of Dositheos about the three steles of Seth, the Father of the living and unwavering race.... (118, 10–13)

4. *Zostrianos* (NHC VIII, 1), the aforementioned, and fragmentary text, mentions "Seth, the father of the immovable race" (51,15).

5. Finally, the term occurs in our initial text, the *Sophia of Jesus Christ* (BG 88, 1–12):

> Because of his (= the Spirit who is) mercy and his love he wished to bring forth fruit by himself, that he might not enjoy his goodness alone but (that) other spirits of the Generation That Does Not Waver might bring forth body and fruit, glory and imperishableness and his infinite grace...

These texts help us to establish a sense of the significance of the immovable race as that of the fulfilled pneumatics. Evidently, Gnostic development strives toward this goal, without ever reaching it, however. "The mana personality," writes Jung,

---

[15] Robinson, *Nag Hammadi Library*, pp. 212, 215, 216.

is a dominant of the collective unconscious, the well-known archetype of the mighty man in the form of hero, chief, magician, medicine-man, saint, the ruler of men and spirits, the friend of God.

This masculine collective figure who now rises out of the dark background and takes possession of the conscious personality entails a psychic danger of a subtle nature, for by inflating the conscious mind it can destroy everything that was gained by coming to terms with the anima. It is therefore of no little practical importance to know that in the hierarchy of the unconscious the anima occupies the lowest rank, only one of many possible figures, and that her subjection constellates another collective figure which now takes over her mana. Actually it is the figure of the magician, as I will call it for short, who attracts the mana to himself, i.e., the autonomous valency of the anima. Only in so far as I unconsciously identify with his figure can I imagine that I myself possess the anima's mana. But I will infallibly do so under these circumstances. (CW 7 §377–78)

Within Gnosticism, the example of Simon Magus nicely illustrates this problem. He is mentioned in the *Acts of the Apostles*:

Now a certain man named Simon has previously practiced magic in the city and amazed the people of Samaria, saying that he was someone great. All of them, from the least to the greatest, listened to him eagerly, saying, 'This man is the power of God that is called Great.' And they listened eagerly to him because for a long time he amazed them with his magic. (8:9–11)

Origen reports sighting various prophets in Phoenicia and Palestine. They claimed to be the most perfect people in this region. They roved in and around the temples, with surprising ease, begging for bread, roaming the cities and fields. According to Origen's *Contra Celsum*, a familiar formula crossed their lips:

> I am God; I am the Son of God; or, I am the Divine Spirit; I have come because the world is perishing, and you, O men, are perishing for your iniquities. But I wish to save you, and you shall see me returning again with heavenly power. Blessed is he who now does me homage. On all the rest I will send down eternal fire, both on cities and on countries. And those who know not the punishments which await them shall repent and grieve in vain; while those who are faithful to me I will preserve eternally. (VII, 9)

This valuable testimony shows that the *archetype of the anthropos* was constellated in that period and subsequently assumed highly diverse forms. Considering the *eschaton* (end-time), Matthew warns that "many false prophets will arise and lead many astray" (24:11). Jesus was not alone in claiming to be the savior. Hence, in his first letter, John warns: "Beloved, do not believe every spirit, but test the spirits to see whether they are from God" (1 John 4:1).

In Book II of his *Stromata* ("Carpets"), Clement of Alexandria engages in a fundamental debate with Simon Magus:

> But the knowledge of those who think themselves wise, whether the barbarian sects or the philosophers among the Greeks, according to the apostle, "puffeth up" (1 Corinthians 8:1). But that knowledge, which is the scientific demonstration of what is delivered according to the true philosophy, is grounded on faith.... And faith is a power of God, being the strength of the truth. For example, it is said, "If ye have faith as a grain of mustard, ye shall remove the mountain" (Matthew 17:20). For the highest

demonstration, to which we have alluded, produces intelligent faith by the adducing and opening up of the Scriptures to the souls of those who desire to learn; the result of which is knowledge (gnosis).... Reason, the governing principle, remaining unmoved and guiding the soul, is called its pilot. For access to *the Immutable is obtained by a truly immutable means* (emphasis added).

These deliberations continue as follows:

> Thus Abraham was stationed before the Lord, and approaching spoke (Genesis 18:22–23). And to Moses it is said, "But do thou stand there with Me" (Deuteronomy). And the followers of Simon wish be assimilated in manners to the standing form which they adore. Faith, therefore, and the knowledge of the truth, render the soul, which makes them its choice, always uniform and equable. For congenial to the man of falsehood is shifting, and change, and turning away, as to the Gnostic are calmness, and rest, and peace. As, then, philosophy has been brought into evil repute by pride and self-conceit, so also ghosts by false ghosts called by the same name; of which the apostle writing says, "O Timothy, keep that which is committed to thy trust, avoiding the profane and vain babblings and oppositions of science (gnosis) falsely so called[16]; which some professing, have erred concerning the faith." (1 Timothy 6:20) (Chapter XI)

First, this plainly reveals the battle between pistis (faith) and Gnosis, which I discussed in the first volume in connection with the controversy between Martin Buber and C.G. Jung. In the last years of his life, Jung returned to this debate on religious belief: "As a responsible scientist I am not going to preach my personal and

---

[16] These words point to the struggles between orthodoxy and Gnosticism.

subjective convictions which I cannot prove." He added, "Either I know a thing and then I don't need to believe it; or I believe it because I am not sure that I know it" (CW 18/II §1589). This, once again, reveals that faith and Gnosis, although mutually exclusive, also complement each other.

Second, these citations clearly establish the dangers inherent in Gnosticism, as the example of Simon Magus proves. The established church would not have persecuted him with such hatred had the same inflation—namely, the identification with the mana personality—not threatened to also take hold of the devout. Jung defines the mana personality as "on one side a being of superior wisdom, on the other a being of superior will." He adds that "by making conscious the contents that underlie this personality, we find ourselves obliged to face the fact that we have learnt more and want more than other people" (CW 7 §396). "And yet Christ, and Paul after him," he continues, "wrestled with these same problems, as a number of clues still make evident" (§397).[17] He concludes that "on psychological grounds, therefore, I would recommend that no God be constructed out of the archetype of the mana-personality. In other words, he must not be concretized, for only thus can I avoid projecting my values and non-values into God and Devil, and only thus can I preserve my human dignity, my specific gravity, which I need so much if I am not to become the unresisting shuttlecock of unconscious forces" (§395).

I shall return to Simon Magus in my discussion of Helen. Simon claimed that he had come to free her, whom he calls *Ennoia* (thought), from the fetters of the world, because, as Irenaeus observes, "he conferred salvation upon men, by making himself known to them" (*Against Heresies* I 23,3).

The "immovable race" of pure Gnostics led us to fundamental reflections on the essence of Gnosticism as opposed to orthodoxy. Let

---

[17] See, for instance, Luke 4:1–13.

us now return to *Eugnostos* and the *Sophia of Jesus Christ*. The spirit declares that he is the imperishable divine, because he has been created by the Father (BG 89,15). Many who failed to make this distinction went astray and perished (BG 89,20). This stance is directed, unequivocally, against philosophy and the material world.

This reveals the tremendous difference between Gnosticism, as a spiritual religion, and alchemy, which believed that the divine mystery inhered in matter, and which also sought it there. In terms of the principle of *enantiodromia*, religions so one-sidedly committed to the spirit as Gnosticism and Christianity risk turning into their repressed opposite. Shunning the outer, material world became necessary for both as a form of rigorous introversion. This, in turn, entailed an unanticipated awakening of the inner world. Sooner or later, however, the eschewed opposite must be recognized once again ("Give therefore to the emperor the things that are the emperor's, and to God the things that are God's," Matthew 22:21). The established church did not shy away from making generous compromises with the world abhorred by the Bible (John 18:36). As far as we know, Gnosticism did not make them. Perhaps this, rather than its persecution by the established church, led to its extinction.

Mary Magdelene raises the question of the difference between impermanence and permanence. The spirit explains this in terms of the various emanations from the Father, which we need not dwell on here, since this question is a matter for specialized scholars of Gnosticism. These reflections lead to the conclusion that everything happens for the "race with kings."

The Gnostics, however, refer to themselves as the "kingless race."[18] The Naassenes derive the totality not from *one* principle, but, as Hippolytus (V 8,2) observes, from three principles: first, the "blessed nature of the blessed, higher person, Adam; second, from the mortal

---

[18] Bergmeier, "Königslosigkeit."

nature of the lower person; and third, from the undominated race without kings (*abasileutos genea*), which is begotten from above...." In the Gnostic *On the Origin of the World* (NHC II, 5), it says:

> There are many others who are kingless and superior to everyone before them... (125,2)... the fourth generation, which is the most, is kingless and perfect. (125, 5–7)

The *Apocalyse of Adam* (NHC V,5) states:

> But the generation without a king over it says that God chose him from all the aeons. He caused a knowledge of the undefiled one of truth to come to be in him. (82,19–25)

Françoise Morard, the editor of the French translation, explains:

> This expression signifies... that the spiritual ones, those whom no servitude ties to any king, rejoice in the liberty of the Spirit, because they are the sons of the One who brings it forth. They must no longer seek their origin in the Illuminator, for they know it is God who has chosen "them from all the aeons," that is, from the divine Pleroma, so that, through him, exists the knowledge of the Truth in its purity. And God himself proclaims his origin: "It is brought forth by a foreign air."[19]

Considering the Simonians, mentioned above, Irenaeus asserts that those who believe in Simon and Helen "being free, live as they please; for men are saved through his grace, and not on account of their own righteous actions." Also, "those who are his should be freed from the

---

[19] Morard, *L'Apocalyse d'Adam*, p. 55—trans.

rule of them [the powers] who made the world" (*Against Heresies* I 23,3).

We have already noted the liberation from the powers of Heimarmene. In the first volume, I commented variously on Carpocrates.[20] There is no need, however, to rehearse those points here even if they belong to our present topic. According to Valentinian teaching, as the *Excerpts of Theodotus* say, human beings can be divided into three categories: "Now the spiritual is saved by nature, but the psychic has free-will, and has the capacity for both faith and incorruptibility... but the material perishes by nature" (56,3).

In *The Search for Roots*, the first volume of this work, I tried to respond to the overbearing hubris of the Gnostics from the perspective of current depth psychology.[21] They are no longer subject to the law as the Jews of the ancient confederation were. They feel privileged due to their direct descendency from the Father. In the individuation process, this corresponds to the dissociation from the collective super-ego (Freud) and to turning toward one's own conscience. Jung writes:

> So, too, our moral reactions exemplify the original behaviour of the psyche, while moral laws are a late concomitant of moral behaviour, congealed into precepts. In consequence, they appear to be identical with the moral reaction, that is, with conscience. This delusion becomes obvious the moment a conflict of duty makes clear the difference between conscience and the moral code. (CW 10 §837)

Gnostic hubris is utterly unnecessary, since it is difficult to take the right decision in concrete situations and to follow one's conscience. It is much easier to follow the collective moral code, provided its principles were imparted to one at an early age. One need not even be particularly

---

[20] *The Search for Roots*, p. 114.
[21] Ibid., pp. 111ff.

conscious of one's decisions, because that code is already deeply ingrained. Thus, the collective moral code is perfectly adequate in most everyday situations. Difficulties arise when obligations clash, when both rules are correct, and when subtle decisions are required. The moral code is a statistical rule, which is correct in most cases, but not in all. Conscience, as an instinctive function, corrects us, if necessary, precisely when we have *not* violated the code. We tend to say, "I have a bad conscience," except that the bad conscience has me and leaves me no peace. This indicates that it is an autonomous function, which is not perturbed whether or not we agree with it.

Gnostic asceticism, which can be observed again and again, suggests that the Gnostics also took conscience seriously and did not recklessly place themselves above the laws of the Old Testament, as the church fathers made out. This is yet another example of how the established church had not completely overcome the old, traditional ways. Especially in the Reformed Church, sermons mostly conclude with the priest admonishing the congregation to lead a good, moral life. Church charities outdo each other with good deeds as if it were a matter of absolving oneself from guilt. Absolving oneself from guilt, and striving for atonement through good deeds, are the eternal cycle of Christianity. Gnosticism succumbed less to this cycle, because its guilt consists solely in remaining unconscious.

Our text continues as follows:

> Now the Unknowable is full of every glory and imperishableness and ineffable joy. And they [men over whom there is no kingdom] all are at rest in him, every rejoicing in ineffable joy in his unchanging glory and the measureless jubilation that was never heard or even known among all the aeons and their worlds until now. (BG 92,16–93,12)

This passage depicts the blissful state of the chosen in the world to come. Such redemption from the material world is typical and recurs throughout the Nag Hammadi scriptures. Although Jacques Menard is an acclaimed scholar of Gnosticism,[22] I disagree with his derivation of Gnostic *anapausis* from Matthew 11:20–30:

> Come to me, all you that are weary and are carrying heavy burdens, and I will give you rest. Take my yoke upon you, and learn from me; for I am gentle and humble in heart, and you will find rest for your souls. For my yoke is easy, and my burden is light.

As I shall try to show, anapausis is a very particular kind of intermission or rest. Along these lines, the previous passage may be compared to Hebrews 4:9–11:

> So then, a sabbath rest still remains for the people of God; for those who enter God's rest also cease from their labours as God did from his. Let us therefore make every effort to enter that rest, so that no one may fall through such disobedience as theirs.

In the *Revelation of John*, it says:

> And I heard a voice from heaven saying, 'Write this: Blessed are the dead who from now on die in the Lord.' 'Yes,' says the Spirit, 'they will rest from their labours, for their deeds follow them.' (14:13)

---

[22] See, among others, his essay "Le Repos, Salut du Gnostique."

To enable the reader thus inclined to gain some idea of the difference between biblical rest and Gnostic *anapausis*, here are some relevant passages. The first is from the *Gospel of the Truth* (NHC I,3):

> And they [= who possess (something) from above of the immeasurable greatness] do not go down to Hades nor have they envy nor groaning nor death within them, but they rest in him [= the perfect one] who is at rest, not striving nor being twisted around the truth. But they themselves are the truth; and the Father is within them and they are in the Father.... (42,17–28)

Meister Eckhart says that a soul that is born in God is not blessed until God is born in the soul.[23] This suggests that in the first case, "God has not yet come into the world," since the world takes his place. The rigorous introversion of the Gnostics devalued and introjected the world to such an extent that for them it became the inner God, the Christ in you. This is the state of genuine rest, when the vicissitudes of the external world do not toss one from one emotion into another. Biblical Christianity, which insisted on the historicity of the savior, failed to seek the *inner God-man*. Despite all assurances to the contrary, resting in faith is deceptive, because doubt never strays far from belief. It is therefore projected onto a state after death:

> ...through the mercies of the Father the aeons may know him and cease labouring in search of the Father, resting there in him, knowing that this is the rest. (24,14–20)

> Who, therefore, will be able to utter a name for him the great name, except him alone to whom the name belongs and the sons of the name in whom rested the name of the Father, (who) in turn themselves rested in his name. (38,24–32)

---

[23] *The Search for Roots*, p. 86f.

The poetic language should not overly confuse us, because this is characteristic of archetypal expression. Our task, instead, is to unearth the basic ideas lying behind the arabesques.

The *Letter to Rheginus, or Treatise on the Resurrection* (NHC I,4) states:

> They [those who are not Gnostics] seek rather their own rest, which we have received through our Savior, our Lord Jesus. We received it when we came to know the truth and rested ourselves upon it. (43,34–44,3)

This passage is interesting, because it illustrates the difference between the members of the established church, who find repose in their belief in the Lord, as the various Bible citations indicate, and the Gnostics, whom the spirit of Christ guides toward true knowledge and who find rest therein. Rather than rejecting the Bible, the Gnostics understand it as addressing an inner reality, not as an outer one. Therefore, Jesus Christ often appears as a spirit, who instructs the Gnostics and, as an inner illuminating authority, guides them toward knowledge.

The final text of the Jung Codex, the *Tripartite Tractate* (NHC I,5) says:

> Not only those who have come forth from the Logos, about whom alone we said that they would accomplish the good work, but also those whom these brought forth according to the good disposition will share in the repose according to the abundance of the grace. (131,14–22)

This passage is interesting, because it concerns the *psychikoi*, the members of the established church. They have freedom of choice. With good works, and due to their good disposition, they can attain the repose of the *pneumatikoi*. Therefore, doing good is important for the *psychikoi*. Ultimately, however, grace is paramount. Another passage in the same treatise states:

> And they first chose for themselves honor, though it was only a temporary wish and desire, while the path to eternal rest is by way of humility for salvation of those who will be saved, those of the right ones. (121,22–29)

The Gnostics, then, did not feel immune to worldly temptations, but needed to overcome such lures to reach the path of genuine humility, which leads to salvation. Importantly, humility can neither be feigned nor conjured up. Ambition belongs to life and is not simply negative. Ultimately, while the libido makes us strive for things, our goal shifts in the second half of life, from the material to the transcendental.

Logion 51 in the *Gospel of Thomas* (NHC II,2) includes a surprising statement:

> His disciples said to him, "When will the rest for the dead take place, and when the new world come?" He said to them, "What you look for has come, but you do not know it." (51, 1–2)

In his commentary on the French edition, Ménard interprets the answer as a reference to the immanence of the event, although in many scriptures it is projected into the world beyond. Despite this difference, we need not doubt the Gnostic nature of this logion. It corresponds to the active role played by the Gnostics in their redemption.

The *Dialogue of the Savior* (NHC III,5)[24] begins with the savior telling the disciples:

---

[24] Emmel, *The Dialogue of the Savior*, p. 41.

> Already the time has come, brothers, for us to abandon our labor and stand at rest. For whoever stands at rest will rest forever. (120,1–8)

This clearly establishes that anapausis should not be understood eschatologically, but ought to be attained in the here and now, because it signifies a state of equilibrium between opposites. Isaiah (65:17–25) describes this eschatological Kingdom of Peace as follows:

> For I am about to create new heavens and a new earth… be glad and rejoice for ever… for I am about to create Jerusalem as a joy, and delight in my people…. They shall not labour in vain… for they shall be offspring blessed by the Lord—and their descendants as well….. The wolf and the lamb shall feed together, the lion shall eat straw like the ox.

Were the Gnostics spelling out Isaiah in striking a similar eulogistic note about the place of rest in the *Sophia of Jesus Christ* (BG 92,16–93,12)? Whoever holds this view, and many scholars of Gnosticism do, has precious little faith in the creative impulse. Even if these passages sound quite similar, they are both genuine. Naturally, the Isaiah passage is ever present in the unconscious inventory of the Gnostics, and it can enter things unconsciously. Gnostic scholarship, however, describes the genesis of a treatise always as if an "ur-text" had existed; as if it had been cobbled together from numerous earlier citations, which were manifoldly formulated and revised until they took on the form known to us today. Frequent attempts were made to reconstruct the "ur-text," because this was believed to represent the "original" version. This myth informs Gnostic scholarship, but it has precious little to do with historical reality. Because they were deeply respected, religious texts are known to have been transmitted very faithfully. If corrections or revisions were made, then that was because the spirit of the age receiving a particular text had changed. While our discussion of the *Sophia of Jesus Christ* (compared to that of *Eugnostos*) has extended previous knowledge about this treatise, it has not revealed any "Christianization," i.e., that Christian ideas were smuggled into the text instead of Gnostic ones.

The above Isaiah passage originates in the prophesying of the coming kingdom of peace:

> The wolf shall live with the lamb, the leopard shall lie with the kid, the calf and the lion and the fatling together, and a little child shall lead them. The cow and the bear shall graze, their young shall lie down together; and the lion shall eat straw like the ox. The nursing child shall play over the hole of the asp, and the weaned child shall put its hand on the adder's den. (11:6–8)

Common to both texts is not the wording, but the archetypal idea of a kingdom of eternal peace, which is described in very different images in the Revelation of John (Chapter 21). This is far from a merely Christian or Gnostic idea, but a universal one. Crucially, the first verse says:

> Then I saw a new heaven and a new earth; for the first heaven and the first earth had passed away, and the sea was no more. (21:1)

This suggests that *metanoia*, i.e., a fundamental change of mind and transformation of the worldview, has occurred. Nothing is as it used to be. Thus the kingdom of peace and rest can now begin. Being at one with oneself is the final repose. This signifies the security and stability of the individuated personality, which the Gnostics call *anapausis*.

In the *Gospel of the Egyptians* (NHC III,2), the notion of rest occurs in a hymnal passage:

> I see thee, O thou who art invisible to everyone. For who will be able to comprehend thee in another tongue? Now that I know thee, I have mixed myself with the immutable. I have become light.... I was shaped in the circle of the riches of the light which is in my bosom.... O God of silence! I honor thee completely. Thou art my place of rest.... Therefore the incense of life is in me.... (66,22–67,23)

This describes the anticipated transfiguration of the Gnostic who has attained his goal.

In the *Gospel of Mary* (BG 1), the soul that ascends to the highest heaven after death replies to the lower world, where wrath resides, as follows:

> What binds me has been slain, and what surrounds me has been destroyed, and my desire has been brought to an end, and ignorance has died. In a [world], I was set loose from a world and in a type, from a type that is above, and from the chain of forgetfulness, which exists in time. From this hour on, for the time of the due season of the age, I will receive rest in silence. (16,17–17,7)

This passage shows that anapausis means overcoming the emotions arising from the conflict between opposites. These are the unconscious fetters that hold the soul captive in the world. I shall discuss this idea further in the next chapter. The soul liberates itself by recalling that it is created in the image of the Father. These shackles, therefore, are merely temporary, whereas rest is timeless.

In an expanded section, the *Sophia of Jesus Christ* repeats this fundamental idea:

Now I have taught you about Immortal Man and have loosed the bonds of the robbers from him. I have broken the gates of the pitiless ones in their presence. I have humiliated their malicious intent, and they all have been shamed and have risen from their ignorance. Because of this, then, I came here, that they might be joined with that Spirit and Breath, and might from two become a single one, just as from the first, that you might yield much fruit and go up to Him Who Is from the Beginning, with ineffable joy and glory and honor and grace of the Father of the Universe. Whoever, then, knows the Father in pure knowledge will go to the Father and repose in Unbegotten Father. (BG 121,13–123,6)

This summarizes and again illustrates how the Gnostic must free himself from the fetters of the archontic powers with the help of the savior. The Gnostic's inner turmoil yields to the unity attained through the knowledge of the Father, who is indeed a Father. This leads to jubilation and repose. This, I hope, establishes how Gnostic anapausis differs from the repose of the pious.

The reader may forgive me for concluding this discussion of the *Sophia of Jesus Christ* as a Christianized version of the *Eugnostos* with a basic point: except for the Christian names given to the characters, this treatise contains no specifically Christian ideas that contrast with Gnosticism. What emerges instead from studying this expanded version of the *Eugnostos* is the compensatory function of Gnosticism in relation to Christianity. I have extrapolated, and highlighted, specific Gnostic ideas to illustrate how they emphasize aspects neglected by orthodox Christianity. As a form of reception, Gnosticism in no way rejects the Christian tradition, but refreshingly adds a symbolic and spiritual dimension to its concretistic conception. Whereas it was perhaps more convincing for people in antiquity to perceive the events surrounding Christ in concrete terms, from a historical distance we realize that the archetype of the anthropos was constellated in the whole of Hellenism and manifested itself syncretistically in the figure of Christ. Over time, the historical figure of Jesus was laden with ever-new traits. Also attributed to parallel phenomena, these features gained increasing ground until the rival cults descended into meaninglessness. A similar battle for power also took place within the various currents of Gnosticism, whose emerging theology assimilated a great deal to eliminate its rivals. This theology succeeded in eliminating its rivals by adjusting better to the prevailing worldly structures, which Gnosticism, due its one-sided stubbornness, wholly rejected. Ultimately, its distinct introversion sealed the fate of this magnificent spiritual awakening. Today, at a time when Christianity is in a profound spiritual crisis, which is dismissed only by those in denial, Gnosticism has much to teach us precisely because of its compensatory function. Only those readers eager to misunderstand me, maliciously, will claim that I am making the case for a Gnostic church. On the contrary, I believe that the study of Gnosticism and its concerns, as an unconscious reaction to the burgeoning fledgling church, could reinvigorate the old-line church by giving it new impulses.

Chapter 8
The Lost Soul and Its Redemption

This chapter discusses an important topic that I have introduced in the previous chapter.[1] It focuses on the *Exegesis on the Soul*, a treatise part of the Nag Hammadi corpus (NHC II,6).[2] This text contains a succinct account of our overall concern: the soul's fall into the material world and its subsequent redemption. This motif is ubiquitous and not specifically Gnostic. The Gnostic traits are scattered across history, through which this motif resonates. The author of this treatise seeks to establish his orthodox inclinations, which explains his use of numerous biblical citations to corroborate his statements. The treatise exemplifies how the emerging church and Gnosticism developed alongside each other, and moved apart only with the formulation of the canon. It would therefore be preposterous or at least blasphemous to brand the Gnostics as apostates, since no "orthodoxy" in the strict sense existed at the time.

Codex II is the most comprehensive, best-preserved, and most carefully written of all Nag Hammadi texts.[3] *Exegesis on the Soul* is related to other Nag Hammadi scriptures which will not be mentioned here. However, an evident parallel exists with the complementary

---

[1] While preparing this chapter, I delivered five two-hour lectures on the topic at the C.G. Jung Institute in Küsnacht (Zurich) in the 1999/2000 term.
[2] Translator's note: this text is sometimes also translated as the *Expository Treatise on the Soul*; see, for instance, Bentley Layton, Nag Hammadi Codex II, 2–7, vol. II, pp.136–169.
[3] I gave a seminar on this text at the Psychologischer Club Zürich from September 23 to October 28, 1995 (a typescript of the seminar was prepared based on the audio recordings).

Authoritative Discourse (NHC VI, 3). On account of its ubiquitous motif, the editor of the French translation of the *Exegesis* has wondered whether this treatise is at all Gnostic.[4] My own view is that this motif enables us to work out the specifically Gnostic characteristics of this text. Thus, for instance, it says:

> The sages who came before us gave the soul a feminine name. She is also feminine in nature, and she even has a womb....
> While the soul was alone with the Father, she was a virgin and androgynous in form. (127, 22–129,5)

There is a long-established tradition that the psyche is feminine. "In place of the parents, woman now takes up her position as the most immediate environmental influence in the life of the adult man," writes Jung, and adds:

> She becomes his companion, she belongs to him in so far as she shares his life and is more or less of the same age. She is not of a superior order, either by virtue of age, authority, or physical strength. She is, however, a very influential factor and, like the parents, she produces an imago of a relatively autonomous nature—not an imago to be split off like that of the parents, but one that has to be kept associated with consciousness. Woman, with her very dissimilar psychology, is and always has been a source of information about things for which a man has no eyes. She can be his inspiration; her intuitive capacity, often superior to man's, can give him timely warning, and her feeling, always directed towards the personal, can show him ways which his own less personally accented feeling would never have discovered. (CW 7 §296)

---

[4] Maddalena Scopello, *L'Exégèse de l'Ame* (NHC II, 6).

> Here, without a doubt, is one of the main sources for the feminine quality of the soul. (CW 7 §297)

In the beginning, the soul is still contained in the pleroma, with the Father. She is a virgin and androgynous. The latter characteristic differentiates itself only in puberty. Until then, boys are male and girls female, but not really. Only in puberty does the young person identify with the one side and suppress, i.e., repress the other side into the unconscious. In homosexuality, this identification does not occur, and the homosexual remains in the androgynous phase. This leads some "modern" Jungians to believe that men also have an animus and women an anima. Normally, an adolescent's female characteristics lapse into the unconscious, just as the male ones do in teenagers. Gnosticism abounds in truly (emphatically!) unconscious psychology. The account of the soul in the *Exegesis* continues as follows:

> When she fell down into a body and entered this life, she fell into the hands of many robbers. These shameless men passed her from one to the other and [violated] her. Some raped her, others seduced her with gifts. (127,25–30)

The incarnation of the soul is depicted here as a falling into the body. Behind this image stands the ancient Greek idea, espoused by the Gnostics, that the body is the prison of the soul. Ordinarily, the predators and the pretentious are the archontic powers, whose leader says about himself: "I am the Lord, and there is no other; besides me there is no god" (Isaiah 45:5). He utters these words without knowing that he is a subordinate god, who does not know the Father. The soul, which is initially so pure and chaste, is at the mercy of Heimarmene, who abuses and sullies it. The Christian cult of male and female chastity springs from the idea of preserving original purity, or as the *Exegesis* phrases it:

> They defiled her, and she [lost her] virginity.
> In her body she became a whore and gave herself to everyone, and she considered each sexual partner to be her husband. (128)

Those who enter life cannot remain innocent, unless they become neurotic. Those who do not pay tribute to life, pay with neurosis. The soul prostitutes itself by following its instincts and desires, and thereby hopes to discover happiness. It binds itself to material goods and other people. The reader will find this as normal as I do and not in the least reprehensible. The Gnostic, as mentioned, beholds the "Great Theater of the World" from the self, from the Father. Therefore, existence, as the existentialists (among others) observed, means to "be thrown into the world," to fall from the bright world of the Father into the gloomy material world.

> After she gave herself to shameless, faithless adulterers for them to abuse her, she sighed deeply and repented. But when she turned her face from those adulterers, she ran after others, and they made her live with them and serve them in their beds as if they were her masters. (128,4–10)

For the Gnostics, adultery (*fornicatio*) seems to be the cardinal sin. But we must ask ourselves what this means in actual life, because the Gnostics always expressed themselves symbolically. It means to devote oneself to the material world, to its pleasures and desires, and to be constantly spellbound, fascinated, and disappointed by them. These images have lost none of their authority in our materialistic times. In the *Authoritative Discourse* (NHC VI,3), it is drunkenness: "That soul will fall into drinking too much.... She has abandoned knowledge and has fallen into the life of an animal" (24,14–22). Drunkenness also occurs as a motif in Philo's *On Drunkenness*, where agnosia is a state of spiritual inebriation and deadens the eye and the ear. Agnosia has the same effect on the soul, since it damages the inner face and hearing. Common in Gnosticism, generally this motif belongs to the emotions or, as the Gnostics say, the passions. The *Book of Thomas* (NHC II,7) states:

> The Savior continued and said: "Oh, unsearchable love of light! Oh, bitterness of the fire! You blaze in the bodies of people and in the marrow of their bones, blazing in them night and day, burning their limbs and making their minds drunk and their souls deranged." (139,32–37)

Commenting on his French translation of this treatise, Raymond Kuntzmann notes that drunkenness was a widespread motif in the Ancient Orient,[5] where it was associated with disorder and symbolized ignorance and enslavement. In the *Ginza Rba* ("The Great Book"), it is the weapon of darkness against Adam. Drunkenness numbs the body and makes the soul inattentive (*agnoia*). Desire plunges the heart into ignorance and the soul into turmoil. The *Gospel of Truth* (NHC I,3) explains:

> He who is to have knowledge in this manner knows where he comes from and where he is going. He knows as one who having become drunk has turned away from his drunkenness, (and) having returned to himself, has set right what are his own. (22,13–21)

A Manichaean Psalm (CCXL VIII 56,15–17) says:

> Come, Lord Jesus, the savior of spirits, who has rescued me from the arrogance and errors of the world.

---

[5] Kuntzmann, *Le Livre de Thomas*, pp. 31 and 83.

As I have repeatedly emphasized, *agnosia*, i.e., unconsciousness, is the cardinal sin for the Gnostics. Whatever induces this state is the work of the devil, whether it is harlotry, drunkenness, the passions that burn the limbs, or the *abaissement du niveau mental* resulting from identifying with objects. The *Exegesis on the Soul* continues thus:

> She was ashamed, and then she did not dare to leave them. For a long time they fooled her into thinking they respected her like faithful, true husbands. But finally they left and abandoned her.
>
> She became a poor lost widow. She was helpless, and no one even gave ear to her in her pain. She got nothing from the adulterers except the filth they left when they had sex with her. (128,12–20ff.)

This passage tells us how the "poor soul" becomes caught up in a vicious circle of attraction, disappointment, and shame, in which it remains trapped. The *Authoritative Discourse*, already cited above, observes:

> When the spiritual soul was cast into a body, it became a sibling to lust, hatred, and envy, that is, to material souls. So the body came from lust, and lust came from material substance. That is why the soul became a sibling to them. (23,13–22)

These treatises reveal why the Gnostics rejected the material world and the body. They believed that the body is the source of all desires and passions, which mesmerize the soul, which mediates between matter and spirit. The soul is free to decide whether it follows one or the other. If it succumbs to the material world, the soul becomes irremediably hylic and forlorn. This shows, as I claimed in the first volume, that hylics, psychics, and pneumatics are not categories determined by fate, but stages within a process.

In the *Exegesis*, the children begotten from fornication, the outcome of unbridled passion and instinct, are deformed:

> The children she had from the adulterers are mute, blind, and sickly. They are disturbed. (128,13–14; 25–26)

This is a harsh verdict. The *Authoritative Discourse* puts it this way:

> For the possessions of the stepchildren are exalted passions, life's pleasures, hateful jealousies, boastful expressions, foolish experiences, reproachful words ... If a soul who is ignorant chooses a spirit of prostitution, he casts her out and throws her into a brothel. He has left her to corruption, because she has abandoned modesty. (23,29–24,10)

Such ideas occur also in the Old Testament, such as in Jeremiah:

> Yet her false sister Judah did not fear, but she too went and played the whore. Because she took her whoredom so lightly, she polluted the land, committing adultery with stone and tree. Yet for all this her false sister Judah did not return to me with her whole heart, but only in pretense, says the Lord. (3:8–10)

Contrary to our text, where the female figure is individual and spiritual, here it is collective and tribal. In earlier times, the drama took place between the Lord and Israel, his bride, whereas now it occurs between the All-Father and the soul, his daughter. This marks the progress of consciousness from the collective to the individual. As I mentioned earlier, the individual was discovered during Hellenism:

> Her Father on high noticed her. He looked down on her and saw her sighing in pain and disgrace and repenting of her

prostitution. She began to call on him for help, and [she sighed] with all her heart and said, 'My Father, save me.' (128, 26–30)

This *metanoia* (change of mind) had announced itself already as sighing and repentance in verses 128,5 and 7. Actual change, however, becomes possible only when one has reached a dead-end and sees no way out. Change never arises from reasoning and insight. In therapeutic practice, it is therefore sometimes extremely difficult to encourage patients to run against a brick wall. One's motherly feelings resist this impulse. It is not, however, until one is lying on the floor rubbing the bruise on one's head that one comes to one's senses. One must even be grateful to have merely sustained a bruise, not a fractured skull.

In the *Gospel of the Egyptians* (NHC IV,2), this change of mind has been hypostatized:

> Because of this, Metanoia came to be. She received her completion and her power by the will of the Father and his approval with which he approved of the great incorruptible race of the great, mighty men of the great Seth, in order that he may sow it in the aeons which had been brought forth, so that through her (= Metanoia), the deficiency (hystérema) may be filled up. For she had come forth from above down to the world which is the image of the night.[6] (III 59,9–20)

Such a change of mind cannot be determined by sheer will. It is autonomous and comes to our aid, or not, out of mercy. Therefore, *metanoia* in this passage is a female figure, which appears by the will of the Father, with whose approval she makes the Sethians come to their senses. This privileged, incorruptible race is saved by Gnosis. The world down here is the image of the night, the place of deficiency.

---

[6] Böhlig and Wisse, *The Gospel of the Egyptians*, pp. 128 and 185.

Another Gnostic term in the previous passage is *Hystérema*.[7] This became a *terminus technicus* only after the Gnostics equated this word with the fallen Sophia and with the material creation brought about by her. The term is unknown in classical Greek and first appears in the *Septuagint*, the Greek translation of the Old Testament. In its Gnostic sense, it occurs in Irenaeus' *Against Heresies* (I, 11,1) when twelve forces—one of which has lapsed and become deficient—emanate from the *anthropos* and the *ecclesia*. Secundus, whose teaching also has a Valentinian character, maintains that a power also fell away from the fruits of the thirty aeons and became deficient (Irenaeus I, 11,2). The demiurge and the material world are the fruits of deficiency (Irenaeus II, 1,1: 9,2; 19,4.9; 28,4.7; 25.5, etc.). Christ and the Holy Spirit arise because of this deficiency. The term also occurs in Hippolytus, in Clement of Alexandria's *Excerpts from Theodotus*, and in the Valentinian scriptures included in the Nag Hammadi corpus (*Gospel of the Truth*; *Letter to Rheginus, or Treatise on the Resurrection, Apocalypse of John*). I shall not, however, trouble the reader by enumerating these passages.

Evidently, the soul that has fallen into the material world suffers from this very deficiency, from the imperfection of the Creation, from which it is meant to be redeemed. In response to the question of how the perfect Father could produce such a deficient Creation, the Gnostics assert that this was an accident, an aberration from harmony. Consequently, the subordinate creator could not possibly have created a perfect world, but instead made "the best world possible." *Metanoia* is meant to redeem the soul from this deficiency, in which it becomes inevitably embroiled.

---

[7] Booth, "Deficiency."

"Look, I shall tell [you how I] left home and fled from my maiden's quarters. Restore me to yourself." For many afflictions have come upon her because she left home.

The holy Spirit prophesies in many places about the prostitution of the soul. (128,34–129,5)

Metanoia consists in the soul, which has turned entirely toward material reality, once again facing the Father. I find it difficult to accept the accusation of hubris leveled at the Gnostics by the established church, quite simply because a profound humility speaks to us from this text. Before its redemption, the Gnostic's soul is caught up in the deficiency of the world. It is, as I emphasized in the first volume, rather the anxious hope or joyful certainty of belonging to the seed of Seth which is rescued from the deficient world.

Our text continues with biblical citations, which are adduced to prove the orthodox character of the myth. We can safely leave aside these references, because they do not further illuminate the text, and continue directly with the myth:

As long as the soul keeps running here and there having sex with whomever she meets and defiling herself, she will suffer what she deserves. But when she perceives the trouble she is in and weeps before the Father and repents, the Father will pity her. He will make her womb turn from the outside back to the inside, so that the soul will recover her proper character. It is not so with a woman. The womb of the body is inside the body like the other internal organs, but the womb of the soul is turned to the outside like male sex organs, which are external.

When the womb of the soul, by the Father's will, turns to the inside, she is baptized, and at once she is free of the external pollution forced upon her, just as dirty [clothes] are soaked in [water and] are moved about until the dirt is removed and they are clean. The soul is cleansed so that she may regain what she had at first, her former nature, and she may be restored. That is her baptism. Then she will begin to rage like a woman in labor, who writhes and rages at the time of delivery. (131ff. etc.)

The image of the vagina turned inside out, which is meant to represent the soul's extraverted behavior in the world, is suggestive. Thus, Bentley Layton travelled to the Nile valley to establish that local women still wash clothes inside out and brush and soap them on stone.[8] This everyday scene obviously suited the author's endeavor to symbolize the repentance and absolution of the Father. Turning the vagina inside represents an introverted attitude, which no longer succumbs to the temptations of the world, but concentrates on the Father. This is the baptism of the soul—a spiritual baptism, a spiritual sacrament. In several steps, the Gnostics reject water baptism as an external action that corresponds to no inner transformation.[9] Many passages, even among the opponents of Gnosticism, reveal that baptism is an inner sacrament, and as such associated with *metanoia*. The Gnostics, then, experience a symbolic action or a symbol as a psychic reality. These actions and symbols appear to the modern person only as signs, whereas they are the primary reality of the psyche. Writing about the Naassenes, Hippolytus remarks:

> For the promise of washing is not any other, according to them, than the introduction of him that is washed in, according to them, life-giving water, and anointed with ineffable ointment (than his introduction) into unfading bliss. (V 7,19)

---

[8] See "The Soul as a Dirty Garment."
[9] For the promise of washing is not any other, according to them, than the introduction of him that is washed in, according to them, life-giving water, and anointed with ineffable ointment (than his introduction) into unfading bliss (V 7,19). Sevrin, *Le dossier baptismal Séthien*.

Further:

> But if any one, he says, is blind from birth, and has never beheld the true light, which lightens every man that comes into the world (John 1:9), by us let him recover his sight, and behold, as it were, through some paradise planted with every description of tree, and supplied with abundance of fruits, water coursing its way through all the trees and fruits; and he will see that from one and the same water the olive chooses for itself and draws the oil, and the vine the wine; and (so is it with) the rest of plants, according to each genus. (V 9,20)

The *Book of Baruch* states:

> ...and he drinks from life-giving water, which is to them, as they suppose, a bath, a fountain of life-giving, bubbling water. For there has been a separation made between water and water; and there is water, that below the firmament of the wicked creation, in which earthly and animal men are washed; and there is life-giving water, (that) above the firmament, of the Good One, in which spiritual (and) living men are washed. (V 27,2–3)

Aqua permanens (i.e., Greek *hydor theion*) plays a major role in alchemy, where it symbolizes the spiritual aspect of the unconscious. Muhammad Ibn Umail, a tenth-century alchemist, writes:

> And his exclamation, "his leaves are the water," means that leaves [of the sages] are white, spiritual water, in which they carry the body's soul. And she ascends with it [water] and breaks forth, just

as the plants break forth. This water embraces the soul, just as the leaves embrace the wood of their plant.[10]

Even more impressive is the following passage from the Latin translation (*Senior de Chemia*):

> Hermes said that a secret and the life of every thing consists of water and that water ingests the food of human beings and other creatures, and that *water contains the greatest secret*. In this way, it makes grain ferment, the olive produce oil, certain trees produce rubber, and conifers make turpentine (in the Arabic text: and this water ferments in the grain, becomes wine in the vine, and turns into olive oil in the olive).[11] Everything begotten has *its origin in water...*[12]

I can spare the reader further Gnostic citations on baptism, which may be found aplenty in Sevrin's *Les noces spirituelles dans L'Evangile de Philippe*. My concern here is to show that the "living water above the firmament" mentioned in the *Book of Baruch* corresponds to the "divine water" (*hydor theon*) of Greek alchemy, and to the "eternal water" (*aqua permanens*) of Latin alchemy.

> But since she is female and cannot conceive a child by herself, her Father sent her from heaven her man, her brother, the firstborn. The bridegroom came down to the bride. She gave up her former whoring and cleansed herself of the pollution of adulterers, and she was restored to be a bride. She cleansed herself in the bridal chamber. She filled it with perfume and sat there awaiting the

---

[10] Vereno, *Studien zum ältesten alchemistischen Schrifttum*, p. 217—trans.
[11] Turab Ali et al., *Three Arabic Treatises on Alchemy by Muhammad ibn Umail*, p. 174; emphases added.
[12] *Theatrum Chemicum* V 219.

> true bridegroom. She no longer went around the marketplace having sex with whomever she desired, but she stayed and waited for him, saying, "When will he come?" And she feared him. For she did not know what he looked like. She no longer remembered from the time she fell from her Father's house. Yet, by the Father's will, she dreamed of him like a woman who loves a man. (*Exegesis on the Soul*, 132,6–27)

The *Gospel of Philip* (NHC II,3) elaborates on this in Logion 122:

> No [one can] know when [a husband] and wife have sex except those two, for marriage in this world is a mystery for those married. If defiled marriage is hidden, how much more is undefiled marriage a true mystery! It is not fleshly but pure. It belongs not to desire but to will. It belongs not to darkness or night but to the day and the light. (81,34ff.)

The mystery of the bridal chamber occupies a significant role in this Gnostic treatise.[13] Valentinian teaching maintains that the union between Achamoth and the redeemer is exemplary:

> When all the seed shall have come to perfection, they state that then their mother Achamoth shall pass from the intermediate place, and enter in within the Pleroma, and shall receive as her spouse the Saviour... that thus a conjunction may be formed between the Saviour and Sophia, that is, Achamoth. These, then, are the bridegroom and bride, while the nuptial chamber is the full extent of the Pleroma. The spiritual seed, again, being divested of their animal souls, and becoming intelligent spirits, shall in an irresistible and invisible manner enter in within the

---

[13] Sevrin, *Les noces*.

Pleroma, and be bestowed as brides on those angels who wait upon the Saviour. (Irenaeus, *Against Heresies* I, 7,1–2)

Logion 125a of the *Gospel of Philip* says:

> The bedchamber is hidden, and it is the holy of the holy. At first the curtain concealed how God manages creation, but when the curtain is torn and what is inside appears, this building will be left deserted, or rather will be destroyed.

This fits with the end of Logion 76:

> There are people in Jerusalem who [do worship] in Jerusalem, and they await [the mysteries] called [the holy] of holies, the curtain [of which] was torn. [Our] bridal chamber is the image [of the bridal chamber] above. That is why its curtain was torn from top to bottom, for some people from below had to go up.

Logion 79:

> A woman is united with her husband in the bridal chamber, and those united in the bridal chamber will not be separated again.

Logion 126c:

> Everyone who [enters] the bedchamber will kindle the [light. This is] like marriages that occur [in secret and] take place at night. The light of the fire [shines] during the night and then goes out. The mysteries of that marriage, however, are performed in the day and the light, and neither that day nor its light ever sets.

The reader thus inclined will have gathered from these passages just how crucial the *Mysterium coniunctionis* is for the Gnostic. It is the hope he embraces during his life, his redemption, the goal of his development. Essentially, he projects this mysterium onto the moment of death, where it is known as the motif of the marriage with death. In

On Dreams and Death, Marie Louise von Franz reports the dream of an elderly nurse. This woman dreamed that she received her engagement announcement, with which she wholeheartedly agreed, although she did not know who the groom was. She awoke and could not make sense of the dream. She fell back asleep again and dreamed that she was wearing a white robe of death and holding a red rose. She went toward the groom, her heart full of desire and joy. When she reawakened, she realized that the groom must be Jesus Christ, and that her dream had prepared her for her death.

Unfortunately, scholars of Gnosticism have no such empirical knowledge to ground their interpretation of Gnostic texts in actual human reality. Consequently, these profound texts remain inaccessible to the layperson and thus also to a wider public. One of my reasons for writing this book is to show that Gnosticism provides unconscious psychology dressed in mythic clothes and can be truly understood only today.

I need to draw the reader's attention to the incestuous nature of this union. Incest always points to an inner relationship between opposites, in that the union occurs with a part that has always belonged to the whole. Alchemy possesses a rich and often devastatingly blunt symbolism in this respect (Jung, CW 14). Our present subject is different because the alchemists understood the union of opposites in the here and now as part of their work. By contrast, this idea is merely hinted at in Gnosticism and Hermeticism. The great union occurs at the end of life. After the change of mind (*metanoia*), the soul finds itself suspended, waiting, detached from the temptations of the world, expecting the heavenly groom.

Unlike in the above dream, in Gnosticism the sexes are reversed: in dreams about the marriage with death, the dying ego as a rule conjoins with the otherworldly soul (the anima or the animus!), whereas in our text it is (emphatically!) *not* the ego that matters, but the transcendent (female!) soul. What does it mean if she unites with her brother? The entire plot is shifted into a sphere that transcends the ego. The Gnostic attaches little or no importance to the material world and the body, nor to the empirical ego. In this respect, Gnosticism is far closer to Eastern philosophies of religion than to Christianity. But this attitude involves such rigorous introversion and negation of the world that it could not survive for long. Such admirable undercurrents, which include Catharism and Albigensianism, have flourished time and again in the European history of ideas, only to disappear quietly after a while.[14] This suggests that the meaning of our existence lies not in the ultimate union of a soul cleansed of the dirt of the world with its otherworldly, immortal redeemer. This also explains why the Gnostics ill-regarded both the psychics, most of whom belonged to the established church, and the hylics, who had fallen victim to the material world. The Gnostic stance is too transcendental. Surely, the fact that the human being is born into this material world must make some kind of sense! In the first few centuries of its existence, Christianity also clung to ascetic ideals.[15] Possibly, Gnosticism and the monastic ideal compensated for the worldly stance, which becomes enslaved to material values all too easily.

Alchemy discovered a third way between these two extremes: it wondered where this fascination with matter comes from. *This question is indeed fruitful, because one should neither evade nor succumb to the numinous residing in matter, the* deus terrestris. Thus, the divine is found not only in the world to come, but also in earthly existence. This probably also explains why alchemy survived for over one and a half millennia, although in seclusion. Although it was also a compensatory undercurrent of orthodox Christianity, it never opposed

---

[14] Quispel, *De Hermetische Gnosis*; Rottenwöhrer, *Katharismus*.
[15] Ribi, *Die Dämonen*, p. 127.

the mainstream, and was never stifled as a result. It considered itself complementary to the Christian work of redemption.[16]

Let us once more return to the *Exegesis on the Soul*:

> Then, by the Father's will, the bridegroom came down to her in the bridal chamber that had been prepared. And he decorated the chamber.
>
> This marriage of the soul is not like a marriage of the flesh. In a marriage of the flesh, those who have sex with each other become satiated with sex, and so they leave behind them the annoying burden of physical desire and [turn their faces] from each other. This marriage of the soul [is different]. When the partners join [with each other], they become a single life. (132,27–35)

Next come several biblical citations, presumably to substantiate the orthodoxy of the passage cited here. For this reason, among others, I believe that Gnosticism developed side by side with Christianity. It did not, as is so often claimed, split off from Christianity. A passage in Irenaeus affirms this view:

> Such, then, is their system, which neither the prophets announced, nor the Lord taught, nor the apostles delivered, but of which they boast that beyond all others they have a perfect knowledge. They gather their views from other sources than the Scriptures; and, to use a common proverb, they strive to weave ropes of sand, while they endeavour to adapt with an air of probability to their own peculiar assertions the parables of the Lord, the sayings of the prophets, and the words of the apostles, in order that their scheme may not seem altogether without

---

[16] C.G. Jung, *Psychology and Alchemy*, especially Part 1, "Introduction to the Religious and Psychological Problems of Alchemy" (CW 12).

support. In doing so, however, they disregard the order and the connection of the Scriptures, and so far as in them lies, dismember and destroy the truth. By transferring passages, and dressing them up anew, and making one thing out of another, they succeed in deluding many through their wicked art in adapting the oracles of the Lord to their opinions. Their manner of acting is just as if one, when a beautiful image of a king has been constructed by some skillful artist out of precious jewels, should then take this likeness of the man all to pieces, should rearrange the gems, and so fit them together as to make them into the form of a dog or of a fox, and even that but poorly executed; and should then maintain and declare that this was the beautiful image of the king which the skillful artist constructed, pointing to the jewels which had been admirably fitted together by the first artist to form the image of the king, but have been with bad effect transferred by the latter one to the shape of a dog.... In like manner do these persons patch together old wives' fables, and then endeavour, by violently drawing away from their proper connection, words, expressions, and parables whenever found, to adapt the oracles of God to their baseless fictions. (*Against Heresies* I, 8, 1)

These remarks are not unjustified, even if implicitly they ridicule Gnosticism. Dogma later employed exactly the same means to produce a coherent system out of the controversial statements in the Bible. But such coherence was intended neither by the prophets, nor by the apostles, nor by the believers. The veracity of the Bible lies in its contradictoriness, because life *is* contradictory. What was true at one time, under certain circumstances, can be utterly wrong at another, under other circumstances. The truth is controversial, and every theological system must take this into account. The Gnostics, therefore, aspired not so much to a literal conception of the Scripture, but rather to understand its underlying spirit. The following verses in 2 Corinthians are not from a Gnostic treatise, but may well have been inspired by the Gnostics:

> Such is the confidence that we have through Christ towards God. Not that we are competent of ourselves to claim anything as coming from us; our competence is from God, who has made us competent to be ministers of a new covenant, not of the letter but of the spirit; for the letter kills, but the Spirit gives life. (3:3–4)

Especially in Paul's case, who never experienced the Lord during his lifetime, we need to ask where his theology comes from if not from divine inspiration, as it does with the Gnostics. Some readers may find this idea blasphemous, but I believe that the Gnostics took their task as seriously as Paul did and that they were just as convinced as he was of its spiritual truth.

> If we truly repent, God, who is patient and abundant in mercy, will hear us. To God be the glory forever and ever.
> Amen. (137,23)

Thus, our treatise concludes as the expression of a profound belief and a strong hope in a merciful God. Why on earth did the established church persecute these men of God with such boundless hatred? Well, because they formulated what the men of the established church thought unconsciously, but which did not fit their conscious notions.

Chapter 9
The Fall of the Soul into Matter

In the previous chapter, we traced the theme of the soul that has fallen into the world in the *Exegesis on the Soul*, one of the ancient texts found at Nag Hammadi (II, 6). I began my discussion by pointing out that the motif of the fallen soul is widespread. Here, I widen that perspective to further pursue this motif. The most famous example of the fall within Gnosticism is the Fall of Sophia in the Valentinian system. In the Ptolemaic Gnostic system, as recounted by Irenaeus, it is told thus:

> But there rushed forth in advance of the rest that Aeon who was much the latest of them, and was the youngest of the Duodecad which sprang from Anthropos and Ecclesia, namely Sophia, and suffered passion apart from the embrace of her consort Theletos. This passion, indeed, first arose among those who were connected with Nous and Aletheia, but passed as by contagion to this degenerate Aeon, who acted under a pretence of love, but was in reality influenced by temerity, because she had not, like Nous, enjoyed communion with the perfect Father. This passion, they say, consisted in a desire to search into the nature of the Father; for she wished, according to them, to comprehend his greatness. When she could not attain her end, inasmuch as she aimed at an impossibility, and thus became involved in an extreme agony of mind, while both on account of the vast profundity as well as the unsearchable nature of the Father, and on account of the love she bore him, she was ever stretching herself forward, there was danger lest she should at last have been absorbed by his sweetness, and resolved into his absolute essence,

unless she had met with that Power which supports all things, and preserves them outside of the unspeakable greatness. This power they term Horos; by whom, they say, she was restrained and supported; and that then, having with difficulty been brought back to herself, she was convinced that the Father is incomprehensible, and so laid aside her original design, along with that passion which had arisen within her from the overwhelming influence of her admiration.

Irenaeus continues:

> But others of them fabulously describe the passion and restoration of Sophia as follows: They say that she, having engaged in an impossible and impracticable attempt, brought forth an amorphous substance, such as her female nature enabled her to produce. When she looked upon it, her first feeling was one of grief, on account of the imperfection of its generation, and then of fear lest this should end her own existence. Next she lost, as it were, all command of herself, and was in the greatest perplexity while endeavouring to discover the cause of all this, and in what way she might conceal what had happened. Being greatly harassed by these passions, she at last changed her mind, and endeavoured to return anew to the Father. When, however, she in some measure made the attempt, strength failed her, and she became a suppliant of the Father. The other Aeons, Nous in particular, presented their supplications along with her. And hence they declare material substance had its beginning from ignorance and grief, and fear and bewilderment. (*Against Heresies* I, 2,2–3)

This passage indicates that the creation of matter was a misfortune. Besides, it is not what we moderns imagine it to be, but the passions of

Sophia. This helps us to understand her place in Gnosticism. In the *Excerpts from Theodotus*, Clement of Alexandria reports:

> But the Aeon which wished to grasp that which is beyond knowledge fell into ignorance and formlessness. Whence it effected an abstraction of knowledge which is a shadow of the Name, that is the Son, the form of the Aeons. Thus the distribution of the Name among the Aeons is the loss of the Name. (31,3–4)

In another passage, he says:

> But he is alluding to the Woman on high whose passions became creation when she put forth those beings that were without form. On her account the Saviour came down to drag us out from passion and to adopt us to himself. (67,4)

Interpreting Gnostic texts is difficult because matters are described quite unemotionally. Precisely in the myth of Sophia we would expect intense emotions to be articulated. Yet for the Gnostic visionary, these are all intuitions. They are emotionally barely accessible, and the Gnostic hardly understands what they mean for his everyday life. I often encounter the same phenomenon among my analysands, who are capable of formulating insights, which, however, are not yet their own, personal, painful truth. This Gnostic myth anticipated a fact that we are becoming conscious of only now: the relationship between psyche and matter.[1]

Marie-Louise von Franz has observed, "matter is merely one archetypal notion among many others." She adds that, "the term goes back to the archetype of the Great Mother." The Gnostics maintain

---

[1] von Franz, *Psyche and Matter*, p. 22.

that this archetype emerged from the Father, the archetype of the Spirit. But spirit and matter are two principles neither of which can have arisen from the other, because they are coeternal. But if the Gnostic view is so one-sided, it upholds the spiritualist hypothesis according to which matter is demonized.[2] Thus, matter remains an autonomous notion in the unconscious, from where it produces ghostly phenomena. This, as it were, is the revenge for non-recognition. On the other hand, this phenomenon exercises a fascination that consciousness is barely able to evade. This is our current predicament.

We succumb to the attraction of materialism because it carries the hope of deliverance. We believe that only what we can experience with our senses is real. Everything that is unconscious is also projected. Consequently, we are unable to recognize the problem as ours, which removes us even further from a solution.

Not only the Valentinian myth of the fall of Sophia, but also the treatise discussed in the previous chapter can be regarded as the *Sophia salvanda* (redeeming wisdom). This is our great task today. But because a depth-psychological approach is avoided at all costs, and dismissed as unscientific, no other solution is found. Instead, one stubbornly follows the path taken, hoping to resolve the problem with materialistic and positivistic means. The result is even greater one-sidedness. We have lost what distinguished the Gnostics: a profound confidence in the reality of the spirit, the *mentis religio* (*Asclepius*, 25.29). We should once again hear the appeal for help of the divine spark trapped within matter to aid its liberation. In the Gnostic treatise *Thunder, Perfect Mind* (NHC VI,2), Sophia exclaims:

> Do not be arrogant toward me
> when I am thrown down on the ground,
> and you will find me

---

[2] Ribi, *Was tun mit unseren Komplexen*, p. 148.

in those [who] are to come.

If you see me on the dung heap,
don't go and leave me thrown there.

You will find me in the kingdoms.

If you see me when I am thrown out
with the disgraced in the most sordid places,
don't mock me.

Don't throw me down violently
with those in need.

I, I am compassionate and I am cruel.
Take care not to hate my obedience,
but love my self-control.

In my weakness do not disregard me,
and do not fear my power. (15,2–21)

This passage ties in neatly with the *Exegesis on the Soul* (NHC II,6), a treatise dedicated to a specific ambivalent figure, namely the dangerous force lurking behind the seemingly weak and humiliated female.

In Chapter 7, I already mentioned the Gnostic Simon Magus, who considered himself the "Great Power of God." Writing about Simon, Irenaeus says:

> Now Simon, the Samaritan, from whom all heresies got their start, proposed the following sort of heretical doctrine. Having himself redeemed a certain Helen from being a prostitute in Tyre, a city of Phoenicia, he took her with him on his rounds, saying that she was the first Thought of his mind, the Mother of all things, through whom in the beginning he conceived in his mind to make the Angels and Archangels. For he asserted that this Thought leaped forth from him, since she knew what her

Father wanted, and descended to the lower regions and gave birth to Angels and Powers, by whom also this world was made. But after she gave birth to them, she was detained by them out of envy, since she did not wish to be considered the offspring of someone else. For he was entirely unknown to them. His Thought, however, who was detained by the Powers and Angels that had been emitted by her, also suffered all kinds of contumely at their hands, so that she could not return to her Father on high. She suffered even to the extent of being imprisoned in a human body and of transmigrating for ages in to other female bodies, as from one vessel into another. For example, she was in the famous Helen on account of whom the Trojan war was fought; for that reason Stesichorus who reviled her in his verses was struck blind, but after he repented and had written what are called palinodes, in which he sang her praises, his sight was restored. Thus, passing from one body into another, and always suffering insults from the body, she was at last a prostitute in a public house. She was the lost sheep. (*Against Heresies* I, 23,2; see Matthew 18:12 and Luke 15:4)

It is no coincidence that the woman accompanying Simon is called *Helen*. She is a *femme fatale*, i.e., a woman who shapes destiny. Ever since Homer, Helen has been depicted as the most beautiful woman, whose abduction precipitated the Trojan War. In Book 3 of the *Illiad*, Homer compares her to a goddess. Indeed, her name derives from the goddess Selene (moon). She was said to be a lunar creature that had fallen to earth. In his poem *Iliuspersis*, Stesichoros (c. 640–555 BCE) depicted Helen as a woman with two or three husbands and as an unfaithful wife. He was punished with blindness and only regained his eyesight when he declared that Paris had merely taken an *eidolon* (image, idol) to Troy. This assertion seems psychologically correct, because men who fall in love with such "anima women" actually fall in love with a divine image, and not with the real person. According to a legend transmitted by Pausanias, Helen later led a demure life with the hero Achilles. In Epode 17, which he called a *palinode* (an ode in which the writer retracts a view or sentiment), the first-century Roman poet Horace wrote: "You chaste, you honest girl will walk about in the stars as a constellation of gold." Nor should we forget Goethe's Helen in *Faust*, where Mephistopheles comments on what happens after one drinks a diabolical potion:

> Once you have this potion down you, you will see in every woman Helen. (Part 1, ll. 2603-4)

Euripides' drama *Helen* offers a psychologically subtle version of Helen as the phantasmagoria that sparked the Trojan War:

> Hermes caught me up in the folds of the air and hid me in a cloud—for Zeus was not neglectful of me—and he set me down here in the house of Proteus, having selected the most self-controlled of all mankind, so that I might keep my bed pure for Menelaos. And so I am here, while my wretched husband has gathered an army and gone over to the towers of Ilion to hunt down and recover me. And many lives have been lost for my sake by the streams of Skamandros; and I who have endured all this am accursed, and have in appearance betrayed my husband and brought a great war to the Hellenes. Why then am I still alive? I heard the god Hermes declare that I would yet live in the glorious country of Sparta, with my husband—for Hermes knew I never went to Ilion—so that I would not go to bed with another man. Well, as long as Proteus saw this light of the sun, I was safe from marriage; but now that he is hidden in the dark earth, the dead man's son hunts after a marriage with me. But I, out of regard to my husband of long ago, am throwing myself down as a suppliant

before this tomb of Proteus, for him to keep my bed safe for my husband, so that, if I bear a name infamous throughout Hellas, at least my body may not incur disgrace here. (31–67)

The opposition between the whore and the saint is integral to the archetype of the anima. The Christian church divided this image into two figures: the immaculate Virgin Mary and Mary Magdalene, from whom seven demons were said to have "gone out" (Luke 8:2), and who the Gnostics were impressed by even more.[3] In the *Pseudo-Clementine Homilies* (2,25,2), Helen is said to have caused the Greeks and barbarians to fight, "having before their eyes but an image of truth; for she, who really is the truth, was then with the chiefest god." Epiphanius also studied the Simonians and reported that Simon had gotten himself a female vagrant from Tyrus named Helen, but did not disclose their relationship. Instead, he told his disciples that his beloved was the Holy Spirit. Simon professed that he was the greatest power of God, and that he had descended to Ennoia, this very woman, who is also called *prunicos* (*Panarion* 21,2,4).

The *Acts of Peter* (Chapter 22) contains a fascinating account of the dispute between Simon Magus and the apostle Peter:

> And Marcellus turned to sleep for a short space, and awoke and said unto Peter: O Peter, thou apostle of Christ, let us go boldly unto that which lieth before us. For just now when I turned myself to sleep for a little, I beheld thee sitting in a high place and before thee a great multitude, and a woman exceeding foul, in sight like an Ethiopian, not an Egyptian, but altogether black and filthy, clothed in rags, and with an iron collar about her neck and chains upon her hands and feet, dancing. And when thou sawest me thou saidst to me with a loud voice: Marcellus the whole

---

[3] See Epiphanius, *Panarion* (8,1–12; 12, 1–4), *Pistis Sophia*, *Pseudo-Clementine Homily* 19; *Gospel of Mary* (BG); see also Marjanen, *The Woman Jesus Loved*.

power of Simon and of his God is this woman that danceth; do thou behead her. And I said to thee: Brother Peter, I am a senator of a high race, and I have never defiled my hands, neither killed so much as a sparrow at any time. And thou hearing it didst begin to cry out yet more: Come thou, our true sword, Jesu Christ and cut not off only the head of this devil, but hew all her limbs in pieces in the sight of all these Whom I have approved in thy service. And immediately one like unto thee, O Peter, having a sword, hewed her in pieces: so that I looked earnestly upon you both, both on thee and on him that cut in pieces that devil, and marvelled greatly to see how alike ye were. And I awaked, and have told unto thee these signs of Christ. And when Peter heard it he was the more filled with courage, for that Marcellus had seen these things, knowing that the Lord alway careth for his own. And being joyful and refreshed by these words, he rose up to go unto the forum.

This story, although merely a dream, is more genuine than the subsequent pious narrative about Peter resurrecting the dead men[4] in the forum, following the pattern established by his master (John 11:41–44; Mark 5:41; Matthew 9:25). But the dream does have the meaning desired by the devout. According to Irenaeus (*Against Heresies* I 23,3), Simon claims to be the "great power of God," and that he has come into the world to "first take her [the fallen Soul, Helen] to himself, free her from her bonds, and then bring salvation to humankind." Moreover, he "pledged himself that the world should be dissolved, and that those who are his should be freed from the rule of them who made the world." The "woman exceeding foul, in sight like an Ethiopian, not an Egyptian, but altogether black and filthy" appearing in Marcellus' dream is the soul whose neck, hands, and feet are chained. Her black, sullied rags suggest

---

[4] In one case, this is typically the "son of a widow" (Luke 7:12); see also Jung, CW 14 §13.

her lowly descent: this is a fitting image for Helen, who needs to be redeemed. But there is also her dark skin, which does not fit Helen. Psalm 74:14 describes the Egyptians as "creatures of the wilderness," who are fed the "heads of Leviathan." Citing this psalm, Epiphanius refers to the Egyptians as "blackened by sin" (*Panarion* 26,16,6). His text reveals that this is a pagan shadow, the spirit that had not accepted Christianity (*denigrati peccato*). In the *Pistis Sophia*, Ariuth, the Egyptian, a female archon, is completely black. Her fourteen demons stir human quarrelsomeness to the point of warfare and murder. She hardens human hearts and incites murderous wrath.[5] Origen states that the Egyptians eat human flesh.[6] In Thomas Aquinas' *Aurora consurgens*, the first parable mentions the Egyptians "of the black earth." He cites Psalm 72:9: "May his foes bow down before him, and his enemies lick the dust" (Vulgate: *coram illo procident Aethiopes et inimici eius terram lingent*).[7]

These amplifications should suffice to establish that from a Christian perspective the Egyptian was rather devilish. From a historical distance, we can understand her psychologically as a more primitive, pagan anima. In alchemy, she is the prime matter and responsible for the alchemist's *nigredo* state. She is the problem to be treated, but which one prefers to ignore and cast aside, because one does not believe that treatment will bear fruit. St. Peter totally suppresses the problem by blending it with the Christian logos. This manifests itself in early Christianity as chastity, which is granted overwhelming importance. Emphasizing chastity is an attempt to eliminate the feared dark female side. The young men resurrected by St. Peter are also meant to lead a chaste life in the service of God. It is an attempt to restore the

---

[5] *Ibid.*, 2,38,21–28; see also Till, *Koptisch-Gnostische Schriften*, column 140.
[6] *Traité de Principes* II, 9,5. SC 252, 363.
[7] Jung, *Mysterium Coniunctionis* III; Marie-Louise von Franz, *Aurora Consurgens*, GW 14/III, pp. 48–49.

state of innocence before the Fall. This attempt is still made by the established church, although with varying success.

Simon Magus approaches the problem of the dark, earthy anima from a different angle: his task, which he does not shun, is to appear in public accompanied by a consort. Since no psychology existed at the time, much was acted out as if in a dream. His Helen is the "fallen soul," which needs to be freed from her embroilment with evil matter. As a sword, the logos is of little use to him, unlike the devoted acceptance of the defiled woman. Her dancing refers to her quickening effect on consciousness. What consciousness fears often bears the greatest potential. But his task has made Simon lapse into typical inflation, which easily happens to men seeking to raise the fallen woman. He overestimates his own virtuousness when he lowers himself to her.

In the alchemical *Super arborem Aristotelis*,[8] which is attributed to Albertus, the Egyptian [male = shadow] appears as a task described as follows: "until the black head, which resembles the Egyptian, is well washed and begins to whiten." In Melchior Cibinesis, the virgin receives the Egyptian in the bathroom: "The Egyptian appears at the bottom of the basin, burned, buried, submerged in his own dampness and slowly calcinating until he emerges from the powerful fire, radiant.... Behold the magnificent restoration or renewal of the Egyptian!"[9] To be sure, this is the male figure of the "black person," i.e., the shadow. But the figure is understood as a task. If Simon Magus regards himself as Helen's "savior," then we do not know what else his work of redemption consists of other than parading her on their wanderings.

The motif of the lost sheep received interesting treatment in Gnosticism, where it often symbolizes the fallen Sophia.[10] For instance, the *Gospel of Truth* (NHC I,3) says:

---

[8] *Theatrum Chemicum* II 456f., 1659—trans.
[9] *Ibid.*, III 760, 1659—trans.
[10] Scholten, *Martyrium und Sophiamythos*.

> He [= Savior] is the shepherd, who left behind the ninety-nine sheep which were not lost. He went searching for the one which had gone astray. He rejoiced when he found it, for ninety-nine is a number that is in the left hand which holds it. But when the one is found, the entire number passes to the right (hand). As that which lacks the one—that is, the entire right (hand)—draws what was deficient and takes it from the left-hand side and brings (it) to the right, so too the number becomes one hundred. It is the sign of the one who is in their sound; it is the Father. (31,35–32,17)

This passage is probably barely comprehensible for the unprepared reader. At the time, one counted to ninety-nine with the left hand and then changed to the right hand to continue counting. Hence the symbolism of left and right becomes relevant. Irenaeus comments as follows on certain Gnostics:

> ...if they call material substances left hand, and claim that those who belong to the left hand necessarily tend to corruption, but that Savior came to the lost sheep that he might transfer it to the right side, that is, to the ninety-nine sheep that were on the saved side, which had not been lost but remained in the sheepfold. (*Against Heresies* II 24,6)

Markos, a second-century disciple of Valentinus, developed an alphabetical and a numerical symbolism that is ridiculed by Irenaeus. If taken seriously, however, this symbolism represents an archaic relationship between the spiritual and the creaturely world through the archetype of the number. After lengthy alphabetical speculation, Irenaeus adds:

> For the lambda [the letter A], as it were, having gone in search of the character like itself, and having found it and snatched it to itself, filled up the place of the number twelve, since the mu is composed of two lambdas. By means of their knowledge, then, they too flee from the place of the ninety-nine, that is, Degeneracy, which is the type of the left hand; however, they strive after the one, who, when added to the ninety-nine, transfers them to the right hand. (*Against Heresies* I 16,2)

In the *Gospel of Truth*, the "one" is the Father, whose knowledge is sought not only by Sophia but also by the Gnostics, who want to be saved. In another passage, Irenaeus comments:

> ...that Achamoth strayed outside the Fullness, was given a form by Christ, and was sought by Savior, he indicated, they claim, when he said that he came to the sheep that had gone astray. For the sheep that had gone astray, they explain, is said to be their Mother. From her "seed," they hold, the Church here below was planted. The straying is her stray outside the Fullness amid all sorts of passions, from which they hold matter was made. (*Against Heresies* I 8,4)

The story of Simon, the arch-Gnostic for Irenaeus, illustrates how profoundly the Gnostics interpreted tales like that of the lost sheep (Matthew 18:2; Luke 15:4) and integrated them into their system. As I showed in the first volume, the church fathers adhere to the sensation function, but the Gnostics to its opposite, intuition. For the former, everything is concrete; for the latter, symbolic.

Simon and Helen must therefore be understood as a syzygy (i.e., union of opposites) between spirit and matter. In *Aion*, Jung offers an extensive discussion of the Gnostic notion of the "universal Ground or Arcanum":

> Psychology takes this idea as an image of the unconscious background and begetter of consciousness. The most important of these images is the figure of the demiurge. The Gnostics have a vast number of symbols for the source or origin, the centre of being, the Creator, and the divine substance hidden in the creature. Lest the reader be confused by this wealth of images, he should always remember that each new image is simply another aspect of the divine mystery immanent in all creatures. My list of Gnostic symbols is no more than an amplification of a single transcendental idea, which is so comprehensive and so difficult to visualize in itself that a great many different expressions are required in order to bring out its various aspects. (CW 9/II §306)

Another symbol of the soul that has fallen into matter is the spark of life (*spinther*). Cited by Irenaeus, the Gnostic Saturnius (or Satornil) of Antioch says:

> But the world and all that is in it was made by certain seven Angels. Man too is the work of angels. When a shining image appeared from above from the sovereign Power and they were not able to hold fast to it because it immediately ascended again, he said that they exhorted each other, saying, "Let us make man after an image and likeness" (Genesis 1:26). When this first-formed man was made and was not able to stand erect because of the weakness of the Angels, but wriggled on the ground as a worm [Psalm 22:7], then the Power on high had pity on him, because he was made after its likeness, and he sent a spark of life which raised him up and set him upright and made him live. This spark of life, then, he claims, returns to its own kind after man's death, and the rest of the things out of which he was made are again resolved into these same things. (*Against Heresies* I 24,1)

The spark covers a wide range of meanings, not merely in Gnosticism, but also in the entire history of ideas.[11] For instance, Hippolytus says about the Sethians:

> When, however, this wave that has been raised out of the water by the wind, and rendered pregnant in its nature, has within itself obtained the power, possessed by the female, of generation, it holds together the light scattered from above along with the fragrance of the spirit—that is, mind molded in the different species. And this (light) is a perfect God, who from the unbegotten radiance above, and from the spirit, is borne down into human nature as into a temple, by the impulsive power of Nature, and by the motion of wind. And it is produced from water being commingled and blended with bodies as if it were a salt of existent things, and a light of darkness. And it struggles to be released from bodies, and is not able to find liberation and an egress for itself. For a very diminutive spark, a severed splinter from above like the ray of a star, has been mingled in the much compounded waters of many (existences), as, says he (David), remarks in a psalm. (V 19,14–16)

In the previous chapter, I discussed the motif of the soul lost in the world. Here the soul is captured in matter (*anima in compedibus*); it is a "severed splinter from the ray" of the uncreated light. Thus, matter is not dead, but contains an imprisoned divine spark, which cannot free itself and cries for help. Jung explains:

> The extension of God as the *anima media natura* into every individual creature means that there is a divine spark, the scintilla, indwelling even in dead matter, in utter darkness. The

---

[11] Tardieu, *Psychaios Spinter*.

medieval natural philosophers endeavoured to make this spark rise up again as a divine image from the "round vessel." Such ideas can only be based on the existence of unconscious psychic processes, for otherwise we simply could not understand how the same ideas crop up everywhere. (CW 11 §152)

We find this motif not only in Hermeticism and Gnosticism, but already in Greek alchemy, for instance, when Komarius tells Cleopatra:

> Tell us how the highest comes down to the lowest and the lowest to the highest, and how the middle approaches the upper and the lower and they become one with the middle, and of what kind of elements they are. And the blessed waters flow down to the dead who are lying there, who are bound and oppressed in the gloominess and darkness of the depths of Hades. And how life's curing element enters in and awakens them, so that they revive for their creators. And how the new [fresh] waters enter into the head of the grave bed and are born in the bed and come forth with the light and the cloud carries them upward. And the cloud which carries the waters rise up from the sea. When the adepts see this apparition, they rejoice.[12]

According to Hippolytus, the Sethians had quite similar ideas, which is hardly surprising because the motif is a principal concern in relation to redemption:

> Since, however, light is above and darkness below, and spirit is intermediate in such a way as stated between these; and since light is so constituted, that, like a ray of the sun, it shines from above upon the underlying darkness; and again, since the

---

[12] Cited in von Franz, *On Dreams and Death*, pp. 28–29.

fragrance of the spirit, holding an intermediate place, is extended and carried in every direction, as in the case of incense-offerings placed upon fire, we detect the fragrance that is being wafted in every direction: when, I say, there is a power of this description belonging unto the principles which are classified under three divisions, the power of spirit and light simultaneously exists in the darkness that is situated underneath them. But the darkness is a terrible water, into which light is absorbed and translated into a nature of the same description with spirit. The darkness, however, is not devoid of intelligence, but altogether reflective, and is conscious that, where the light has been abstracted from the darkness, the darkness remains isolated, invisible, obscure, impotent, inoperative, (and) feeble. Wherefore it is constrained, by all its reflection and understanding, to collect into itself the lustre and scintillation of light with the fragrance of the spirit. (V 19,2–6)

Here the spirit occupies a middle position, just as the soul does. There is considerable overlap between the two concepts, which both denote what animates the dead body. For Gnosticism, as a spiritual religion, the liberating force also leads to consciousness. Light and darkness are interdependent, i.e., one cannot exist without the other. Light, and thus also the spark, is always related to consciousness, so that darkness, its opposite, is the unconscious. This is understood not as a *privatio lucis* (absence of light), but as a being in its own right, which even entertains its own thoughts. This substantive notion of the unconscious is also advocated by the alchemists. In this regard, Gnosticsm, Hermeticism, and alchemy share very similar conceptions. This points to a lively exchange of ideas among the various currents. Thus, not so much trouble was taken to distinguish oneself from neighboring disciplines than to absorb everything helpful in formulating one's own ideas.

In the *True Book of Sophe the Egyptian* [= Cheops], a Greek alchemistic treatise with an Egyptian element, it says:

> For those who rescue and purify the divine soul entrapped in the elements or rather the divine breath commingled in the texture of the flesh, the chemical symbol emerges from the creation of the world in exemplary fashion.[13]

Alchemy imitates the creation while it also attempts to rectify or perfect what the demiurge has botched or left incomplete. But why did the alchemists not perform their work on the human being, like all other redemptive religions, but instead on unknown chemical substances? The work of redemption, which is also the alchemist's goal, does not happen in the conscious person. The unconscious is ubiquitous or rather it is not tied to any place. It is not, as we believe nowadays, located only *in* the human being, but also in objects and substances. What is unconscious, is also projected. For this is not the personal unconscious, which belongs to an individual, but the collective unconscious, which belongs to humanity. The alchemist does not labor to redeem himself in the first instance, but the world. The fact that he did not succumb to a grandiose inflation as the "savior of the world" must be attributed to his humility, religious attitude, and unawareness of his own actions. Thus, not everyone who lives the "Christ in you" (Romans 8:10) necessarily becomes inflated as modern theologians fear. One can also see oneself as a modest tool of the *opus magnum*.

Curiously, the tenth-century Arabic alchemist ibn Umail formulates matters similarly in his brief treatise *Silver Water and Starry Earth*.[14] Reading this work, we need to realize that ibn Umail was very familiar with Greek alchemy:

---

[13] Festugière, *La Révélation d'Hermès Trismégiste* I 261—trans.
[14] Turab et al., *Three Arabic Treatises on Alchemy*, pp. 152 and 174.

But Mary said: the water... is the king who has descended from heaven and the earth absorbs it with her moisture and holds back the heavenly and earthly waters... and honors it because of its sand.... The divine water, which is the soul, is also called the king, because it is spiritual and has been extracted from the earth and rose up to heaven.

A later passage states:

Hermes said that the secret and the life of every thing is water... and that water contains the greatest secret.

Water, as is generally known, occupies a central role in alchemy, because it symbolizes the destructive and life-enhancing aspects of the unconscious. And since redemption is about becoming conscious, water, as a symbol, is always involved in this process. So why, we may wonder, did the alchemists not express themselves in clearer and simpler terms? They claimed to possess a secret that must be concealed from the uninitiated. Similarly, the Gnostics maintained that their treatises were intended for the chosen only. This is not secretiveness, but the secret of the soul, which can convey itself only symbolically, through images. Moreover, it was not until the sixteenth century that the alchemists began to realize that the philosopher's stone that they were creating was something within themselves. This withdrawal of the projection from matter also heralded the end of alchemy. The ancient alchemists conducted depth psychology in the guise of chemistry, just as the Gnostics did in that of theology.

Water is not only holy and eternal. It is also the secret. Thus, in medieval alchemy, it is the mysterious figure of Mercurius (CW 13 §239ff.) that comes to occupy the place of the Gnostic spirit between light and darkness. The difference, however, is that for the Gnostics this is the world-spirit, whereas the alchemists attempt to contain it in a bottle. This signals the progressive attainment of collective consciousness. The creative form of Gnosticism foundered in antiquity whereas alchemy survived for over one and a half millennia. While Gnosticism endured for centuries, it hardly brought forth new ideas.[15]

The alchemists, as the citation from Komarius shows, move back and forth between the highest and the lowest cosmic spirit and the microcosmic event of birth in a retort. In their creative fantasy, these events reproduce a cosmic event on the smallest possible scale. Indeed, our absolute standards fall short as regards "what is greater than great and smaller than small," as the Upanishads put it (Chandogya Upanishad 3,14,3). In effect, unconscious processes are at work everywhere, irrespective of our dimensional notions. The alchemist observing these processes in the retort, as the house of the world, is himself transformed along with his transformative substance. His creative fantasy, which sympathetically accompanies the material transformations, is the transformative agent. It is what Jung later called the *active imagination* ("The Transcendent Function," CW 8 §131ff.). It is an active intervention of consciousness in the emerging unconscious fantasies.

Depth psychology does not destroy the secret of the soul, as some choose to believe. On the contrary, I hope that the many cross-references in this book convey a sense of the complexity and the magnitude of the soul. Psychology does not "explain" the unconscious, which would be grossly presumptive, since consciousness, as an offspring, can never rise above its origin, but instead points to parallel manifestations. This amplification illuminates and clarifies contents. This involves painstaking effort, which unfortunately I cannot spare the reader. The numerous citations gathered here are meant to enable readers to form their own opinion of these contents, so as not to rely blindly on my interpretations.

---

[15] Quispel, *De Hermetische Gnosis*.

An asymmetry exists in Hermeticism and in Gnosticism, where light exists above and darkness below; what is above is qualified in positive terms, and what is below in in negative ones. In alchemy, by contrast, above and below have a symmetrical meaning. The so-called *Tabula Smaragdina* says: "*quod est superius est sicut quod est inferius.*"[16] From this arises a circular process, in which the upper forces are meant to be brought down, and the lower ones lifted up: "It ascends from earth to heaven and returns to earth and takes up the superior and inferior forces." This marks considerable progress compared to the earlier currents, in that the lower sphere (i.e., darkness, the bedeviled matter) is awarded the same meaning in the work as the upper sphere (i.e., light, the spirit). Spiritually, we have still not developed so far as to also live this truth with all its consequences. We still seek the "ideal world" in light and are reluctant to behold our shadow. Thus, we contribute to darkness gaining the upper hand. Jung repeatedly emphasizes that the God-Man has still not become fully incarnated, because Christ is unlike any mortal human. He lacks the shadow, which adheres to us ancestrally, just as the tail belongs to the animal.

The mass has repeatedly been compared with the alchemical opus, which was considered blasphemous. Jung comments on the alchemical paraphrase of Melchior Cibinensis, a Hungarian chaplain (CW 12 §480ff.). In his extensive alchemical work, Pierre-Jean Fabre (1588–1658) attempted to establish the parallels between Christianity and alchemy. He dedicated his *Alchymista Christiana* (1642) to Pope Urban VIII. Its tenth chapter is entitled "The spirit descending from heaven onto earth for the preservation of the life of the sublunar is in some measure a symbol of the Lord Jesus Christ, who in the Holy Communion descends to preserve the life of all believers." Its ninth chapter is entitled "The natural ascent of the Spiritus Mundi to heaven as to his fountain represents the figure of Christ's ascent and his

---

[16] Ruska, *Tabula Smaragdina. Ascendit a terra in coelum, iterumque descendit in terram, et recipit vim superiorum et inferiorum.*

ascension to heaven after his father as his true and veritable fountain." At the end of his book, however, the author still feels compelled to account for his peculiar undertaking. He writes that the secrets of the established church cannot be compared in the least with the profane operations of alchemy, because the former are supernatural. Nevertheless, Christ himself had shown him this path:

> For he frequently refers to himself as a vine-stock or a vine-branch, a vineyard, a lion, an immaculate lamb, indeed even a stone [all well known alchemistic symbols]. And although only an inferior equality exists between Christ and these examples of natural things, he nevertheless maintains that to some extent he imitates these natural things, because a symbol and a shadowy figure is found in these things.

Such inadequate attempts to harmonize Christianity and alchemy seemingly arise less from a need to establish harmony than from a *sentiment d'incomplétude* (sense of incompleteness). Christianity has remained one-sided, whereas alchemy, as a undercurrent, sought to rectify that deficiency.

The Greek alchemist Olympiodoros transmits Mary's exclamation as follows:

> If you do not render incorporeal the corporeal substances and if you do not render <corporeal> the <incorporeal> substances, and if you do not make the two <bodies> into one, none of the expected <results> will occur.[17]

This is alchemy's *opus rotatorium*, one of the key procedures for sublimating solid substances and solidifying ephemeral ones. In the

---

[17] Berthelot, *Collection des Anciens Alchimistes Grecs*, vol. 3, p. 101. The terms occur most certainly in reverse order in the second part of the sentence.

analytical process, sublimation, as the spiritualizing of the concrete body, is a well known procedure, in which concrete facts are perceived symbolically. This is exactly what the Gnostics did with the biblical message. The reverse process, in which spiritual contents become concrete, is the realization of an idea. In the alchemical opus, as in the analytical process, this must be repeated time and again. Both parts are equal, and the process symmetrical. The first part involves the cleansing and liberation of the divine soul that commingles with the elements, as the *Book of Sophe the Egyptian* says. Psychologically, the *extractio animae*, as the alchemists called it, is the withdrawal of the projection from external reality. This painful and tedious procedure has an awakening and a redemptive effect. One is no longer compulsively attached to the outside world and disappointed if it does not behave as expected.

Gerhard Dorn, the seventeenth-century alchemist, formulated this in succinct terms:

> The body must hence be dissolved in the spirit, and the spirit brought back into the body.[18]

In one of his aphorisms, Hermes says:

> If you do not disembody the bodies, and if you do not render corporeal the incorporeal, the expected result will not occur.[19]

The unprepared reader may find the process of making bodily things immaterial odd. In terms of everyday language, however, this seems perhaps less peculiar, such as when we say that "we are *attached* to a piece of furniture, a garment, a piece of jewelry, or a person." Being

---

[18] "Physica Trismegisti," *Theatrum Chemicum*, vol. 1, p. 383—trans. *Corpus igitur in spiritum solve necessarium, et spiritum in corpus redigi.*

[19] Festugière, *La Révélation*, vol. I, p. 242—trans.

attached to something, which in itself is perfectly natural, means that we have blended with that object, unconsciously and necessarily. Indeed, "our heart *clings* to something or someone," so that we lose it if we lose the object or the person. We can detach ourselves only by considering what that object or person means to us symbolically. We can dissolve our dependency by tearing ourselves away from the object or person, because this means losing that part of our soul that has been attached. We are able to regain part of our soul from the outside world only if we consider what that person or object means to us. This, too, is the deeper meaning of the Gnostic *Exegesis on the Soul* (NHC II 6). In the world, we lose our soul to objects and must extract it from them again in the second half of life (!). In contrast, the first half of life must incarnate itself in the world and become embroiled in a myriad of things. Those who do not embrace this task, who remain outside, and who do not wish to sully themselves with the "dirty" world, pay the price of neurosis.

We do not know how the Gnostics and Hermetics understood their writings. Their symbolic language resembles the dreamer's, which enables us to translate their works into psychological language and to understand them. There have been and still are people who have direct access to the unconscious, as children do. Were these perhaps the pneumatics? They require no translation. But most people's consciousness is so far removed from the unconscious that translation serves them as a bridge. Later alchemy had already approached consciousness to such an extent that its writings are more comprehensible.

The *Rosarium Philosophorum* ("The Rosary of the Philosophers"), a sixteenth-century alchemical treatise, cites Senior (i.e., ibn Umail) as follows:

> I am Luna, increasing moist and cold, and thou art Sol, hot and moist (otherwise dry). When we shall be coupled in equity of

state (*aequitas*) in a mansion which is not made otherwise but with light fire [...] when we shall be conjoined we shall be emptied in the belly of the house being shut, I will by flattery take thy soul from thee, if thou take away my beauty and comely shape (*decoram figuram*), we shall rejoice and shall be exalted by the rejoicing of the spirit when we shall ascend the order of the aged (*ordo seniorum*), then the light of thy light (*lucerna*) shall be poured into my light, and of thee and me there is a commixtion made of wine and sweet water, and I forbid my melting (*fluxus*) after thou shalt have put on blackness with my colour, which is like ink (*atramentum*) after my solution (*solutio*) and coagulation (*coagulatio*). When we shall enter into the house of love (*domus amoris*), my body shall be coagulated and I shall be in my emptiness (*vacuitas*).

Sol answers saying: If thou do this and wilt not hurt me (*nocumentum*), O Luna, my body shall be changed (*revertetur*) and afterwards I will give unto thee a new virtue of penetrating (*penetratio*) by which thou shalt be mighty in the virtue of the fire of liquefaction (*liquefactio*) and purging, out of which thou shalt go forth without any diminishing (*diminutio*) or blackness, as copper and lead, and thou shalt not be resisted (*rebellis*), when as thou art not weak.[20] (III 143–144)

Here the opposites have become equal. Traditionally, the soul is attributed to the moon, while the sun symbolizes consciousness. They unite in their abode, a hermetically sealed vessel. Luna loses her beauty, which means she becomes an empty moon. This is the blackness of the moonless night, when Luna is closest to the sun. The light of the sun flows into that of the moon like wine and water, so that they become

---

[20] The square brackets indicate an incomprehensible passage in the Latin.

indistinct. This is a clear reference to the mass, about which Jung says in "The Sequence of the Transformation Rite":

> The mixing of water with the wine originally referred to the ancient custom of not drinking wine unless mixed with water. A drunkard was therefore called *akratopotes*, an 'unmixed drinker.' In modern Greek, wine is still called κρασί (mixture). From the custom of the Monophysite Armenians, who did not add any water to the Eucharistic wine (so as to preserve the exclusively divine nature of Christ), it may be inferred that water has a hylical, or physical, significance and represents man's material nature. The mixing of water and wine in the Roman rite would accordingly signify that divinity is mingled with humanity as indivisibly as the wine with the water. (CW 11 §312)

The union of opposites, so the text, is complete and not merely an admixture or a solution. The term *solutio* is ambiguous: it refers both to a chemical procedure and to the unraveling of a riddle. *Coagulatio* is the opposite of *solutio*, namely, concretization. The soul (*luna*), which was ephemeral, has now become a solid function. The *sol* (sun) confidently anticipates this transformation and believes it will suffer no damage, even though it is darkened in an eclipse. Rather, it appeases Luna, upon whom "a new virtue of penetration" will be conferred. *Penetratio* is a characteristic trait of the spirit, which again reveals the proximity between soul and matter. The remaining parts of the passage are somewhat unclear. What can be established is that after the union the product resists fire and is cleansed. Lead, a "base metal," belongs to the initial stage of the work (I mentioned copper and verdigris earlier).

Our motif reaches its peak here: the fundamental opposites are no longer projected outward, but are instead united within the human being, in the hermetically sealed vessel. The genuine union of opposites transforms both opposites. This is the great novelty of alchemy. All previously discussed currents regarded the human being as what is to be transformed and the divinity or the God-Man as the initiator of that transformation. This principle finds complete formulation in the Valentinian myth of Sophia (Irenaeus, *Against Heresies* I, 2,2ff.), where the Father, through Monogenes, emanated Horos to rescue Sophia. Horos cleanses and fortifies the fallen Sophia, and returns her to her consort (*syzygos*). He detaches and crucifies the *enthymesis* (intention) along with her passion (I 2,4).

Such a rescuing intervention does not transform the rescuer, but the incongruous is cast out of the pleroma (the perfect higher order). Alchemy embraced this expelled *prima materia*, precisely because it belongs to the totality. Christianity cannot be spared the accusation that its ideal of perfection makes it neglect and leave unconscious too much of what actually belongs to the totality. Although Gnosticism is also obsessed with cleanliness, at least it attends to the fallen soul (Ex.am.). There, too, the brother sent forth to rescue her is not blackened.

The ancient *Dicta Alani* state:

> The water of Mercurius is absorbed by the soul of the sun and the moon. What was concealed, namely, the soul, now becomes visible. Conversely, the visible, Mercurius, is concealed. Thus occurs the extraction of the soul (*extractio animae*) through the spirit of Mercurius, not just once and at the same moment, but many times.[21]

The *extractio animae* is the common denominator of all intellectual currents that emerged during Hellenism. Although their methods are

---

[21] *Theatricum Chemicum* III, p. 725—trans.

very different, they all seem to agree that the extraction of the soul is the central element of redemption.

Chapter 10
The Role of the Redeemer

While the redeemer appeared in one form or another already before Hellenism, he became the *central figure* of redemption only in the Hellenistic religions. In classical antiquity, the distance between gods and humans was still so great that veneration, i.e., the cult, was enough to instill in humans a sense of security through the protection afforded by the gods. In mythology, the sacred narratives about the gods, we find much that is human, indeed too human, without this diminishing the depth of reverence in the slightest, however. We must therefore conclude that the gods were an incommensurable factor for humans, true to the saying "Quod licet Jovi, non licet bovi" (*What is permitted to Jove is not permitted to an ox*). People in antiquity, after all, were completely at the mercy of the fate meted out to them at whim by the gods. In the *Iliad*, the gods gamble for their favorites or their allegiance, which spells a bloody fate for humans. This was the prevailing attitude in antiquity.

In Hellenism, an invisible revolution radically transformed this stance. The "Father" is still the unattainable *deus absconditus* (hidden God), who stands above everything, unrecognizably. Now, in his place, his *son* mediates with humans. The *Son of God* becomes the central *figure of redemption*. He becomes the redeemer through his mediatory function: as the son he is equal to God or at least knows the Father while at the same time he is human or at least resembles humans. Jung called this figure of the self in human form the *archetype of the*

Anthropos.[1] He borrowed this term from the Gnostics. In the *Apocryphon of John*, the demiurge Jaldabaoth is instructed as follows:

> The Man [Anthropos] exists and the son of Man [filius Anthropi]. (47,16)

The highest divinity is called *Anthropos*. Primarily, this refers not to an anthropomorphic conception of God, but the opposite: if God created the human being in his image, as Genesis 1:26 says, he must have the same form as his creature, save that his is more perfect. The figure of the Anthropos plays a significant role in Gnosticism.[2]

Gnosticism is not a doctrine of self-redemption, as is often falsely claimed. But, as I have repeatedly emphasized, the redeemer performs a different function in Gnosticism than in orthodox Christianity. In his commentary on "The Golden Flower," Jung writes:

> The West lays stress on the human incarnation, and even on the personality and historicity of Christ, whereas the East says: "Without beginning, without end, without past, without future." The Christian subordinates himself to the superior divine person in expectation of his grace; but the Oriental knows that redemption depends on the work he does on himself. The Tao grows out of the individual. The *imitatio Christi* has this disadvantage: in the long run we worship as a divine example a man who embodied the deepest meaning of life, and then, out of sheer imitation, we forget to make real our own deepest meaning—self-realization. As a matter of fact, it is not altogether inconvenient to renounce one's own meaning. (CW 13 §80)

---

[1] Ribi, *Anthropos*.
[2] Schenke, *Der Gott "Mensch."*

The essence of Gnosticism and Hermeticism lies in *knowledge as that which redeems*. The content of Gnosticism is the Gnostic's knowledge of three essential questions: "where from," "where to," "what for"; these questions concern the extra-worldly sphere and the return to the pleroma.[3] This finds impressive formulation at the end of the "Poimandres," after the visionary has received the instructions:

> First, in releasing the material body you give the body itself over to alteration, and the form that you used to have vanishes. To the demon you give over your temperament, now inactive. The body's senses rise up and flow back to their particular sources, becoming separate parts and mingling again with the energies. And feeling and longing go on toward irrational nature.
>
> Thence the human being rushes up through the cosmic framework, at the first zone surrendering the energy of increase and decrease[4]; at the second evil Machination, a device now inactive; at the third the illusion of longing, now inactive; at the fourth the ruler's arrogance, now freed of excess; at the fifth unholy presumption and daring recklessness; at the sixth the evil impulses that come from wealth, now inactive; and at the seventh zone the deceit that lies in ambush.
>
> And then, stripped of the effects of the cosmic framework, the human enters the region of the Ogdoad; he has his own proper power, and along with the blessed he hymns the father. Those present there rejoice together in his presence, and, having become like his companions, he also hears certain powers that exist beyond the ogdoadic region and hymn god with sweet voice.

---

[3] Voorgang, *Die Passion Jesu*.
[4] First the lunar zone, second Mercury, third Venus, fourth sun, fifth Mars, sixth Jupiter, seventh Saturn; according to Walter Scott, *Hermetica* I 129.

> They rise up to the father in order and surrender themselves to the powers, and, having become powers, they enter into god. (CH I 24–26)

This passage reveals the ascetic stance: the Hermetists cannot prevent the ruler of the planetary sphere from bestowing upon him a typical trait at birth. Yet on his ascent through the various spheres, he returns that trait "unused," and thereby evades its rule. He thus reaches those who truly are, who receive him joyfully. He becomes equal to them and the powers, and ultimately enters into God. The prospect and hope for a blessed end affords him the strength to endure his ascetic lifestyle. But the actual redemption is projected into the phase after death. Life is preparation for a blessed end. In this sense, a lifestyle that abstains from passions and desires is an accomplishment whose fruits are reaped in the world to come.

The *Apocalypse of Adam* (NHC V,5) says: "The men will be like those angels, for they are not strangers to them. But they work in the imperishable seed" (76,3–8). The immortal seed are the chosen, who are guaranteed salvation. In the first volume, I indicated that everyone probably contains a part of this seed and takes heart from it for their particular end.

The *Tripartite Tractate* (NHC I, 5) says: "Now, the spiritual kind will receive complete salvation in every respect" (119,16–17).

Only the chosen will enjoy complete salvation, which goes as far as a union with God (*unio mystica*). The *Exegesis on the Soul* (NHC II, 6), discussed above, emphasizes that "No one can come to me [the Son] unless my Father draws and brings that one to me. I myself will raise that one on the last day" (135, 1–4). Thus, there is no salvation, but instead the concealed Father chooses his people, guides them, and resurrects them through his son. The redeemer's function is described in Clement of Alexandria's *Excerpts from Theodotus*:

> Therefore when the Saviour came, he awakened the soul and kindled the spark. For the words of the Lord are power. Therefore he said, "Let your light shine before men." (3,1)

The resurrection takes place not only beyond the grave, as in Christianity, but also in life, with the awakening of the soul and the kindling of the soul-spark. It plays a major role in the alchemical opus, where it means the *metanoia* (change of mind). It is the secret of the death of the Old Adam and the resurrection of the *corpus glorificationis*.

In the Greek alchemical treatise, Komarius, the philosopher and high priest, explains mystical philosophy to the erudite Cleopatra:

> Tell us how the highest comes down to the lowest and the lowest up to the highest, and how the middle approaches the upper and the lower and they become one with the middle, and of what kind of elements they are. And the blessed waters flow down to the dead who are lying there, who are bound and oppressed in the gloominess and darkness of the depths of Hades. And how life's curing element enters in and awakens them, so that they revive for their creators.

Cleopatra replies:

> The penetrating waters revive the bodies and the bound, weakened spirits (*pneumata*). For they have suffered renewed afflictions and have been hidden again in Hades. After a short time they begin to grow and to come forth and clothe themselves in splendid, bright colors, like the flowers in spring. And Spring rejoices and indulges herself in the beauty which clothes them.[5]

---

[5] Cited from von Franz, *On Dreams and Death*, pp. 28–29.

In spring, dead nature awakens and blossoms anew. This occurs analogously to the dead bodies when they are doused with *aqua permanens* or *hydor theon*. Here redemption takes place through the *blessed water*, which liberates the fettered dead from Hades. Alchemy knows no personal redeemer; according to its materialistic character, it is the special water, which has a thousand names, or medicine, the *alexipharmakon*, the elixir in Arabic, the *pharmakon phoneuton* in Greek, which pervades bodies and kills them. In the Arabic age, the word *iksir* (elixir) is not used until the alchemy of Gabir. It actually means poison. But it is unclear whether, as Friedemann Rex claims, it means the poison of poisons (*samm as-sumum*), the "poison" against every illness, or whether, as Marie-Louise von Franz believes, it is all-pervasive poison that kills the ego.[6]

Alchemy is in search of the panacea (*panpharmacon*) rather than the redeemer, but the former is difficult to find. The thirteenth-century Arabic alchemist Abu'l-Qasim writes in his *Kitab al-'ilm al-Muktasb*:

> ...the Elixir is taken from a single tree which grows in the lands of the West. It has two branches, which are too high for who seeks to eat the fruit thereof to reach them without labour and trouble.... The blossom of one of the two is red, and the blossom of the second is between white and black.... And this tree grows on the surface of the ocean as plants grow on the surface of the earth. This is the tree of which whosoever eats, man and jinn obey him; it is also the tree of which Adam... was forbidden to eat, and when he ate thereof he was transformed from his angelic form to human form.... And this tree may be changed into every animal shape.[7]

---

[6] Rex, *Theorie der Naturprozesse*, p. 115; von Franz, *ibn Umail's Hall ar-Rumuz*, p. 86.

[7] Holmyard, "Abu' l-Qasim al-Iraqi."

The elixir is the *elusive treasure*, which can only be reached only with difficulty. The remedy takes the place of the redeemer. It makes its fortunate owner whole and healthy. Salvation is found in the magnificent *arbor philosophica*, which occupies a significant role in alchemy (Jung, CW 13 §350ff.). The magical tree in our text has mythological echoes: Hesperidian apples, the Tree of Knowledge of Good and Evil (Genesis 3:5), the alchemical process, whose fruits bear the shades of the black, white, and red. This again shows how the human imagination took from the great body of Hellenistic culture what suited it best. The golden apples of the Hesperides in the Western land, which Gaia gave to Zeus and Hera as a wedding gift, are the elusive treasure that Heracles had to steal from the hundred-headed dragon Ladon, which symbolizes the terrible aspect of the unconscious, and which immortalized Heracles.

The above passage in the Komarius text continues as follows:

> But when the dark, fetid spirit (*pneuma*) has been removed, so that no smell and no color of the darkness is perceptible any more, then the body is illuminated and soul, body and spirit rejoice that the darkness has retreated. And the soul calls back to the illuminated body: "Wake up from Hades and stand up from the grave and awaken from the darkness. For you have clothed yourself in spirituality and divinity. For the call of resurrection has sounded and the medicament of life (*pharmakon tes zoes*) has entered into you."[8]

The summons, i.e., the trumpet, is the signal that awakens the soul in Hades. Here occurs a fundamental difference between alchemy and all other mysteries of redemption: the latter always consist of a *unio*

---

[8] von Franz, *On Dreams and Death*, p. 120.

mentalis (Jung, CW 14/II §335), i.e., a union of spirit and soul achieved through overcoming the body. This psychic balancing of opposites leads to a tranquility beyond the body's affective and instinctual state. To attain a higher level, however, alchemy idealizes the dark body in a total union of opposites, which involves the reunion of the spiritual position with the bodily sphere. Thus, it turned toward the material world rather than remaining a purely spiritual current. The union with the body was believed to have an indispensable healing influence.

In the dialogue between Komarius and Cleopatra, it says:

> And all were united in love: body, soul, and spirit—they became one, in which the [unity] of the mystery is concealed. Their union completes the mystery.[9]

Thus, the earliest forms of alchemy knew about the complete union of opposites. In ibn Umail, it says:

> The king lives; he rises from his grave, puts on the purple royal garments and places his crown upon his head, which his feet have brought to his head.

"His feet" refers to the lower part of the vessel while "upon his head" means the upper part.

The union of the *mens*, as Gerhard Dorn calls the product of the union of spirit and soul, and the body, the second level of the union of opposites on the path toward resurrection, is a mystical wedding, a "chemical wedding." Given the meaning of "mystical" here, this marriage can be achieved neither with willpower nor with consciousness. The negative attitude toward matter and the body in all Hellenistic religions probably prevented the complete union of

---

[9] Vereno, *Studien*, p. 213—trans.

opposites. Alchemy was known to be an undercurrent of Christianity, although there were frequent attempts to reconcile them, as I have briefly shown above. Christianity, it must be noted, was one of many Hellenistic mystery religions; its essential character has not changed in the last two thousand years. In the first five centuries, however, its spirit was still in a state of flux, so that it could have developed further. But the development of systematic theology cut Christianity off from its roots, from its primary experience. All institutions and organizations face the danger that their spirit will hypostatize itself. I dare not decide whether this would not have happened if Gnosticism had not been stifled. The fact that Gnosticism is taken notice of today certainly provides languishing Christianity with new blood, provided one engages with this other spirit. As far as I can tell, established scholars treat Gnosticism merely as a subject of research, without asking what it might mean for their own life.

Already the mystical masters of Islam had understood alchemy as a transformation process occurring in the alchemist's psyche. The thirteenth-century scholar and Sufi Ibn Arabi remarks: "It seems evident to you that 'the transmutations are an absurdity'.... It is an act of divine perception which, among us, is 'imaginary' (Khayali)."[10] This perspective marks a certain progress, but it also explains why more and more Sufi masters gave up laboratory work and instead devoted themselves to the "mystical" part of alchemy. In the West, late alchemy ended in mysticism in the seventeenth century, which coincided with the rise of the natural sciences at the time and prompted a renewed split between spirit and body.

Like Avicenna, the tenth-century Arabic philosopher Al-Kindi referred to the power of intimate thoughts, which can even "move mountains" (Matthew 21:21), and thus influence matter. *De Radiis* maintains that the highest God is unmoved and beyond influence. And

---

[10] Ruspoli, *Muhammad ibn Arabi: L'alchimie du bonheur parfait*, p. 94.

yet prayers, together with intense desire, could affect matter, provided that the plea coincided with heavenly harmony.

The alchemist's *active imagination*, which accompanied his handling of unknown substances, might account for numerous analogous coincidences of matter with the adept's expectations. Published under the name of Zosimus, one Arabic treatise contains the interesting story of Alexander the Great's mirror:

> As soon as a man looked at himself in this mirror, it would prompt him to examine and purify himself, from head to foot.
>
> Afterwards the mirror was brought to the priests, into the temple they called "The Seven Gates." These mirrors were made to fit the size of men and revealed unto them that they had to purify themselves. This manifested itself in the form of a mystery...
>
> The mirror had not been made for this goal, that a man should behold himself materially therein; because as soon as he left the mirror he forgot what he looked like. So what, then, was this mirror? Listen.
>
> The mirror represents the divine spirit; when the soul contemplates herself, she beholds her shame, and rejects it; she makes her tasks vanish and remains blameless. As soon as she is purified, she imitates and models herself on the Holy Spirit; she, too, becomes a spirit; she possesses tranquility and keeps turning to this higher state, where she is known (God) and where she knows. Now, without any task, she detaches herself from any ties and from those who share her bodily state, and rises toward the Omnipotent. What does the word of philosophy say? Know thyself. It thus points to the spiritual and intellectual mirror. What, then, is this mirror, if not the divine and primordial spirit (of the Father)?

As soon as man looks into this mirror and sees himself, he turns away from the gods and demons and, attaching himself to the Holy Spirit, he becomes a perfect man; he sees God, who is within him, through the mediation of the Holy Spirit.[11]

Up to this point, the story follows the ancient Delphic maxim "Know thyself," which leads to the discovery of the divine spark within the human being. To this extent, this process is no different from the common Hellenistic one, and one wonders what its alchemical aspect might be. Its discovery requires a precise knowledge of alchemical symbolism. At the beginning, Alexander talks about a secret recipe for producing electrum, an alloy of gold and silver, which already represents a union of the ultimate opposites. In one land, lightning never ceased to strike the earth and each year it destroyed the fruits of the earth and its dwellers, so that only very few survived. This is the *terra damnata* (cursed earth). Alexander knew about this and invented this alloy. This gleaming metal protected the land and the people against lightning. Alexander made coins out of it and distributed these among the population. From that time on, there was no more lightning. The people who found the coins sown by Alexander used them as amulets.

Sowing coins in the soil is an alchemical process. We can marvel at the Emblema VI in Michael Maier's *Atalanta Fugiens*: "Sow your gold in the white foliated earth." The philosophers should do this for the farmers (*ruricolae*) and cast their gold into the earth, because like wheat, as the explanatory epigram says, it has a life of its own and grows.

Self-knowledge through reflection (the mirror) is the gold that must now be subjected to everyday experience (the earth), where it will grow like wheat and yield diverse fruit (John 12:24). The Hermes citation is a common saying; it is found, among other sources, in the

---

[11] Berthelot, *Collection des Anciens Alchimistes Grecs* II, pp. 262–263—trans.

work of Muhammed ibn Umail. In the Hermetic treatise XIV, Hermes Trismegistos explains to Asclepius how God created the world:

> If you want to learn how he makes, how things come to be that come to be, it is given to you. Consider this lovely image that is very like him: See a farmer casting seed upon the earth, here the wheat, there the barley, elsewhere seed of some other kind; see him planting the vine and the apple and other kinds of trees. In the same way, god sows immortality in heaven, change in the earth, life and motion in the universe. (CH XIV, 9–10)

Discussing this passage, Marie-Louise von Franz remarks that the act of sowing goes back to the mysteries of Osiris:

> It points to a post-mortal process of resurrection or regeneration in which many are produced from one and there is a secret identity of things that are "like." The potential unity of the cosmos is indicated in the seed motif, but it also has an intrapsychic meaning as the germ of conscious realization of the self.[12]

The Arabs were eclectics, who chose from Gnosticism, Neo-Platonism, and Greek and Christian philosophy those elements that best suited their purposes. Ibn Sina (Avicenna in Latin) says in *Havy b. Yaqzan* that "through self-knowledge and knowledge of the surrounding world you will attain knowledge of God."[13] In the Gnostic *Gospel of Truth* (NHC I, 3), it says:

> The gospel of truth is joy for people who have received grace from the Father of truth, that they might know him through the

---

[12] von Franz, *Aurora Consurgens*, p. 401 (§583 in GW).
[13] Affifi, *The Influence of Hermetic Literature on Moslem Thought*, p. 845.

power of the Word. The Word has come from the fullness in the Father's thought and mind. The Word is called "Savior," a term that refers to the work he is to do to redeem those who had not known the Father. (16, 33–37)

Jacques Ménard, the editor of the French translation, comments on this passage as follows:

> The supernatural knowledge revealed by the Logos leads to salvation, as we shall see, by the realization of this spiritual seed, which each one of us bears: it is above all a knowledge or recognition of the superior "self." Common to Hermeticism and Gnosticism, salvation is the reascent to the Principle, to the condition that each of us becomes aware of as the "us" existing within each of us and that, returning to ourselves, we return to the Father."[14]

Here, the function of the Gnostic redeemer becomes plainly evident as the Logos, which leads human beings to self-knowledge, which is identical with knowing the Father. The *Gospel of Philip* (NHC II, 3) says:

> The upper realm was opened for us in the lower realm, that we might enter the hidden realm of truth. This is what is truly worthy and mighty, and we shall enter through symbols that are weak and insignificant. They are weak compared to perfect glory. There is glory that surpasses glory, there is power that surpasses power. Perfect things have opened to us, and hidden things of truth. The holy of holies was revealed, and the bedchamber invited us in.

---

[14] *L'Evangile de Vérité*, pp. 43 and 76—trans.

> As long as the seed of the Holy Spirit is hidden, wickedness is ineffective, though it is not yet removed from the midst of the seed, and they are still enslaved to evil. But when the seed is revealed, then perfect light will shine on everyone, and all who are in the light will [receive the] chrism. Then slaves will be freed and captives ransomed. (85, 11–17; 22–28)

Here, the redemptive power is the perfect light, which rains upon all slaves and prisoners. Light symbolizes the illuminating consciousness. In the above citation, it replaces the Logos and reveals the function of the Gnostic redeemer as the one who guides human beings to liberating knowledge. This is the fundamental difference to the Christian redeemer, who takes upon himself the sins of humankind through his passion.

Various redeemer figures exist in Gnosticism (Seth, Noah, etc.) and have the same function. In the *Concept of our Great Power* (NHC VI, 4), it says:

> Then, in this aeon, which is the psychic one, the man will come into being who knows the great Power. He will receive (me) and he will know me. He will drink from the milk of the mother, in fact. He will speak in parables; he will proclaim the aeon that is to come, just as he spoke in the first aeon of the flesh, as Noah.... And he opened the gates of the heavens with his words. And he put to shame the ruler of Hades; he raised the dead, and he destroyed his dominion.
>
> Then a great disturbance took place. The archons raised up their wrath against him. They wanted to hand him over to the ruler of Hades. Then they recognized one of his followers. A fire took hold of his soul. He (Judas?) handed him over, since no one knew him (Jesus?) [Luke 22:57]. They acted and seized him. They brought judgment upon themselves. And they delivered him up

to the ruler of Hades. And they handed him over to Sasabek for nine bronze coins. He prepared himself to go down and put them to shame. Then the ruler of Hades took him. And he found that the nature of his flesh could not be seized, in order to show it to the archons. But he was saying: "Who is this? What is it? His word has abolished the law of the aeon. He is from the Logos of the power of life." And he was victorious over the command of the archons, and they were not able by their work to rule over him.

The archons searched after that which had come to pass. They did not know that this is the sign of their dissolution, and (that) it is the change of the aeon.... And after these things he will appear ascending. And the sign of the aeon that is to come will appear. And the aeons will dissolve.

And those who would know these things that were discussed with them, will become blessed. And they will reveal them, and they will become blessed, since they will come to know the truth. For you have found rest in the heavens. (40,24–42,31)

This passage is typical of Gnostic reception. The redeemer is the anthropos who announces the new aeon. He knows his father, the great force, which Simon of Samaria saw himself to be. He will overcome the earthly aeon that Noah has heralded and will open the gates of heaven (Genesis 28:17). He will resurrect the dead and break the power of hell. All of a sudden, the story of the redeeming anthropos follows that of the Passion of Christ with Judas' betrayal. Offering himself to the powers of the underworld as the "fish-hook," however, he sows confusion among these powers and dissolves their rule.

The Gnostics, whenever they mention the Passion of Christ, emphasize that Christ on earth only seemed to suffer. This doctrine is known as docetism. Typically Gnostic is the laughing Christ, who leads the powers of darkness a merry dance by foisting upon them another body for crucifixion, for instance, Simon of Cyrene's (Matthew 27:32). Because it held the Passion of Christ to be the central work of redemption, the established church became very agitated about Gnostic docetism, which took many different forms.[15] Docetism can be understood only in terms of the entirely different function of the Gnostic redeemer. Those who have understood the truth, to whom the anthropos has announced a new aeon, are saved and enter repose (*anapausis*). This blissful state, as I have shown above, is free of opposites.

The *Apocalypse of Adam* (NHC V, 5) speaks of the "illuminator," which is probably the most fitting expression for the Gnostic redeemer:

> Once again, for the third time, the illuminator of knowledge will pass by in great glory, in order to leave (something) of the seed of Noah and the sons of Ham and Japheth—to leave for himself fruit-bearing trees. And he will redeem their souls from the day of death. For the whole creation that came from the dead earth will be under the authority of death. But those who reflect upon the knowledge of the eternal God in their heart(s) will not perish. For they have not received spirit from this kingdom alone, but they have received (it) from a [...] eternal angel. (76, 8–27)

Gnostic redemption is often understood as a gathering together (*syllexis*), whether of souls or pneumatics in the *ecclesia spiritualis* (spiritual church), or of the remaining coming of light among the Ophites, but above all through the gathering and liberation of light in Manichaeism.

The redeemer is concealed and manifests himself in various forms: as light, as a voice, and as the word concealed in the

---

[15] Voorgang, *Die Passion Jesu*.

"unspeakable silence." In the *Paraphrase of Shem* (NHC VII, 1), the redeemer says about himself:

> For this is my appearance: for when I have completed the times which are assigned to me upon the earth, then I will cast from me [...] And my unequalled garment will come forth upon me, and also all my garments which I put on in all the clouds which were from the Astonishment of the Spirit. For the air will tear my garment. For it (i.e., my garment) will shine, and it will divide all the clouds up to the root of the Light. The repose (*anapausis*) is the mind and my garment. (38,28–39,11)

Unlike Christ, the Gnostic redeemer appears in many different forms. The *Tripartite Treatise* (NHC I, 5), states:

> Now, the Savior in fact was a bodily image of something unitary, namely the All. Therefore he preserved the model of indivisibility, from which is derived impassibility. (116)

Thus, the Gnostic redeemer is an image of totality and unity. An image is not a copy, but an inner image, an inner reality. "The inner image is a complex structure," writes Jung, and adds:

> made up of the most varied material from the most varied sources. It is no conglomerate, however, but a homogeneous product with a meaning of its own. The image is a condensed *expression of the psychic situation as a whole*, and not merely, nor even predominately, of unconscious contents pure and simple. It undoubtedly does express unconscious contents, but not the whole of them, only those that are momentarily constellated. This constellation is the result of the spontaneous activity of the unconscious on the one hand and of the momentary conscious

situation on the other, which always stimulates the activity of relevant subliminal material and at the same time inhibits the irrelevant. Accordingly the image is an expression of the unconscious as well as the conscious situation of the moment. The interpretation of its meaning, therefore, can start neither from the conscious alone nor from the unconscious alone, but only from their reciprocal relationship. ("Definitions," CW 6 §690)

Readers unfamiliar with Jungian psychology will be asking themselves why I am citing so many different sources. This, as Jung explains, serves what he calls "amplification":

> In dealing with the products of the collective unconscious, all images that show an unmistakably mythological character have to be examined in their symbological context. They are the inborn language of the psyche and its structure, and, as regards their basic form, are in no sense individual acquisitions. Despite its pre-eminent capacity for learning and for consciousness, the human psyche is a natural phenomenon like the psyche of animals, and is rooted in inborn instincts which bring their own specific forms with them and so constitute the heredity of the species. Volition, intention, and all personal differentiations are acquired late and owe their existence to a consciousness that has emancipated itself from mere instinctivity. Wherever it is a question of archetypal formations, personalistic attempts at explanation lead us astray. The method of comparative symbology, on the other hand, not only proves fruitful on scientific grounds but makes a deeper understanding possible in practice. The symbological or "amplificatory" approach produces a result that looks at first like a translation back into primitive language. And so it would be, if understanding with the help of

the unconscious were a purely intellectual exercise and not one that brought our total capacities into play. (CW 10 §646)

This brings us back to the theme of collection, of gathering together! The orientalist Valentinian school, whose representative works include Clement of Alexandria's *Excerpts from Theodotus*, asserts that "Wisdom, he says, put forth a receptacle of flesh for the Logos [i.e., the Savior], the spiritual seed; clad in it the Saviour descended" (1,1). Irenaeus says: "And this spiritual element, they say, is the salt... and the light of the world [Matthew 5:13]" (*Against Heresies* I 6,1). Theodotus adds: "The visible part of Jesus was Wisdom and the Church of the superior seeds and he put it on through the flesh" (26,1). In typically Gnostic fashion, the redeemer's incarnation is understood simultaneously in spiritual terms, as the seed brought down to be saved. We need not dwell any further on the differences between the two Valentinian schools. Crucially, the redeemer brings with him what is to be redeemed. Theodotus formulates this as follows:

> The Cross is a sign of the Limit in the Pleroma, for it divides the unfaithful from the faithful as that divides the world from the Pleroma. Therefore Jesus by that sign carries the Seed on his shoulders and leads them into the Pleroma. For Jesus is called the shoulders of the seed and Christ is the head. Wherefore it is said, "He who takes not up his cross and follows me is not my brother." Therefore he took the body of Jesus, which is of the same substance as the Church. (42, 2–3)

Collection refers to those who are destined for redemption. But the term also has a psychological meaning, namely, collecting oneself. "When, however, all the offspring have attained perfection," says Irenaeus,

> ...they say that Achamoth, their Mother, will withdraw from the intermediate region and will enter the Fullness and receive Savior as her spouse, who was made out of all [the Aeons], that the conjugal union between Savior and Wisdom, that is, Achamoth, may take place. These are the bridegroom and the bride, but the bridal chamber is the entire Fullness. The spiritual persons, moreover, having put off their souls and having become intellectual spirits, will enter the Fullness without being apprehended or seen, and will be given as brides to the angels who surround Savior. (I 7,1)

Here we encounter the image of the seed again, and related with it maturation. This harvest is gathered by the redeemer, who is the first to perform the "Sacred Wedding" (*hieros gamos*). Maturation indicates new development within the Gnostic. Such indications are rather sparse, so that we need question whether any development occurs at all. Ultimately, though, all apocalyptic descriptions serve to guide the Gnostic's development. In the curious *Letter of Peter to Philip* (NHC VIII, 2), found at Nag Hammadi, Peter tells his fellow disciples:

> My brothers, listen to my voice. And he was filled with a holy spirit. He spoke thus: "Our illuminator, Jesus, came down and was crucified. And he bore a crown of thorns. And he put on a purple garment. And he was crucified on a tree and he was buried in a tomb. And he rose from the dead. My brothers, Jesus is a stranger to this suffering. But we are the ones who have suffered through the transgression of the mother. And because of this, he did everything like us." (139,14–26)

Notably, this citation reverses the usual interpretation: not Jesus suffered for all of us, but he is the prototype of *our* suffering. His example encourages the Gnostic to "take up his cross" (Matthew

10:38). The danger of the established church, as Jung explains in a letter to the Reverend Dr. Dorothee Hoch of July 3, 1952, is that one assumes that

> Christ and *his* cross deliver us from our conflict, which we simply leave alone.... Instead of bearing ourselves, i.e., our own cross, ourselves, we load Christ with our unresolved conflicts. We "place ourselves under *his* cross," but by golly not under our own. Anyone who does is a heretic, self-redeemer, "psychoanalyst," and God knows what. The cross of Christ was *borne by himself* and was *his*. To put oneself under somebody else's cross, which has already been carried by him, is certainly easier than to carry your own cross amid the mockery and contempt of the world... Whoever imitates Christ and has the cheek to want to take Christ's cross on himself when he can't even carry his own has in my view not yet learnt the ABC of the Christian message. (*Letters* II, p. 76)

The Nag Hammadi text strikes me as a first step, and as a mark of considerable progress for those times.

Those alchemists who, while making no compromises with Christian salvation, nevertheless felt obliged to complete the uncompleted work of redemption pursued this direction steadfastly. As much as this made them assume the role of the redeemer themselves, of which they remained unaware, they were saved by a curious redemptive figure, which we shall turn to at the end of this chapter: the legendary Hermes Trismegistus (thrice-greatest Hermes).[16]

The Greek Hermes underwent a peculiar transformation in Hellenism, becoming a kind of revelatory god invoked by Hermeticism. In Egypt, he was associated with Thoth, the god of scribes who became

---

[16] Fowden, *The Egyptian Hermes*.

a god of wisdom. His role as a psychopomp (i.e., guide of souls) stood him in good stead. The Greek settlers identified him with Hermes, so that he became a syncretistic figure. Like other, similar figures, he stands between humans and gods, and thus belongs to the anthropos figure like Heracles, Dionysus, Asclepius, and Orpheus. In the stories told about him, he preserves his Egyptian origin. Asclepius, to whom a treatise is devoted in the *Hermetica*, is not the classical Greek god of healing, but a syncretistic figure along with the legendary Egyptian architect and physician Imhotep, who served during the Old Kingdom. Without dwelling on the other figures resembling him, Hermes is already described as follows in the Hermetic treatise *Kore Kosmou*:

> Such was all-knowing Hermes, who saw all things, and seeing understood, and understanding had the power both to disclose and to give explanation. For what he knew, he graved on stone; yet though he graved them onto stone he hid them mostly, keeping sure silence though in speech, that every younger age of cosmic time might seek for them [...] Hermes, however, made explanation to surrounding space, how that not even to his son, because of the yet newness of his youth, had he been able to hand on the Perfect Vision. But when the sun did rise for me, and with all-seeing eyes I gazed upon the hidden mysteries of that new dawn [*aurora consurgens!*], and contemplated them, slowly there came to me—but it was sure—conviction that the sacred symbols of the cosmic elements were hid away hard by the secrets of Osiris. Hermes, ere he returned to Heaven, invoked a spell on them, and spake these words. For 'tis not meet, my son, that I should leave this proclamation ineffectual, but rather should speak forth what words our Hermes uttered when he hid his books away. Thus then he said: "O holy books, who have been made by my immortal hands, by incorruption's magic spells.... free from decay and incorrupt from time! Become unseeable, for

every one whose foot shall tread the plains of this our land, until old Heaven doth bring forth meet instruments for you, whom the Creator shall call souls." (Stobaeus, Excerpt XXIII)

This story explains the *arcanum* (secret), which also plays a significant role in the Hellenistic mysteries. Here lies the difference between Hermetic and profane philosophy, which is accessible to everyone. As the passage cited above from Jung shows, the collective unconscious not only possesses a rational aspect, but also a feeling aspect, an emotional value. Therefore, no secretiveness is involved, nor any deliberate obfuscation, but a genuine state of possession by the secret of the soul. Time and again, it is emphasized that the secret may not be divulged to any unauthorized person. Considering that alchemical treatises were accessible in countless books, this warning makes little sense, unless the alchemists themselves did not really know the nature of the secret.

Ever since this story in the Hermetic treatise *Kore Kosmou*, innumerable stories were told about mysterious discoveries in concealed writings, whose sole objective was to emphasize the *mystery*. In the *Life of Adam and Eve* (49), Eve admonishes her descendants to write down her life and her father's on tablets of stone and clay, because she knows that the Lord, in his wrath, will annihilate the human race with water and fire. Since these stories are so common, I would not dare trace them to either a Gnostic or a Jewish source.[17]

Among the Nag Hammadi scriptures is the *Apocalypse of Adam* (NHC V, 5), which I have cited several times. It contains Adam's revelation to his son Seth, who occupies a major role among the Gnostics. Epiphanius explains this as follows:

> Two men came into existence right at the beginning, and Cain and Abel are the sons of the two. The angels quarreled about

---

[17] Festugière, *La Révélation d'Hermès Trismégiste*, vol. 1, p. 321.

them and went to (war with) each other, and thus caused Abel to be killed by Cain. For the angels' quarrel was a struggle over the human stocks, since these two men, the one who sired Cain and the one who sired Abel, (were at odds). But the power on high, whom they call Mother and Female, was the winner.... Since the power who is called Mother and Female won, they say, she reflected—finding that they had killed Abel—caused the generation of Seth, and put her power in him. In him she planted a seed of the power from above, and the spark that was sent from above for the first planting of the seed, and the Origin (of it). And this is the origin of righteousness, and the election of a seed and a stock, so that the powers of the angels who made the worlds and the two primordial men would be purified through this origin and by this seed. For this reason the stock of Seth, which is elect and distinct from the other stock, is derived separately from this origin. (*Panarion* 39, 2,1–6)

Adam tells his son Seth that the Gnosis was lost due to the demiurge's jealousy and his attempt to destroy humankind through the flood and through fire until the arrival of the third redeemer, the "illuminator":

When God had created me out of the earth, along with Eve, your mother, I went about with her in a glory which she had seen in the aeon from which we had come forth. She taught me a word of knowledge of the eternal God. And we resembled the great eternal angels, for we were higher than the god who had created us and the powers with him, whom we did not know.

Then God, the ruler of the aeons and the powers, divided us in wrath. Then we became two aeons. And the glory in our heart(s) left us, me and your mother Eve, along with the first knowledge that breathed within us. (NH V,5 64,6–28)

The text ends thus:

> These are the revelations which Adam made known to Seth, his son. And his son taught his seed about them. This is the hidden knowledge of Adam, which he gave to Seth, which is the holy baptism of those who know the eternal knowledge through those born of the word and the imperishable illuminators, who came from the holy seed. (85,19–29)

These words of the highest god were not written down for later generations, but preserved on a high mountain, the rock of truth, as the "Words of Imperishability and Truth (85, 5–18).

Now, this knowledge always remains original. Due to the corruption of the world, however, it must be transmitted secretly until the pure seed, which will find this knowledge, is born.

In his apocryphal testament, Adam also predicts to Seth the coming events, which he has heard about through his direct communication with God:

> He spoke to me about this in Paradise [saying]: "Adam, Adam do not fear. You wanted to be a god; I will make you a god [John 10:33–36], not right now, but after a space of many years. I am consigning you to death, and the maggot and the worm will eat your body".... And I, Seth, wrote this testament.... And we sealed the testament, and we put it in the cave of treasures with the offerings Adam had taken out of Paradise, gold and myrrh and frankincense. And the sons of kings, the magi, will come and get them, and they will take them to the son of God, to Bethlehem of Juda, to the cave.[18]

---

[18] Charlesworth, *The Old Testament Pseudepigrapha*, vol. 1, p. 994.

This suggests that concealment is intended to safeguard the message for the elect. It was deplored that Gnosticism had an elitist trait. This is not a defect, however, but a privilege, just as alchemy or analytical psychology is not for everyone. Each is a destiny, a calling, rather than a matter of choice.

One of Zosimus' writings, which has survived in Arabic as "Risālah fī bayān tafrīq al-adyān wa-tafarruʿ al-ʿibādāt wa-al-diyānāt wa-al-iʿtiqādāt" (*The Explanation of Differences of Religions and the Variation of Religious Observances, Professions of Faith, and Beliefs*) also begins with the legend of Adam, who, after his expulsion from Paradise, carried with him all kinds of books about astrology, medicine, magic, and the creation of gold and silver. He passed on this knowledge to Seth, who was the first prophet, who passed it on to Idris (i.e., Hermes). Engraved on clay, wooden tablets, and stone, these sciences were spared extinction in the flood. Due to a misunderstanding, the Persians, Indians, Sabians, Manicheans, and Christians developed these sciences into different religious systems.

The Arabic author Abu' L-Qasim Al-Iraqi describes the traditional transmission of alchemy in his text *Risala' Maghush al-Maghribi* as follows:

> Alchemy was revealed by God to Adam (peace be upon him!), then to his son Seth, then to Hermes, then to Noah, then to Shem, then to Ham, then to Falagh, then to David, then to Solomon, then to Alexander (Iskander), then to Hippocrates, then to Pythagoras, then to Socrates, then to Aristotle, then to Galen, until it reached to Islam by [various] means, and was spread abroad among the prophets.[19]

---

[19] Holmyard, p. 407.

Thus, the Arabs took little interest in historical connections, which might explain why countless alchemical treatises were transmitted to the Latin Middle Ages under fantastic pseudonyms. One also speaks of "the Aristotle" and other imputed writings, which is incorrect in that these were not forgeries, but evidence of ahistorical understanding.

The Arabic epistle *qabas al-qabis fī tadbīr Harmas al-Harāmis* equates Hermes with Ahnūh (i.e., Enoch) and Idris. Hermes, according to this letter, is Syrian for "the knowing one," which is a reference to his wisdom. "Ahnūh, praise be unto him,"

> ...had migrated from upper to lower China; then he entered the land of India, in the valley of the River Sarandib (Ceylon), until he reached the Darandib mountains, unto which Adam—praise be unto him—had descended [Adam Peak]. From there he reached the cave replete with treasures, which he called the Cave of Treasures, because it contained the treasures and precious metals of science; remember this! So after Ahnūh—praise be unto him—had reached and entered this place, he found tablets, on which the treasures of science were written. Then he took the most beautiful, the briefest, and the most important from each science, until he stood before the science of the noble art. Therein, he also found many stones and for each stone manifold procedures. Among these stones he found a stone that was the most noble and most important, whose effect was the strongest of all, the most colorful, and the easiest to use.... This is the mother and the father of all procedures, and this is the work of nature, and the work of our Lord Adam—praise unto him—whose procedures we have described in various treatises.[20]

---

[20] Siggel, "Das Sendschreiben"—trans.

In the Syrian *Book of the Cave of Treasures*,[21] the cave is said to be Adam's grave, in which all descendants must serve before the dead body and may not withdraw from it. When the flood approached, Noah took Adam's dead body onto the ark. Later, a tree grew upon the grave, upon which eventually the cross came to stand. It is the center of the earth and where Adam and all his children are redeemed.

Such reports have offshoots in Latin alchemy. Bernardus, Earl of the Mark of Treviso, writes in his *Liber de Alchemiae*:

> Since its establishment, the Father of this art is called Hermes, as in all books of the Hermetic Turba, which used to be called Pythagorean.[22] No matter how many will perform this art, they will be known as the sons of Hermes. It is said, in the scriptures, that he was the first to set foot in the valley of Hebron, where he found seven stone tablets, on which the sages had engraved the seven free arts before the flood, which they alone had known from the beginning, so that they would not be forgotten.[23]

After his expulsion from Eden, Adam is said to have come to the Valley of Hebron, where he found the tablets. Hermes had written on other tablets, which he called the *Tabula Smaragdina* ("The Emerald Tablet of Hermes"), which begins with the words: "This is true and remote from all cover of falsehood" (*Verum, sine mendacio, certum et verissimum*) (*Theatrum Chemicum*, IV).

What comes from the beginning of the world, and perhaps even from the Creator himself, is the original truth, which has survived intact, unfalsified by human beings. This truth claims the highest credibility. In human beings, it represents the instinctive truth from the deep layers of the psyche, whose age is immeasurable, and which we

---

[21] Bezold, *Die Schatzhöhle*, p. 27.
[22] Actually, the "Assembly of Philosophers"; see Ruska, *Turba Philosophorum*.
[23] *Theatrum Chemicum* I (1659)—trans.

even share with our animal ancestors. These stories tell the tale of a *pre-existent knowledge*, which is happily distinct from modernity.

The seventeenth-century Frankfurt physician, Paracelsus, and alchemist Gerhard Dorn formulates this as follows in his *Congeries Paracelsicae chemica De transmutationibus metallorum*:

> Adam, the first teacher and inventor of the arts and their knowledge, conferred upon him by divine light, which he possessed of all things before the fall, prophesied that the earth will be renewed by water, or come within a hair's breadth of being annihilated. Hence his descendants should erect two stone tablets, upon which the natural arts existing since the beginning of time should be engraved in hieroglyphic signs, to ensure that his prophecy would reach all his descendants so that they could face the dangers of future ages with the necessary precaution. Noah found one of the tablets after the flood, by the River Ararat in Armenia; described thereupon where the proportions of the upper firmament and the lower spheres and the courses of the planets.[24]

Wilhelm Christoph Kriegsmann, a seventeenth-century Hermetic author, offers a slightly different account of this story in his commentary on the *Tabulae Hermeticae*[25]: in the centuries after the flood a woman named Zara had to be taken out of the hands of the dead body of Hermes at the entrance to the town of Hebron. It was not known whether this woman was Sarah, Abraham's wife.

There is a story of the *Sacro Catina*, an emerald tablet, which the Queen of Sheba reportedly gave to King Solomon. The tablet had served Christ as a dining table. It was stolen by the crusaders during the conquest of Caesara in 1101 and taken to the cathedral of Genova.

---

[24] *Theatrum Chemicum* I (1659), p. 543f.—trans.
[25] Manget, *Bibliotheca Chemica Curiosa* I, p. 384.

These stories are often related to the Egyptians, which suggests close contact with Egyptian culture and the Greco-Roman origins of alchemy.[26] Throughout this volume, I have repeatedly emphasized that Hellenism was a great spiritual "reservoir," from which the unconscious drew those images and ideas that best suited it. In one of these stories, the various wisdoms are said to have been buried in hieroglyphic signs. In Hellenistic Egypt, pictographic writing was no longer understood, thus making it even easier to infer all kinds of wisdom traditions in these temple inscriptions. One such story concerns Pseudo-Democritus, an authority on Greek alchemy, who purportedly came from Egypt:

> Indeed, I, too, come from Egypt, to which I bring the science of the occult virtues.... But because our master (Ostanès) died before our initiation was completed, leaving us totally preoccupied with the task of recognizing matter, I tried to evoke it from Hades, as they say. So I set to work and, as soon as it appeared, I asked it: "Do you not give me anything in return for what I have done for you?" No matter what I said, it remained silent. But when I addressed it in the most beautiful terms, and asked how I could engage with the natures, it told me that it found it difficult to speak, since the demon forbid it from speaking. It simply said: "The books are inside the temple." Turning around, I set off to investigate in the temple, to see if I could lay my hands on the books—for it had not said anything about any descendants and had died intestate, according to some after taking a poison to separate the soul from the body, according to its son after swallowing the poison inadvertently; it had taken precautions, before its death, to ensure that its son would not recognize these books if he survived the first age: however, none of us knew

---

[26] Lindsay, *Les Origins de l'Alchimie dans l'Egypte Gréco-Romaine*.

anything about these matters.... When we were inside the temple, all of a sudden, a column opened in the middle. At first sight, however, it was empty. But Ostanès (the son) told us that it contained his father's books.... Bending forward, we were surprised to see that nothing had escaped us, apart from a helpful formula: "One nature is charmed by another, one nature defeats another, one nature dominates another." Our admiration that so much of the Scripture was gathered in so few words was great.[27]

Like the *Tabula Smaragdina*, this story encapsulates the essential mnemotechnic verses, which are repeated countlessly in alchemy. It lends more weight to the seemingly harmless, yet infinitely profound sayings, which, for the alchemists, represent the essence of their work.

In his *Final Account*, Zosimos refers to the story of Democritus.[28] At the time of Hermes, natural colorations were reportedly found in a book bearing the same title. The ancients, however, above all Hermes, were accused of never expounding these methods, whether publicly or secretly. Democritus alone had described them in his work. But the ancients had engraved the procedures in symbolic signs upon a stele standing in the shadows of the temple. This was done so that anyone who sought to gain unauthorized knowledge in the darkness of the sacred place could not understand the signs, despite his temerity in entering the sacred precinct.

The theme of the book that is hidden and rediscovered is so common that it is impossible to reproduce all the corresponding passages.[29] Pebechios, who had found hidden books belonging to the divine Ostanes in Egypt, tells an interesting and instructive story. The books were written in Persian, which he could not understand. Pebechios consulted the Persian magician Osron, who told him the

---

[27] Festugière, *La Révélation d'Hermès Trismégiste*, vol. I, p. 228—trans.
[28] Berthelot, *Collection des Anciens Alchimistes*, vol. 3, p. 233.
[29] Festugière, *Ibid.*, p. 321.

following story: some of Hermes' pupils unraveled one of the king's spells and were thus able to explain the writing on the stele. They showed the king the true art. In return, he erected secret places in Egypt, where either he or the philosophers engraved the divine and unspeakable art on seven tablets. He built seven doors as entrances to the secret place. On one door, he had the serpent Ouroboros and symbolic pictures painted. He decreed that the doors should be opened only to those of high descent and to the adepts of the master. Thus, the priests concealed the secrets and returned to their homeland.

The ancient sages, of course, knew the sacred Egyptian places, and the magnificent images contained therein, from inside. Since they no longer understood their meaning, they interpreted the images in terms of their secret. At least they knew that these places were royal tombs, in which the dead bodies await their resurrection. This suited the work of the ancient sages, who expected the same process to take place in the retort. Hence, the temple largely contained the same mystery as the Hermetic vessel. I have referred to several texts to elucidate the awakening of the dead in Hades by the descending holy waters, so that readers will understand the parallel drawn by the alchemists. The temple, moreover, was a sacred place of the mysterium, just as the Hermetic vessel was for practicing the divine art. Both exerted a fascination that finds expression in our naive stories. For the Egyptians, moreover, matter was sacred and male (Geb); this suited the alchemists insofar as they believed that matter contained a divine mystery.[30]

Transmitted in the Arabic tradition,[31] the *Book of Cratès* includes a wide-ranging story of discovery, from which I cite only the most important passages:

In a vision, the author is raised up onto the path of the sun and the moon. In one hand, he holds a scroll of parchment entitled "He

---

[30] von Franz, *ibn Umail's Three Arabic Treatises on Alchemy*, p. 25ff.
[31] Berthelot, *La Chimie au Moyen Age*, vol. 3, pp. 44–75.

who dispels darkness and makes clarity appear." Several figures, representing the seven heavens, the two large glinting orbs, and the five wandering planets, which are moving in the opposite direction, are drawn on the parchment. The author then sees an old man seated on a chair. He is the most beautiful of all human beings, clad entirely in white garments, and is holding a book lying on a lectern with his right hand. Before the old man lay the most magnificent vessels that the author had ever seen. When he asked the old man for his name, he said it was Hermes Trismegistus; he explained that the book is among those that elucidate the mystery that is hidden away from human beings. The author was told to remember the contents of the book so that he could describe it to his own kind.

The figure of the old man seated on a throne recurs in other tales of discovery. Here this figure is called Hermes Trismegistus (Thrice-Greatest Hermes). He owns the mysterious book, *the* book of alchemy. A similar illustration can be found in Senior's *De Alchemia*; Senior is the Latin translation of Arabic *Zadith*, the wise man. He holds a book with the two large orbs before him and is surrounded by a group of philosophers. Five birds are aiming a bow and arrow at the book, which symbolizes the directedness of the process. The individual stages of the process are described in Ibn Umail's text.[32]

The visionary in Cratès' account of his mystic experiences is bending over a volume held by Hermes, in which two figures are described: one is concerned solely with the goods of the world and its pleasures, the other with virtue, wisdom, peace, and benevolence, according to the principles of the revealed religion (Islam!). This is the theme of Heracles at the crossroads, which represents the correct attitude toward the work. Among the people, the alchemists are mostly known as gold-makers. But their writings contain enough hints that precisely this is not the correct attitude toward the work. The

---

[32] Turab et al., *Three Arabic Treatises on Alchemy by Muhammad ibn-Umail*, p. 146.

materialist and the spiritualist are discussing this question: the latter asks the former whether he knows his soul completely. Because if he did, and if he knew how he might improve it, he would realize that the philosophers' words are not reliable, because no one was prepared to accept the designations used by his precursors. This had greatly confused the art.

This confusion springs from the use of so-called pseudonyms. Each alchemist claims to be employing secret names to prevent the unauthorized from accessing the secret. The true secret, however, has no name, and therefore is given a thousand names. No specialist language exists for the secret of the soul, because it is a genuine mystery, which can be expressed only symbolically. "The living symbol formulates an essential unconscious factor," writes Jung,

> and the more widespread this factor is, the more general is the effect of the symbol, for it touches a corresponding chord in every psyche. Since, for a given epoch, it is the best possible expression for what is still unknown, it must be the product of the most complex and differentiated minds of that age. But in order to have such an effect at all, it must embrace what is common to a large group of men. This can never be what is most differentiated, the highest attainable, for only a very few attain to that or understand it. The common factor must be something that is still so primitive that its ubiquity cannot be doubted. Only when the symbol embraces that and expresses it in the highest possible form is it of general efficacy. Herein lies the potency of the living, social symbol and its redeeming power.
>
> All that I have said about the social symbol applies equally to the individual symbol. (CW 6 §820–21)

Its symbolic nature and pseudo-chemical idiom render the language of alchemy extremely difficult to understand. Hermes tells Cratès:

> Know, O heavenly Cratès, that not one single philosopher has not done everything in his might to reveal the truth. The difficulty that they have experienced in illuminating these matters for the ignorant has led them to prolixity. They have said what ought to be done, and what not. The ignorant treated these books as a matter of fun; they derided them and rejected them as evil, disheartening, saddening, and laughable, as far as the knowledge of the truth is concerned.

Although unprecedented numbers of books are printed nowadays, we have lost the kind of respect expressed in the above passage. Books have become profuse, commonplace. We are critical of their contents, but they no longer serve as a vessel of truth. Nevertheless, we still succumb to what is printed "in black and white," as if it were the final word. Choosing books or manuscripts based on their quality was indispensable in earlier times due to the effort involved in their production. Books were not readily accessible and could be read only by the educated. This explains why the book, as the memory of humankind, exercises such fascination.

Pseudo-Manetho[33] claims that the Gnostic books were found in the *Dayta* (the most sacred place) of the Egyptian temples, where Hermes had placed them. He had written these books on stone tablets, and hence they survived the flood. Afterwards, the second Hermes had written them in books and on scrolls of parchment, and even later they were translated from Egyptian into Greek. This indicates the sacred character of these writings, which could be kept safe, but only at a sacred place. The time-honored age of these books bears witness to their veracity. In an unpublished manuscript, one of Hermes' medical recipes is written on golden tablets entrusted to the priests of Ptah in Memphis, on the condition that their existence be kept secret. This

---

[33] Festugière, *Corpus Hermeticum*, vol. 3, p. CLXIII; Scott, *Hermetica*, vol. 3, 491–493, and A3.

secrecy was breached only when a Roman emperor suffering from gout needed the remedy. Thus, the sacred ancient texts also contain the remedy for the soul, which is what the alchemists were seeking.

The story of Cratès has also survived in the Arabic tradition, although under other names.[34]

Numerous different traditions have shaped the figure of Hermes, which explains why he took on increasingly fabulous traits. Another figure that had already become legendary in antiquity, and which alchemy adopted for its purposes, was Apollonius of Tyana (Balinus in Arabic). He was a Neopythagorean in Cappadocia and the subject of controversy already during his lifetime. Empress Julia Domna, the wife of Septimus Severus, commissioned the Sophist Philostratus of Lemnos to author an eight-volume biography of the life of Apollonius, which has very novelistic features. Apollonius was known as a magician and miracle-worker (*thaumaturgos*); he could heal the sick, exorcize demons, and awaken the dead. He possessed the gift of prophecy, understood the language of animals, and communicated with the gods and the remote heroes. He bears unmistakable parallels with the anthropos figures of the Hellenistic mystery religions. There was even a proper Apollonius cult, who was said to be a pupil of Hermes Trismegistus and a temple servant in the asclepeion at Epidaurus, the most celebrated healing center of the classical world. Philostratus reports that Apollonius had spent seven days in the oracular cave of the god Trophonius, where he wrote the *Pythagoron doxai* (the words of Pythogoras). He is therefore regarded as the transmitter of Hermetic texts. In one occult text, "Alexander's Treasure" (*Dahirat al-Iksander*), Alexander is supposed to have recovered Hermes' original text from a hiding-place in the sea. Yet another book, the *Book about the Secrets of Creation* (*Kitab Sirr al-haliqa*), is (mistakenly?) attributed to Apollonius. It contains the following story of discovery:

---

[34] Ruska, *Arabische Alchemisten*, vol. 1, pp. 16–18.

In Tyana, the hometown of the poor orphan Balinus, a statue of Hermes stood on a column, whose inscription declared that beneath the image lay concealed the secret of the Creation and the representation of nature. While the people of Tyana did not understand the meaning of the inscription and stared at the foot of the statue in vain, Balinus, as soon as he had grown up, understood that he needed to dig up the earth at the foot of the statue. Digging, he discovered the entrance to a dark vault; he was unable to enter the place, because fierce winds kept extinguishing his lamp. Exhausted from his futile attempts, he fell asleep. In his dream, perfect nature advised him to shield the flame with a glass jar. When he entered the temple, he saw an elderly man who sat on a golden throne; this figure held an emerald tablet bearing the inscription, "The Representation of Nature"; before the man lay a book titled "The Secret of Creation." Balinus owes his knowledge of the structure of the world to his discovery of these two texts in the cave.[35]

Evidently, a book in which the story of creation is recorded is not merely precious but also sacred. These narratives seek to express nothing less than this, but thereby avoid any conflict whatsoever with established religion. The book's title encapsulates both the intention and the objective of the alchemical opus. While prevailing religion seeks the divine mystery in heaven and in the spirit, Balinus searches beneath the feet of the statue of Hermes, i.e., in the chthonic sphere. Thus, prevailing religion and alchemy never came into serious conflict, because each searched for the divine mystery in another sphere. Alchemy sought the god who had sunken into matter as compensation for all other religious currents. Hermeticism and Gnosticism, from which alchemy adopted a great deal, paved the way.

---

[35] Weisser, *Das "Buch über das Geheimnis der Schöpfung" von Pseudo-Appollonius von Tyana*, pp. 74–75; Ruska, *Tabula Smaragdina*, p. 113—trans.

In the *Kitāb al-Fihrist* ("Book of Records"), Ibn al Nadīm (987 CE) reports that the pyramid is the tomb of the Babylonian Hermes. He cites the story of an Egyptian viceroy who was eager to find out what stood at the top of the pyramid. Eventually, he found a man from India who was prepared to climb up to the capstone. When he returned, the man described what he had found:

> There was in the middle of this platform a fine cupola, and in the midst of it something like a tomb. At the end of this tomb stood two stone slabs of perfect workmanship and beauty, and rich in colours. On each of them was a statue of stone, one representing the figure of a man and the other that of a woman; they had their faces turned to one another. The man held a tablet with an inscription on it in his hand, whilst in the hand of the woman was a mirror and a golden instrument like a chisel. Between the slabs there was a stone-vessel covered with a golden lid. He says: I tried to remove it, and eventually I succeeded in doing so; and I saw in it something like pitch that had become dry, but without its smell [= nigredo]. He says: I put my hand into it, and there was in it a golden casket; I opened its lid, there was fresh blood in it, which coagulated as soon as it met the air as blood usually does, and which had already dried up when I was ready to descend. He says: On the tomb there were stone covers which I repeatedly tried to remove, until at last I managed to lift one of them. There was a man lying on the back of his head, well preserved, but absolutely dried up (mummified); the shape of his body was clearly recognizable, and his hair still visible, and at his side a woman of the same appearance. He says: And this platform had a cavity about the height of a man, and, round about, some thing like semi-oval recesses with stone vaults on which there were figures partly lying, partly standing, and pictures as well as utensils of unknown shape. But Allah knows best (if this be true).

The story continues as follows:

> In Egypt there are buildings called Barabi (Temples), built of huge stones, that surpass all measures. Such a temple consists of apartments of various shape in which there are places for grinding, pulverizing, dissolving, coagulating, and distilling, which shows that the temple was erected for (carrying out) the Alchemical Art. In these buildings there are paintings, and inscriptions of unknown purport in the Chaldean houses, wherein these sciences were written on parchment treated with lime, on (papyrus made of) bast from the white poplar such as are used by the bowmakers, on plates of gold and copper, and on stone, Hermes composed on the stars, on Magic and on the Pneumata.[36]

Even Athanasius Kircher (1602–1680) states that Albertus Magnus believed that Alexander the Great, during his military campaigns, had discovered the tomb of Hermes, the father of all philosophers. The tomb, so states Magnus, was filled with treasures. These were not made of metal, but of gold, and written on the *Tabula Zadati* (i.e., emerald tablet).

The pyramid, this magnificent yet incomprehensible structure, provided the Arabic descendants with a superb projection screen, upon which they rediscovered all their alchemical ideas. Already in antiquity tomb raiders in search of the *aurum vulgi* had plundered some of these edifices, so that the contents of these buildings became known. The contents were interpreted in alchemical terms, and the pyramid became an alchemical laboratory as a result. In terms of alchemy, everything was curiously linked with everything else, which rendered the entire opus intelligible.

---

[36] Fück, *The Arabic Literature on Alchemy*, p. 51.

Based on a series of dreams, I would like to provide the reader with some insights into how the "book" manifests itself in a modern analysand. In this case, the analysand is a young male academic, aged about 30, who took a strong interest in science and had entered Jungian analysis about two months earlier.[37]

> June 30: A large number of papers and books written by alchemists are piled up in a room. Two colleagues of mine claim that no important alchemists existed anymore; everything now emerging was the work of "para-alchemists," who—the narrator is visibly struggling to express himself and points to his heart—rely on the voice of the heart alone and write down what they hear. I have three penises and hence constantly feel like emptying my bladder. Each time I urinate in another room, but take care I do not wet the papers.

Until then, the dreamer had never taken an interest in alchemy. "Para-alchemists" is an invented term and refers to a secondary current of ordinary alchemy, which is more feeling-toned, as suggested by the reference to the heart, where feelings are usually localized. The three penises are a quirk of nature, a hypertrophy of the creative imagination. Ordinary alchemy takes feelings too little into account.

> July 4: I am looking at various animals in a fifteenth or sixteenth-century castle. Afterwards I am browsing in an antiquarian bookshop and find a dark-blue book whose spine measures about 50cm. I take it off the shelf, because I want to find out how many

---

[37] I have shortened the dreams to highlight their essential motif. Also, I have preserved the first person singular, in which the dream narratives were jotted down by the analysand.

pages this fat book contains. I am disappointed when I discover that there are only 948. I look for translations of Latin authors and find none. The new leather-bound books are standing in a bright light.

Latin alchemy reached its peak in the 15th and 16th centuries. The castle is a place of introversion, where one comes into contact with one's instincts. In an antiquarian bookshop, a recurring theme from this point, the treasures of the past are preserved. Only the expert considers them valuable. In earlier times, books were leather-bound, and there appears to be a renaissance of such old books. Jung, as a matter of fact, bought his alchemical books from an antiquarian bookshop at little expense. Ever since many people have been collecting such books, and prices have soared to exorbitant heights. But many old standard works are now being reprinted. Suddenly, a knowledge of Latin, to be able to study these texts, is in demand. A blue book cover is rather unusual. Dark blue refers to a hidden spirituality. Indeed, before Jung's time, no more than a historical approach to alchemy existed. Only Jung opened up the spirit of alchemy.

> August 6: To reward someone for a good turn, I give that person a book, whose pages I find myself turning. I realize that from its middle the text is in reverse order. The cover bears a dedication written by a former owner of the book, which is secondhand. I ponder where I might write my dedication.

Midway, the book of life is turned by a hundred and eighty degrees. Although the dreamer has not reached the middle of his life, the dream prepares him for this reversal of values.

> October 10: A railwayman is working on the lines at a station. Suddenly, he notices a train travelling at considerable speed

toward him. He positions himself so awkwardly between the tracks reading a book, that the train has to stop to avoid a collision.

The dreamer's fascination with books has made him turn away from the world, so that he can no longer follow the pace of everyday life.

November 11: I am at the court of a king in a foreign, non-European country. By the lake many books are standing on long shelves. The king will celebrate the midnight ritual and is wearing colorful, gold-embroidered clothes. He is taller and fatter than us and sings in a nasal voice. Then he sits down and calls me over to him. He promises me an elephant if I cure his mechanic of his chronic bronchitis.

The many books are unable to replace life, which is represented by this primitive, nature-bound king. The midnight ritual is the lower turning point in the "Amduat," the Egyptian book about the afterworld, wherein the greatest dangers lie. Alchemy never contented itself merely with the spiritual side of the opus, but considered concrete practical work just as worthy. The king's mechanic, a practical craftsman, suffers from a chronic respiratory illness that impairs his pneumatic system. The elephant offered by the king as a prize for his cure embodies the utmost value.

February 2 of the following year: We are walking through many gloomy rooms in a communist museum, when suddenly my torch goes out. According to the catalogue, this room is called "Base of the Skull." In the autumnal evening sun, some colleagues are talking about Professor X's plan to introduce communism already as early as 1936. I am browsing in an antiquarian bookshop full of beautiful, partly leather-bound books, also encyclopedias, but find nothing that appeals to me. The bookseller knows me from earlier times and praises my exactitude.

Communism is an ideology that diminishes the individual and glorifies the collective as the state. In such an era, the light of the individual goes out. The vegetative functions are located at the base of the skull. Human beings are reduced to their primitive function. This is Augustine's "evening knowledge."[38] Professor X was a Nobel Laureate, the author of a thousand-page textbook, and always wore a black suit and a choker, and used a walking stick: he was the epitome of the dignified old-fashioned professor. He is committed to this collective mentality. Bookish knowledge is misplaced, since here it is a matter of cultivating individual values. Books can have not only a preceptive effect but also a collective one. The alchemists eschewed this inasmuch as they cited those passages from their precursors' books that coincided with their own experience. Thus, they eluded the suggestive influence that all books have. Instead, one's own work matters greatly, because books convey another person's spirit and consciousness, which can have devastating effects if one fails to engage creatively with the writer's thoughts. In consumer society, engaged reading is yielding increasingly to superficial consumption. Today, we avoid mental effort and prefer to be entertained. Consequently, book culture is in decline. In science, "one knows more and more about less and less." We lose ourselves in the myriad forms of evening knowledge and no longer seek genuine food for the soul.

August 12: A crane is lifting large square blocks of stone onto a sea mole. A tidal wave caused by rockfall is surging across the lake. We come to a bulwark; it's the stock exchange. There are

---

[38] Ribi, "Morgenerkenntnis und Abenderkenntnis."

many books inside, and I browse through them. To my surprise, their contents are psychological.

A rockfall had occurred recently on Lake Lucerne, causing great anxiety among the locals. It symbolized a strong emotional convulsion of the collective. A sea breakwater offers protection against the emotions breaking forth from the unconscious, the lake. One needs a safe haven where one can seek refuge from a storm. The stock exchange is the extraverted side of international business, a barometer of its current state. The surprising aspect of this dream is its peripeteia, i.e., the dreamer discovering many psychology books at the stock exchange. In his "Face-to-Face Interview" with the BBC (1959), Jung said:

> People didn't think of a war, and therefore it was rather clear what the dreams meant. Nowadays no more so. We are so full of apprehensions, fears, that one doesn't know exactly to what it points. One thing is sure. A great change of our psychological attitude is imminent. That is certain.
>
> [Interviewer:] *And why?*
>
> Because we need more—we need more psychology. We need more understanding of human nature, because the only real danger that exists is man himself. He is the great danger, and we are pitifully unaware of it. We know nothing of man, far too little. His psyche should be studied, because we are the origin of all coming evil.[39]

Psychology is not only a matter for specialists. All of us should be interested in acquiring consciousness, wherever we stand in life. The

---

[39] *C.G. Jung Speaking*, p. 422.

stock market and its fluctuations, provide seismographic indications of how unstable collective consciousness is, just how easily the smallest convulsions can unsettle it, and how fancifully it responds to all kinds of insinuations. Consciousness ought to become a stable bulwark, but this requires the individual to confront his or her psyche. There is no universal ready-made recipe that can be applied instead of the long and tortuous (Herculean) process involved in becoming conscious. No one else can do this for us.

> February 11 of the following year: I am browsing in a bookshop filled with rows and rows of shelves. I find a volume belonging to a ten-volume work about animals in Christianity. Otherwise there is little of interest. We visit a book exhibition to see the complete edition. We start with the encyclopedias.

A ten-volume work about animals in Christianity is tremendously exaggerated, because animals are no more than secondary in Christianity. Such a work enhances the previously neglected role of animals, a task to which the alchemists dedicated themselves. Christian redemption is centered exclusively on humans. Some Hellenistic mystery cults concerned themselves more with this instinctive sphere. Examples include the Mithras cult (bull sacrifice; the appearance of lions, snakes, and scorpions on public monuments), the redemption of Lucius the donkey in Apuleius' *Metamorphoses*, the cult of Cybele, and many others.[40]

The reader might object that animals are indeed present in Christianity: in the stable at Bethlehem, as evangelical symbols, and in the Revelation of John. These instances, however, lack the sacredness and the positive role of the animal still common in Egyptian religion.

---

[40] Cumont, *Die orientalischen Religionen im römischen Heidentum*.

Alchemy addressed this neglected chthonic sphere, and animals subsequently played an important role in the history of alchemy. Thus, its *Filius Makrokosmi* (Son of the Great World) also includes our roots in the animal world. The instincts are exactly that unconscious sphere that connects us with animals. In Christianity, this sphere has been ousted by the cultural instinct to the extent that it finds vehement expression, for instance, in the "sexual revolution." But even living sexual life to the full has not had the desired soothing effect. Spirit and instinct must remain in proper harmony if one-sidedness is not going to lapse into pathology. "Too much of the animal distorts the civilized man, too much civilization makes sick animals," writes Jung (CW 7 §32).

> February 13: I am walking home, a breadknife is tucked under my arm. I turn to Jung's book for guidance about one question.

The knife symbolizes discerning reason. Bread is everyday food. Each day we must decide how much of the animal side is necessary and how much culture, which domesticates the animal, is conducive. On the path toward ourselves this involves walking a very fine line. Jung's books provide orientation. They are like a lighthouse amid the vast ocean of the world.

> March 2: All the members of my family are on their way to the theater accompanied by two servants, a young healthy fellow from the countryside and his friend. At the thought that the play might contain a sad passage the boys begin to cry and remain standing outside the playhouse. I don't know which play I have received an invitation for. A large poster announces a gala evening featuring a travelling company. When I raise the poster, I find antiquarian books. I don't find anything of interest. But my sister is very excited and keeps looking through the books. I reach

a small alley in the old town, where I find a bookshop full of old books. They are all over-sized, a format I have never seen before. Most of them are leather-bound, some have large titles on their spines: a great, voluminous work on ethics, a multi-volume work on ethnology. I am fascinated most by a display case containing many slender over-sized volumes by C.G. Jung, their covers made of very old gold plates. I inquire about the price, which I am told is 1,600 Swiss francs. I object that they ought to be cheaper, because the *Collective Works* are about to appear. The bookseller hands me a catalogue, a black book with golden letters, so that I can see for myself. Each author has a page of his own. I look for "Jung," but cannot find his name. Meanwhile the bookseller disappears. I have been moved to a new class and have brought along my Latin book. A young teacher comes in and his questions suggest that this is a school for physiotherapists. He asks me a question about a dermatological disease that I am unable to answer. I leave the room and meet C.G. Jung at a table. He is about 50 years old. His head is round, his hair sparse and white. He is wearing a pale-grey summer suit and looks a bit like my father. He is holding a notebook bearing the insignia of the bank where my father worked. He says little, soon gets out of his chair, and leaves. He has made a great impression on me, although he looks like the average man his age. My classmates are romping about down by the lake and jumping into the water from a boat. I feel left out. Snow has fallen overnight, as I gather from looking at the hills on the other side of the lake. Instead of the lido there is a long art nouveau villa to my left, probably a hotel. We are crossing a square in a foreign city. An older woman wearing heavy make-up is carrying a clothes rack with a long white dress. I think it's a dancer heading over to the theater. My companion makes some lewd remarks. Even a nun joins the ribaldry and refers to it ambiguously as a matter of duty and as playing a sexual game with a man. At the nearby newsstand I see illustrated magazines that fit the nun's goings-on.

The theater is the "Great World Theater" of life, on whose stage the dreamer is at once spectator, actor, and director. In alchemy, the young servants are the auxiliary spirits (*paredroi*), natural, feeling-toned boys. The dreamer's feelings are still natural, undifferentiated. This explains why he resists sad events in the play. Beneath the theater poster appear antiquarian books, which fascinate only the dreamer's feminine side. The theater symbolizes the concrete life, the antiquarian books as it were its abstraction. The truly numinous books are located in the oldest part of town. At the time the dreamer did not know that such book formats existed; he later found them in the Central Library. As far as the contents are discernible in the dream, the books are about ethics, ethnology, and Jung's writings.

In the first volume, commenting on Buber's allegation that Jung was a Carpocratian, I touched on the role of ethics in the individuation process. Ethnology is important for understanding the psyche because archaic ways of functioning play a significant role in our unconscious, which is still in its primordial state and upon which a cultural varnish has laid itself. Jung's works are very precious, and the dreamer hesitates whether he is prepared to make such a large investment. Even the catalogue is valuable. Subsequent events reveal to the dreamer that he has not reached the pinnacle of his knowledge and still has much to learn. Instead of bothering with abstract Latin, he must learn how to cure the body, which must here be understood as the *corpus* in the alchemical sense. Then he meets C.G. Jung in person, whom he has never met in real life. He is a father figure, and no different in appearance than the ordinary man. The mana-personality makes a great impression on the dreamer, who is now certain that his psychology is the person and his life his psychology. Only when the work is congruent with life, and life with the work, is a book really true. This insight isolates the dreamer, just as Jung's experiences separated him from his classmates. The snow represents emotional distance. Art nouveau is a playful period of art, in which one delighted in beautiful ornaments. And thus one can amuse oneself on the edge of the stage, if one no longer accepts the world as the absolute truth. Even a nun can play tricks and still remain faithful to her inner truth.

> January 1 of the following year: I am on duty at the clinic over the Christmas season and therefore have an announcement to make at three shops that have been entrusted to me. The baker's no longer sells bread, but is full of bookshelves. Then a fourth task demands my attention.

Books, as we have seen in an earlier dream, provide intellectual nourishment, which becomes more and more important toward the midpoint of life. Then the problem of three and four is hinted at, which Jung elaborates on in "A Psychological Approach to the Dogma of the Trinity":

> Here we meet, at any rate in veiled form, the dilemma of three and four alluded to in the opening words of the Timaeus. Goethe intuitively grasped the significance of this allusion when he says of the fourth Cabir in Faust: "He was the right one / Who thought for them all," and that "You might ask on Olympus" about the eighth "whom nobody thought of".... We can now see that it was nothing less than the dilemma as to whether something we think about is a mere thought or a reality, or at least capable of becoming real. And this, for any philosopher who is not just an empty babbler, is a problem of the first order and no whit less important than the moral problems inseparably connected with it. (CW 11 §183–184)

We have already come across the moral problem in the dream on March 2 of the previous year, in the context of the great, voluminous work on ethics. The problem recurs here in a general and more concealed form. The breadknife from the earlier dream had long implied intellectual nourishment. This motif weaves its way subtly through the dreams:

> July 12: I am in a shop, where, among many other books, I find very old dictionaries, including one of the Tibetan language. The chief physician comes in, recognizes me, and says: "By the way, about dying from depression…. I recently had two cases…. A young glider pilot arrived completely exhausted; digitalis injections are helping him." I see a silver-grey glider. I go up to the pilot, who has two small, paddle-shaped wings to fly with.

Here we find someone who is reluctant to put his feet on the ground and exhausts himself as a result. Digitalis is a medicinal product that strengthens the heart muscle. Depression means that the man ought to come down. As a rule, we resist this with all our might, which leads to exhaustion. The dreamer is still too much "up in the air." Being introverted, he shirks reality. The dictionary helps him translate one language into another, for instance, the language of the unconscious (Tibetan) into that of consciousness. The symbolic language of the unconscious requires translation to render it comprehensible to consciousness. This is an ancient art.

> March 3 of the following year (4th year): After masturbating, I let my wife masturbate me again while I kiss another woman. I call for a supervisory authority. A woman accompanied by many people appears and finds me in this compromising situation. They say that this entitles my wife to file for divorce immediately. Then I am standing outside a bookshop, embarrassed. Everyone

knows what I have done. I step inside. On a shelf, the gold-lettered black volumes of Jung's *Mysterium Coniunctionis* catch my eye. I find a copy that Marie-Louise von Franz used for the third volume of the work.

Here the moral question is unmistakably raised. At the time, the dreamer was confronted with an extra-marital affair. The dream answers this question in the clearest possible terms, but it points the dreamer toward the even greater problem of the union of opposites. *Mysterium Coniunctionis* is Jung's most mature work, his *opus magnum*, his late work, in which he drew the conclusions from his study of alchemy. The conjunction is the central operation in the alchemical opus. A unified personality can come into being only if the manifold oppositions of human nature are united. Consciousness cannot afford this operation, because as the breadknife suggests, it must discern. Only eros is the transcendental force that can accomplish the miraculous union of opposites. The dreamer very much admires the work of Marie-Louise von Franz on alchemy.

> March 27: I am walking down an unfamiliar street and through subway stations toward a square with a French refugee child. There is a bookshop with beautiful antiquarian books. I buy a French edition of Alfred Adler's *The Nervous Character*. Then I look for a reference work on world religions.

In the war, many starving children came to Switzerland from occupied France, the country where feeling and eros are cultivated. In this regard, the dreamer's feminine side is still very underdeveloped and undernourished. He must attend to this side, affectionately and patiently. In *Concerning the Nervous Character*, Alfred Adler studied the human power complex as a mechanism that triggers neuroses. Commenting on Adler, Jung writes:

> Where love reigns, there is no will to power; and where the will to power is paramount, love is lacking. The one is but the shadow of the other: the man who adopts the standpoint of Eros finds his compensatory opposite in the will to power, and that of the man who puts the accent on Eros. (CW 7 §78)

When one principle prevails, the other is overshadowed, because they exclude one another in consciousness. In the previous dream, we saw the problem of eros, and here we are confronted with the problem of power as the cause of neurosis. Freud and Adler reduced the problem to human endeavor, ultimately to sex or power. This biological power perspective is unsatisfactory, because it neglects the numinosity of both instincts. To achieve completion, a religious dimension is needed, for only this affords human life meaning and dignity. In the previous dream, this was expressed by the mysterium and here by the study of religions. The alchemists performed their work with a religious attitude. Next to the laboratory stood an oratory, where the process was accompanied by meditation. [Figure 2] The starving child within the dreamer can recover only if it receives patient attention.

> January 1 (six years after the first dream): I am standing outside a large library. It is my father's, which he inherited from his ancestors. It is comprised of small and large volumes. I take a large old volume and start browsing. It is an old encyclopedia with a clearly legible font and beautiful old illustrations.

This dream occurred after the dreamer had delivered his first talk at a renowned association. His father was an extraverted practitioner fully immersed in life, and who took no interest in books. Also, the dreamer could not recall any book-collecting ancestors: they are the dreamer's inventions.

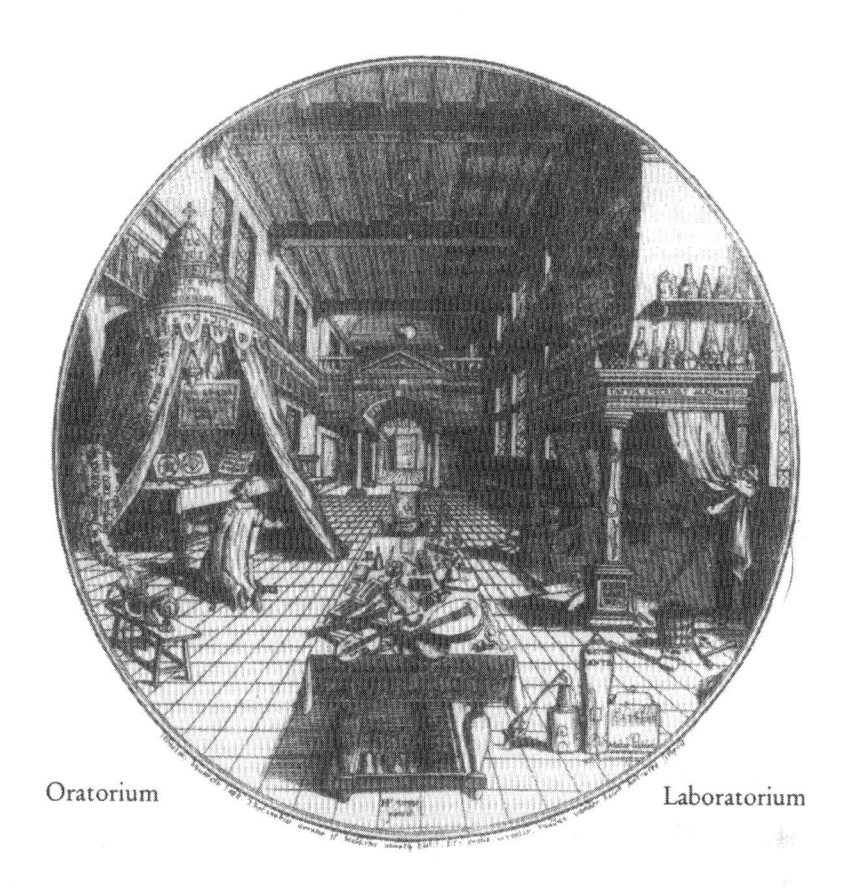

Figure 2. Henricus Khunrath, *Amphitheatrum Sapientiae Aeternae*, 1608

The father represents the dreamer's intellectual side. He has inherited a large treasure. The old encyclopedia stands for the treasure trove of intellectual history, which this volume has offered a glimpse of.

This wealth represents our unconscious roots: it concerns a fundamental question—"where do we come from?"—which the Gnostics sought to answer. There is no simple answer to the questions asked by the Gnostics: "where do you come from?", "where are we going?", and "what for?" On the contrary, one must painstakingly study the entire encyclopedia of the history of ideas.

> February 2: I step into a bookshop on Kreuzplatz. It is a nice antiquarian bookshop filled with old works consisting of multiple volumes. I take down some linen-bound books, which look like Jung's seminar protocols, but are actually old photocopied volumes. I inquire about books by Jung. A woman who is looking for books with her husband overhears my question. I ask her whether she is also interested in Jung's work. She replies that she is. I emphasize how difficult studying his work is. Then I find a multi-volume work about dream interpretation, especially a volume about this practice among the Babylonians. I want to buy all five volumes. They cost 199 Swiss francs. I consider that this type of dream interpretation is obsolete, but that the Jung Institute ought to purchase these books for historical reasons.

The Kreuzplatz, which occurred in many earlier dreams, is where the opposites converge. Here the opposites are united. Dream interpretation was alluded to already in the dream about the dictionary. It is the core of analysis, because the unconscious and its intentions should be considered. It has a long history, stretching back to the Babylonians. Today, we obviously no longer interpret dreams in the same way, but it is impressive to see that people have taken this voice, the "Voice of God," seriously since time immemorial. The connection was not severed until the Renaissance, after which human beings relied increasingly on reason. The discovery of the unconscious in the twentieth century compensates for the one-sided overestimation of consciousness, similar to the relation of alchemy to Christianity. We must once again approach an archaic attitude, one which considers the unconscious, but find this very difficult.

> May 29: Someone tells me that it is possible to build supersonic planes. I agree. At the Central I come past a school. I see teachers

and students entering, among them my former Latin teacher. We are eating in the parlor, where there is a colorful hustle and bustle. A former chief physician is sitting in the bay window. It's hot and he takes off his sweater. Underneath he is wearing two more sweaters, a waistcoat, another sweater, and a white shirt. I believe this is where schemes are plotted and decide to speak up against them. Down on the lower Mühlesteg there is an antiquarian bookshop that sells old encyclopedias. One is entitled "You can't teach an old dog new tricks..." I am surprised that the shop is open so late. The new publications of an acclaimed science publisher are displayed on one shelf.

The theme of "flying" recurs here in a more modern form, not as gliding but as technically sophisticated air travel. The problem of three to four seems to have become more subtle. The dreamer has drawn closer to the center of personality. As an introvert, he is confronted with the extraverted world, where life is lived and where schemes are plotted. The introvert tends to flee this world into the world of books. This is not legitimate. His shadow, in the guise of former chief physician, isolates itself too much, and does not expose itself to the surroundings. But he is already shedding his insulating layers. The introvert faces the danger of retreating to a glass house. His decision to confront the plots and schemes is a sign of progress, because these are made not only in the outside world but also inside. This is a lifelong learning process. One often hears the prejudice that the individuation process makes people egotistical and egocentric. This dream shows that the opposite is true. The center is not the ego, but the whole world. The ego must learn that the world mirrors all the unconscious parts of the personality. Without confronting the world, no consciousness can be attained, or as Jung succinctly put it: "One cannot individuate on Mount Everest." The Central is a lively square in Zurich, where many tramways and streets intersect. The Mühlesteg, where mill wheels stood in former times, crosses the River Limmat not far from the Central. The mill is one of the first machines that made human work easier. In the course of life, these wheels turn day and night. Here the dreamer finds the old encyclopedia, significantly entitled "You can't teach an old dog new tricks...." Individuation is a lifelong process, but important points are switched already in the first half of life. What one would need to know to take decisions at that stage, one discovers only later.

> September 8: I find myself in the company of a friendly gentleman at the Paradeplatz. My father passes us and turns around several times. He is wearing a strange-looking felt cap. We cross a little hill and come to a small back alley where we find an antiquarian bookshop selling old engraved illustrations. Then I am being shown round the Pestalozzi Library. In a large hall is the Goldmann Library. When I return, I realize that the person who has shown me around is an acquaintance. I take her under my coat and cuddle her. Then I am in the army, where old things are being tidied up. Dr. R. is standing in front of me and says that the blue (or red?) fish provided the most light as *abat-jours* [skylights]. Together with other people, I behave impossibly so that they want to throw me out. Eventually, though, I am accepted nevertheless.

The Paradeplatz is where the dreamer's father, an epitome of law and order, used to work. The felt cap comes from an animal and, as *a pars pro toto*, it represents instinct as a guiding principle, namely, the power principle. The striving for power belongs to the survival (i.e., self-preservation) instinct. It is not negative in itself, and becomes so only when it hypertrophies. This echoes the "Alfred Adler" motif observed previously. It is the superiority of the ego that prevents individuation and makes human beings neurotic. For this reason, the dreamer must be on his way and reaches the old part of town, which looks back on a long history and bears many treasures. The soul did not come into being today or yesterday, but carries within itself a history stretching back thousands of years, which explains why it feels at ease in the old town. Here archaic images can arise. The Pestalozzi Library is a public library and serves general education. The "Goldmann Library," whose euphonious name impresses the dreamer in particular, is a publisher of inexpensive editions of books. The dreamer now has to deal not only with scientific topics, but also with matters of general knowledge. These stem from the same intellectual curiosity as the rest. The military stands for uniformity. Everyone is like everyone else and subject to the same disciplinary code. Dr. R., the dreamer's analyst, is a high-ranking officer. The light comes from above, through a fish-shaped window. The fish is the content of the unconscious, a spiritual principle. Blue and red are opposites, and it is not clear whether the archetype merely represents the spiritual or also an image of the unconscious. The dreamer clashes with his surroundings due to his inappropriate behavior. This transitional phase is necessary when one begins to shed one's persona, the social role demanded at the Paradeplatz.

> January 19 (7th year): A party in a large, high-ceilinged hall. I must climb a ladder to the upper floor, where I must arch my back to lift the entire ceiling. In a room filled with people the walls are full of shelves lined with works from the history of ideas. I go over to another room where I find thick volumes, but which are only telephone books. From there I see other rooms with books. I discover long pieces of furniture containing technical equipment for microscoping purposes. It is the histological collection of the Pathology Department, where all sections are catalogued. Further on lies the hospital laundry. Finally I am in a small alley outside a museum bearing the sign: Local Museum for Rare Stones.

The dreamer must arch his back to lift the entire ceiling, just as Atlas lifted the celestial globe. Our intellectual and spiritual heritage means that, unknowingly, we carry the burden of all humanity. The entire pathological heritage, from which humanity suffers and which makes it ill, is also part of our inventory. One ego would not be able to carry this on its own. The rare stones, this fascinating collection, points to the miraculous stone of alchemy, which the alchemists called the *salvator mundi* (the savior of the world). It is the *alexipharmakon* (universal remedy), the panacea for all diseases. The alchemists expected this particular "philosopher's stone" to achieve everything that the ordinary person was incapable of. It is the symbol of the Self, that inconceivable and yet promised wholeness of the human being. The alchemists were on the scent of this factor, which is both psychic and bodily, and neither one nor the other, yet which stands above this opposition.

> January 1 (eight years later): In the first part of this dream an unfamiliar chief physician shows me how he is siphoning off an effusion in the thorax of a tuberculosis patient. Then I have to identify those refugees in an underground passage who should be saved. In the third part of the dream, a woman is looking after me. She leaves behind a book, which is dedicated to my previous analyst. He seems to have stimulated this work, which was not completed until after his death. The book cover contains strange signs of wonder. The book is titled "The Mystification of the Physician by Evil." It contains magnificent old copper engravings, and the topic is explored through the study of alchemical texts. The table of contents is written in ancient letters, as on a marble slate. My analyst tells me that my previous analyst had repeatedly drawn the attention of the historians to this topic, but had fallen victim to the problem himself. He was far from finished with it when he died.

This is the so-called "Great Dream," a dream that conveys not simply a message to the dreamer but to humanity as a whole (Jung, CW 3 §525). It concerns medical practice, the physician's activities, in general. Tuberculosis used to be a very severe chronic and almost incurable disease. It mostly occurred in patients unaware of their own state of resignation or depression: they did not breathe freely! The physician is always confronted with the decision about which patients he can help and which he cannot not. He or she must take a decision that exceeds his or her moral faculties, because his or her strength is limited. Physicians are always combatting death and the devil; the somatic physician confronts death, the psychiatrist the devil and evil.

The alchemists, many of whom were physicians, grappled with this problem for centuries. In contrast to Christianity, their god Mercurius had integrated all aspects. Mercurius is said to have been good with the good, and evil with the evil (Jung, CW 13 §267ff.). He is simultaneously a substance, i.e., mercury, and a spirit. His nature is most controversial and as difficult to grasp as the metallic liquid. In his image one recognizes the reality of matter. In him, moreover, evil is a reality and not merely the absence of the good.

By taking upon himself part of the evil that the sick cannot cope with, the physician is wounded himself. Jungian circles frequently, and somewhat all too readily, speak of the "wounded healer." The dream shows that this is partly true, but in a deeper sense. For the physician suffers not only from his problems, but also from those of humanity in general. This defines his calling. But there exists the danger that the physician's passion makes him forget that he must also take himself into consideration. Many gifted doctors have died an early death. I know a surgeon who dropped a scalpel on his foot during an operation. He ignored this mishap and died of sepsis. Jung (CW 14 §140 A 157) touches briefly on this theme in his discussion of the alchemical text "De sulphure," which is contained in the *Musaeum Hermeticum* (1678). There, sulfur is not only "medicina" (remedy) but also "medicus" (doctor). Like the *corpus*, the doctor is pierced by the lance of *mercurius*, in order to be transformed.

Psychologically, alchemical sulfur denotes volition on the one hand, and drivenness as the great secret of human fate on the other. This unconscious component prevails over the conscious will and characterizes the gifted doctor. It is the dynamis, the driving force, of the anthropos. It is hardly accidental that an important Hermetic treatise is titled *Asclepius*. The book in the dream seems very mysterious, as regards both its typeface and the peculiar signs of mystification, which look like Chinese characters.

> February 11 (eight years later): I am in a schoolroom and must teach a class. The alchemical texts are the Bible. I am unprepared.

At the time, the dreamer had many profound dreams about alchemy, which forced him to study this field in depth. Comparing alchemy with the Bible sounds blasphemous, unless the unconscious, or rather the self, wants to see things this way. Unknown to the dreamer, a similar instance has occurred previously.

Franciscus Patricius, thus his Latinized name, was born in 1529 on the Croation island of Cres (Italian "Cherso"). After an adventurous youth, he arrived in the German town of Ingoldstatt aged 17, where he acquired his first knowledge of Greek. Until the age of 25, he studied medicine in Padova, and then philosophy, which acquainted him with Ficino's *Theologia Platonica*. He made many friends, who later proved useful. His first, Platonized work appeared in 1553 in Venice. At the age of 28, he began travelling around Italy again and published a poetic work, which he dedicated to the House of Este. Several works appeared within the space of a few years. He spent some years on Cyprus, where he amassed a rich collection of Greek codices, which financial difficulties later forced him to sell to the Spanish King Philip II for the Escorial. He did not settle down until the age of 48, when he was appointed Chair of Platonic Philosophy in Ferrara, where he began publishing widely. Eventually, in 1591, his opus magnum, dedicated to Pope Gregory XIV was published. He had known the pope, who had also initiated his appointment at the Sapienza University of Rome, since his student days. But it was not until Pope Clement VIII that Patricius actually came to Rome.

His first work sought to ground his own philosophizing in "ancient" philosophy (*prisca sapientia*), namely, the Hermetic writings, the Chaldean oracles, and the so-called Theologia Aristotelis, which he believed to be older than Plato and Aristotle. The *Theologia Aristotelis* is a translation from Arabic of some of Plotinus' enneads. His principal work, *Nova de universis philosophia*, earned Patricius great acclaim. His inaugural lecture in 1592 was attended by all of Rome's dignataries and notables. But his criticism of Aristotle incurred displeasure, and his work was reported to the Congregation of the Index. Although Patricius attempted to disprove the accusation that his work contradicted Christian belief, it was banned in 1594. Disappointed and lonely, he applied for admission to the Confraternity of the Holy Hieronymous, to which he was admitted in 1596, and where he died on February 2, 1597.

Unlike Giordano Bruno, who was burned on February 16, 1600 on the Campo de Fiori in Rome by the same pope, Patricius could not be accused of any heresies, but merely of divergent philosophy. Today, he is recognized as the best interpreter of Platonic philosophy of the second half of the sixteenth century. At the Council of Trent (1545–1563), the primacy of Aristotelian philosophy at Catholic educational centers had been widely recognized. Patricius tried to demonstrate that Aristotle had adopted the ideas of his teacher Plato and those of other ancient, especially pre-Socratic authors. He therefore argued that Plato's teaching was more compatible with Christianity. The overriding principle is the All-One (*unomnia*), which contains everything in undivided form. The first production (*productio*) brings into existence diversity, which is held together, however, by the love for a second All-One. In this perspective, he maintained, Zoroaster (*Oracula Chaldaica*), Plato, and the Christians would converge. The whole world is governed by the reasonable world-soul.[41]

Patricius was profoundly enthusiastic and believed that Hermeticism could resolve the crisis engulfing the established church during the Reformation. Aristotelian philosophy, he reasoned, had no faith in God, but was hostile to God and his Church. This philosophy, he maintained, negated God's omnipotence and providence. Hermes, by contrast, emphasizes that true piety is impossible without philosophy. Therefore a truer philosophy must be discovered if one seeks to return to God. "I hope," Patricius writes in his introduction to *Nova de universis philosophia*, dedicated to Pope Gregory XIV,

> that You and Your successors will accept this new and renewed religious philosophy and will dispose that it is studied everywhere.... The treatise *de pietate ac philosophia* (Stobaeus *Excerpt* II B) by Hermes contains more philosophy than all of Aristotle's works. The "Poimandres" encompasses almost as much as Moses' Creation of the World and Man. He conveys the trinity much more clearly than Moses. Many books by Hermes are full of piety and true philosophy, whereas those by Aristotle are supposedly not religious. Many of Plato's dialogues should be taught publicly without any threat of paganism and as a strong support for piety.... Thus, it is my wish, O Holy Father, that You, and all future popes, command that some of the books that I have mentioned are taught everywhere, just as I taught them for fourteen years in Ferrara. You will thus make all excellent men of Italy, Spain, and France friends of the Church and even the German protestants might follow their example and return to the

---

[41] Überweg & Heinze, *Grundriss der Geschichte der Philosophie*, vol. 3, p. 44.

Catholic faith. It is much easier to regain their faith in this way than with violent measures.... If You do so, You may expect to receive great fame in future. I ask You to accept me as Your aid in this undertaking.[42]

In his introduction to that part of the book containing the Hermetica, Patricius says: "It seems as if this Hermes Trismegistus is the same age as Moses, even a bit older perhaps.... The books and fragments of Hermes display a pious philosophia toward God and are in harmony with most dogma."[43]

Not only is it astonishing that the unconscious of a dreamer who knew nothing about these events in Renaissance Italy brings into conscious view a similar notion. It is also amazing that Hermeticism might lead to truer piety than Aristotelian philosophy. The Hermeticists, Gnostics, and alchemists were all "possessed." Given the evidence we have for the spread of Christianity, I am convinced that the Christians, too, were "possessed," like the followers of the other mystery religions. When Christianity began, from the second century, to formulate a theology and to distinguish itself from competing subcurrents, it moved away increasingly from primordial experience. This alienation from such experience threatens all spiritual movements with dogmatism. Patricius, incidentally, also opposed scholasticism, which he considered even more dangerous than the Reformation, because it revealed the dilemma between knowledge and faith.

His subtle perception struck at the heart of the matter, because wherever the numinous represents genuine experience, no such dilemma occurs. But if one no longer knows which experience the articles of faith refer to, this raises a fundamental question: *credo ut*

---

[42] Introduction to Patricius, *Discussiones Peripateticae*—trans.

[43] Scott, *Hermetica*, I, pp. 36–40; on the role of Hermeticism in the sixteenth century, see Yates, *Giordano Bruno and the Hermetic Tradition*, esp. pp. 181–184.

intelligam? ("Do I believe so that I may understand?") In a letter written to Dr. Bernhard Lang in June 1957, Jung says:

> Let us take as an example the believing person who has Buber's attitude to belief. He lives in the same world as me and appears to be a human being like me. But when I express doubts about the absolute validity of his statements, he expostulates that he is the happy possessor of a "receiver," an organ by means of which he can know or tune in the Transcendent. This information obliges me to reflect on myself and ask myself whether I also possess a like receiver which can make the Transcendent, i.e., something that transcends consciousness and is by definition unknowable, knowable. But I find in myself nothing of the sort.... So when the believer assures me that I do not possess the organ he possesses, he makes me aware of my humanity, of my limitations which he allegedly does not have. He is the superior one, who regretfully points out my deformity or mutilation. Therefore I speak of the *beati possidentes* of belief, and this is what I reproach them with: that they exalt themselves above our human stature and our human limitation and won't admit to pluming themselves on a possession which distinguishes them from the ordinary mortal. I start with the confession of not knowing and not being able to know; believers start with the assertion of knowing and being able to know. There is now only one truth, and when we ask the believers what this truth is they give us a number of very different answers with regard to which the one sure thing is that each believer announces his own particular truth. Instead of saying: To me personally it seems so, he says: It is so, thus putting everybody else automatically in the wrong. (*Letters* II, p. 376)

What Jung remarks about the individual believer applies, in slightly modified form, also to the collective, the established church, which claims to possess the only organ capable of perceiving absolute truths. This assertion needs to be qualified, because an organization never has an organ. Only individuals ever claim to have one. This affirms, once more, what Jung says in the above letter. Not even a dogma that attributes such an organ to chosen individuals changes this. The only definite reality is primordial experience. Everything else is an interpretation of that experience. Jung's letter to Dr. Lang continues thus:

> Though I am sure of my subjective experience, I must impose on myself every conceivable restriction in interpreting it. I must guard against identifying with my subjective experience. I consider all such identifications as serious psychological mistakes indicative of a total lack of criticism. For what purpose am I endowed with a modicum of intelligence if I do not apply it in these decisive matters?.... Knowing means seeing a thing in such a way that all can know it, and for me it means absolutely nothing if I profess a knowledge which I alone possess. Such people are found in the lunatic asylum. I therefore regard the proposition that belief is knowledge as absolutely misleading. What has really happened to these people is that they have been overpowered by an inner experience. They then make an interpretation which is as subjective as possible and believe, instead of remaining true to the original experience. (*Letters* II, pp. 376–77)

These admonishing words apply not only to the established church, but also to Hermeticism and Gnosticism. To the extent that both were *ecclesia spiritualis* (spiritual churches), the danger of a one-sided, absolutizing interpretation of experience was small. Nevertheless, there were attempts within Hermeticism to establish secret circles, which face the same danger. Whenever one moves too far away from experience, the spirit disappears; and whenever *a* particular experience is believed to be universally valid, dogmatism looms. Hence, the solution proposed by Patricius would not have ensured that the established church could have helped it to avoid its present dilemma. The Gnostics cannot be spared the accusation of striving to absolutize their truth, but we must take into account that they possessed no theory of knowledge. However, they exercised no power with their ideas, at least not as far as we know. Those who felt in good hands with these ideas, clung to them. The threat of power occurs whenever anyone believes that they alone possess the truth. Only alchemy escaped this danger, because it never established itself as a church, but consisted of individuals who saw themselves as pursuing the same path. For this reason, alchemy never posed a serious threat to the established church. Each alchemist sought his own individual path. Obviously, they noticed certain parallels between their work and that of others, whom they cited. Consequently, ugly battles over dogmatism remained largely absent.

Like myself, I am sure the reader would like to become better acquainted with Hermes, this mysterious figure, upon whom all Hermeticism is based. In the above-cited *Kitāb al-Fihrist* ("Book of Records"), Ibn al-Nadīm begins the tenth discourse thus:

> The adepts of the art of alchemy, which is the art of producing gold and silver without mining these metals, assure us that the science of this art was first discussed by Hermes, the sage, the Babylonian, who came to Egypt after the human race was scattered at Babel and became king. They also say that he was a sage, a philosopher, and experienced in the art, about which he wrote several books. He speculated on special characteristics and mental powers. He was successful in his researches and in the science of the alchemical art and knew how to make talismans. He wrote many books on these subjects.... Nobody can succeed in philosophy, nor be called a philosopher, if he has not previously been introduced to the art of alchemy, so that he thus becomes

independent while everyone needs his knowledge and implements.

Another group of alchemists says that this science, which comes from Allah—praised be His name!—was revealed by some of the adepts of this art. Yet others say that this art was revealed to Moses, the son of Amran, and Aaron—peace be with them!—whom Korah looked after.... In another part of his book, AR-Razi emphasizes that many philosophers, Pythagoras, Democritus, Plato, Aristotle, and finally Galen practised this art.[44]

This final remark refers to the famous Turba Philosophorum, the assembly of philosophers. The Arabs plainly thought highly of the art, which they knew from the Greeks. Only its practice makes the practitioner a sage, whose knowledge and skill (*techné*) are superior to everyone else's. He is independent and needed by all. This art was revealed at the beginning of time and recorded by Hermes in many books. For this reason, an adept would substantiate a truth he had discovered with a Hermes citation, just as a theologian would cite the Bible. Hermes is the arch-authority.

How could Hermes rise to this function? He is a typically syncretistic figure, whose traits are indebted to its Greek origin and Egyptian influences. In Egypt, he merged with the god Thot (Tat in Hermeticism), the scribe of the gods. Since time immemorial, he has been associated with the moon, the ruler over the stars, the seasons, months, and years, time in general, and consequently individual destiny. He is the origin of the cosmic order and of religious and political institutions. As a scribe, he presides over ritual texts and formulae and over the arts of magic. He is the lord of wisdom, the inventor of writing, the sciences, knowledge, and language.[45] In the Edict of Edfu (II,16), it

---

[44] Fück, *The Arabic Literature on Alchemy according to* an-*Nadīm*, I, p. 88—trans.
[45] Fowden, *The Egyptian Hermes*, p. 22.

says: "That which is, began upon his command—only little came to be without his word."[46] This is similar to John 1:1–3. In Roman times, these pre-conditions made these two figures coalesce into Hermes Trismegistus.[47] He thus became an *anthropos*, who, being human, receives divine revelations on the one hand, and reveals divine secrets to humans serving their salvation on the other. As an anthropos, Hermes, as we have seen, is associated with a series of other figures typical of mystery religions: Dionysus, Heracles, Asclepius, Orpheus, Mithras, and so on.

In the Arabic "Great Circular Letter of the Spheres" (*Risala al-falakiya al kubra*), Hermes speaks the following words:

> Those who have served the Supreme Light for a long time, for them things will go according to their wishes. I am the Lord of Wonders and have risen through the seven spheres. I have seized power over the resplendent sun and the shining moon and have planted the light-filled tree of knowledge. Those who eat its fruits will never go hungry [again]; they will need no [more] food and drink. They will become a divine spirit, whose knowledge never wanes and whose salvation never ends.
>
> I am the one who made glass, which bends just as lead bends due to its softness; and it shines more brightly than pure silver. And [I have built] the boat that guides itself, which travels across the waters ahead of the wind and will never sink thanks to the power of the god in heaven.
>
> I am the one who built the temple and filled it with wisdom. In it, I have erected the statue of Artemis, who has four faces and whose signs indicate what is happening in the four regions of the earth.

---

[46] Mahé, *Hermes en Haute-Egypte* I, p. 2 A8.
[47] *Ibid*, I, p. 1ff.

Figure 3. Hermes Trismegistus, Cathedral of Siena

I am the one before whom the arduous stones of the soul have bowed and humiliated themselves, so that I have settled them among their own kind with the help of the god of truth.[48]

This is the introduction to an alchemical procedure, which Hermes describes in the first person singular. He is a superhuman figure, who directs the adept and assists him in his work. Each of his actions pertains to the alchemical opus. From experience is the *vitrum*

---

[48] Vereno, *Studien zum ältesten alchemistischem Schrifttum. Auf der Grundlage zweier erstmals editierter arabischer Hermetica*, p. 160—trans.

malleabile (malleable glass), which I long considered meaningless until I had a corresponding dream, in which the brittle glass was plastic and shapeable. Now I understood what the alchemists were saying and that their metaphorical language came from Hermes. In Latin alchemy, he became Hermes-Mercurius or simply Mercurius, who continues to play an outstanding role. But the boundaries are blurred between Mercurius as a person, which Hermes always is, and mercury as an element (Jung, CW 13 §278ff.).

Hermes-Mercurius is the actual *redeemer figure of alchemy*. He is the *prima materia* to be redeemed and transformed, like the complete end-product, the *filius makrokosmi* (Son of the Great World). But he is also the spirit who guides the work (*spiritus rector*) and plays tricks on the alchemist. According to the Tabula Smaragdina, which is attributed to him, Hermes unites the upper and the lower spheres. In "The Spirit Mercurius," Jung writes:

> So it is not a question of a one-way ascent to heaven, but, in contrast to the route followed by the Christian Redeemer, who comes from above to below and from there returns to the above, the filius macrocosmi starts from below, ascends on high, and, with the powers of Above and Below united in himself, returns to earth again. He carries out the reverse movement and thereby manifests a nature contrary to that of Christ and the Gnostic Redeemers, while on the other hand he displays a certain affinity with the Basilidian concept of the third sonship. Mercurius has the circular nature of the uroboros, hence he is symbolized by the circulus simplex of which he is at the same time the centre. He can therefore say of himself: "I am One and at the same time Many in myself." This same treatise says that the centre of the circle in man is the earth, and calls it the "salt" to which Christ referred when he said: "Ye are the salt of the earth" [Matthew 5:13]. (CW 13 §280)

The attentive reader will have noticed that Hermes-Mercurius is a more complete redeemer figure than his Christian counterpart. Especially the paradox, that he is both the beginning and end of the work, and at the same time the work itself, as well as the spirit in the work, indicates the paradoxical nature of the self, of human wholeness. Alchemy's many confusing symbols carry considerably fewer meanings once one has understood that every single process and symbol is based on the totality. This becomes plainly evident in the Arabic circular cited above.

When he recommended Hermetic philosophy to Pope Gregory XIV, Patricius may have intuited precisely this fact, even if he was probably unaware of it. Perhaps he intuitively realized, as the alchemists did, that the Christian idea of redemption was somehow flawed. Laid a hundred years earlier, the mosaic on the floor of Siena Cathedral (1488) shows that Patricius' request to the pope was not completely far-fetched. The mosaic depicts Hermes Trismegistus as a contemporary of Moses and an adept of his Soror mystica. In the book that he proffers to the adept with his right hand, it says: *Suscipte or licteras (sic. litteras) et leges egiptii* ("Take up the books and laws of the Egyptians"). The tablet carried by the two sphinxes alludes to Chapter 8 of the Hermetic *Asclepius*: *Deus omnium creator secum deum fecit visibilem et hunc fecit primum et solum quo oblectatus est et valde amavit proprium filium qui appellatur sanctum verbum* ("God, the Creator of the universe, created a visible god and made him the first and only one in whom he took delight and whom he loved like his own son, who is called the Sacred Word"). The passage in *Asclepius* reads:

> Listen, then, Asclepius. When the master and shaper of all things, whom rightly we call god, made a god next after himself who can be seen and sensed..., then, having made this god as his first production and second after himself, it seemed beautiful to him since it was entirely full of the goodness of everything, and he loved it as the progeny of his own divinity. (CH Asclepius 8)

Most probably, the author of the text in the Cathedral of Siena did not possess a copy of the Latin Asclepius, but Lactantius' citation from the Greek, which accounts for the slight deviation from our translation. This is important for understanding Lactantius' citation from Cicero's *de natura deorum* (III,22), where Hermes is said to have taught the laws and books to the Egyptians (*Aegyptiis leges et litteras tradidisse*).[49]

This image, and the accompanying text, illustrates how easily parallels between the Hermetic text and Christian persuasions could be drawn at the time, while the differences were graciously ignored. In 1471, Ficino's translation of "Poimandres" had initiated a new age, one which discovered true teaching in the *prisca philosophia* and was eager to discover new sources. Because its authority seemed older than Moses, it was accorded greater importance. Today, the dating seems mistaken and the arguments based thereupon irrelevant. But this is a malaise, since by then theology had moved too far away from primordial experience and genuine piety no longer existed among the Princes of the established church. This was the inept yet well-intentioned attempt to return to the sources. It is evident again today that theology is still reluctant to recognize the primacy of the soul as the place from which all true religion originates. Neither Hermeticism nor Gnosticism, nor any of the mystery religions can claim to have discovered the system of true religion. And yet in their own way they all revealed the true source for a certain time. They have all contributed, inalienably, to the colossal work of Western humanity gaining consciousness. Alchemy survived for over one thousand five hundred years because through Hermes-Mercurius it came closest to the living source. We must continue to build on these foundations!

---

[49] Yates, *Giordano Bruno and the Hermetic Tradition*, pp. 24–43; Scott, *Hermetica* I, p. 32; Copenhaver, *Hermetica*, p. 222.

Chapter 11
The Path of the Gnostic

In *Die feindlichen Brüder* (1993), I tried to explain that people experience the world very differently depending on whether they are extraverted or introverted. The extravert is drawn to the outside world, the introvert primarily to the inside world. Now, this does not mean that introverts do not perceive the outside world or are unable to orient themselves there. Instead, for the introvert, the value of that world is measured in terms of inner standards. The outside world is devalued as an external fact, to the degree that it is no more than a parable of deeper values. Thus, at the very end of Goethe's *Faust* (Part 2), the Mystic Choir sings:

> All that is transient
> Is but a parable

Goethe's lines capture the medieval frame of mind. It was not until the Renaissance that the extraverted attitude asserted itself in our culture and helped science and technologies embark on their triumphant march, which our age is currently witnessing. We easily succumb to the illusion that this attitude is more successful and more valuable. And yet we forget the merits of earlier centuries, because we assess them one-sidedly by our extraverted standards. It is exactly in this spirit that Gnostics scholars have sought to understand those old testimonies. To understand Gnosticism, we must attempt to feel our way into the largely introverted mentality of the first centuries after the turning of the ages. I would like to illustrate this approach with the example of the Gnostic Heracleon.

Barbara Aland's essay "Erwählungstheologie und Menschklassenlehre" (1978) makes a remarkable contribution to this topic, and I have benefitted greatly from her work.

Unfortunately, our knowledge of Heracleon is scant. Occasionally, Origen cites him verbatim in his *Commentary on the Gospel of John*, which serves our present purpose very well. Heracleon is also cited by Clement of Alexandria (*Eclogae Propheticae* 25,1; *Stromateis* IV, 9,71–72). He is probably the most important disciple of Valentinus (c. 150) besides Ptolemy.

Heracleon's first fragment, on John 1:3, leads to the heart of the matter. "All things were made through him": He understands this assertion in his own particular way when he says:

> "All things were made through him" means the world and what is in it. It excludes what is better than the world. The Aeon (i.e. the Fullness), and the things in it, were not made by the Word; they came into existence before the Word...

But his actual words are:

> "All things were made through Him," means that it was the Word who caused the Craftsman (*Demiurge*) to make the world, that is it was not the Word "from whom" or "by whom," but the one "through whom (all things were made)."...It was not the Word who made all things, as if he were energized by another, for "through whom" means that another made them and the Word provided the energy.

From a psychological perspective, Origen's seemingly highly complicated and differentiated formulation reflects a typically introverted attitude, which withdraws libido from the object and introjects it. The overwhelming external object is devalued as far as possible while the subject is enhanced. This basic feature pervades Gnosticism, which, as is well known, is no unified system of teaching, but a richly faceted collection of ideas. Put differently, the visible world is just the reflection of an invisible higher world, the *mundus archetypus*. Thus, what we grasp with our senses is merely superficial; it is not the actual, true world, not the pleroma, not the fullness of being. This world lies behind all manifestations as the invisible, unrecognizable *unus mundus*, the One World. This is the invisible, unrecognizable "Father," who is the origin, but not the creator of everything and the universe. Whereas John 1:3 says "All things were made through him," Heracleon employs this *panta* (i.e., everything) to distinguish the cosmos from creation. The whole is the irrational sum of the created and of the eternal, the pre-existent.

Heracleon's first fragment shows that the Gnostic idea of the world is radically introverted and contrasts starkly with that of the established church. Introversion and extraversion are two hostile brothers yet also two complementary attitudes to the world. The extraverted attitude had the advantage in the struggle for primacy, because it coped better with the world and led to the organization of the established church and the papacy, as I explained in the first volume. It could be called *extensive*, and the other *intensive*, in that it facilitated the rapid spread of Christianity and took hold of the masses with its simple confessional formula.[1] The introverted Gnostic attitude was suited to the in-depth exploration of the revelation and possessed, as mentioned, elitist traits.

Heracleon's second fragment deals with John 1:4, "What was made in him was Life." In this respect, Origen appears to have misunderstood Heracleon when he assumes that the pneumatic had already received the salvific gift during the creation. I completely agree with Barbara Aland that Heracleon is actually saying that "only what

---

[1] *Enchiridion Symbolorum Definitionum et Declarationum*: Denziger-Schönmetzer, ed. *Symbola Fidei Primitiva*, pp. 17–19.

came into existence in the image of the Logos was life." This view is thoroughly Neoplatonic! Psychologically, this means that life and meaning prevail in the archetypal, i.e., the primal image. Thus, as we shall see, the pneumatics evidently have a sense of the archetypal, while this is completely alien to the hylics or, psychologically speaking, the sensation type. In this sense, the pneumatics correspond roughly to the intuitive type, and the ideal Gnostic is an introverted intuitive (Jung, CW 6 §834 and 730ff.).

Heracleon's third fragment interprets the words, "No one has ever seen God," as spoken not by John the Baptist, but by a disciple. To understand this, we must consider the entire verse and Origen's interpretation. The Baptist was said to have exclaimed:

> From his [= Christ = Logos] fullness we have all received, grace upon grace. The law indeed was given through Moses; grace and truth came through Jesus Christ. (John 1:16–17)

The pre-Christian prophets received their gift from the fullness of Christ (the Logos) and were guided by the Spirit. This was the first act of mercy. The second, more important act, however, becomes possible only with the appearance of Christ, since "it is his only Son, who is in the bosom of the Father, who has transmitted the knowledge."

As I have noted, the position of the redeemer in Gnosticism differs significantly from the customary orthodox conception. According to Heracleon, the appearance of the Logos is absolutely essential for knowledge to occur. All tidings of the unrecognizable Father prior to the incarnation of the Son, who alone knows the Father, were merely provisional knowledge. Heracleon clearly distinguishes two kinds of knowledge: the knowledge of the prophets, which is conveyed, is "hearsay," whereas genuine knowledge involves being seized by the truth oneself; it is an inner experience, an encounter with the "Christ in you" (Colossians 1:27). What the Gnostics call "knowledge," i.e.,

Gnosis, is not a matter of the intellect but instead of experience in the sense of self-knowledge. This does not mean, as is often misunderstood, self-knowledge, but a process toward knowing the divine core within the individual, i.e., the self (in distinction to the ego), or one's objective reality.

These comments on Heracleon's third fragment suggest that the Gnostics, most of all Valentinus, were disguised psychologists, who formulated their insights in theological terms. They possessed no psychology and projected their knowledge of the soul into theology. This, in turn, provided them with a framework within which they formulated their ideas.

The case of Heracleon plainly reveals that while the Gnostics accepted the Gospel—just as the Valentinians embraced the Gospel of John above all, as Irenaeus asserts in *Against Heresies* (III. 11,7)—they found their own truth therein. Comparing Heracleon and Origen is especially interesting, because, as Barbara Aland suggests, this passage shows "just how close these two theologians were."[2] Thus, the orthodox notion is by no means, as she claims, the only one to be inspired by the Holy Spirit, but it was simply more assertive. Hence, it is worth one's while to pursue unfamiliar Gnostic thinking. Unquestionably, the Gnostics also unearthed "truths," albeit others than orthodoxy. In this respect, we should not forget the influence that orthodoxy exerted on two thousand years of Christian culture. But precisely its one-sidedness brought forth a Gnostic undercurrent, not only during the first Christian centuries but throughout Western thinking.[3] This compensated for the one-sidedness of collectively sanctioned theology, which had never been entirely serious about "the experience of Christ." For theology, Christ remained largely a "historical figure," to whose work the gospels bear witness. But the experience of Christ does not mean the imitation of Christ, nor empathizing with his suffering on the

---

[2] Barbara Aland, "Gnosis und Kirchenväter," pp. 158-9—trans.
[3] Quispel, *De Hermetische Gnosis*.

Stations of the Cross, but, as Jung wrote in his letter of July 3, 1952 to the Reverend Dr. Dorothee Hoch, "to carry [one's] own cross amid the mockery and contempt of the world." Moreover:

> Whoever imitates Christ and has the cheek to want to take Christ's cross on himself when he can't even carry his own has in my view not yet learnt the ABC of the Christian message. (*Letters* II, p. 76)

In fragment 4, on John 1:21, Origen reproaches Heracleon for not distinguishing *the* prophet, i.e., Christ, from *a* prophet, when the priests and the Levites asked John, "if you are not Christ, are you a prophet. Are you the prophet?" He replied, "No, I am not."

This corresponds to what Origen explains in fragment 5: the prophet and Elijah are merely an exterior, a piece of clothing; they are, however, never characteristic of John, whose "attributes, like clothes, were other than himself." Psychologically, then, Elijah or the prophet is an external role, i.e., a persona. The priests and the Levites would like to fit the unknown man dressed in clothes made of camel's hair, who subsists on locusts and wild honey (Matthew 3:4), into their idea of the world. As we shall see, they resist baptism and evangelization (fragment 6 on John 1:25).

Fragment 8 on John 1:26 is aligned with and further elucidates the previous fragments. Heracleon emphasizes that the words spoken are "there stands among you one," not "He is already here, and he is in the world and among human beings, and he is already manifest to you all." Thus, Origen asks when was the Logos not present, not in the world, because afterwards there is mention of "one whom you do not know" (John 1:26). "Yet the world did not know him" (John 1:10). In Isaiah, however, God says: "I was ready to be sought out by those who did not ask, to be found by those who did not seek me" (65:1). According to Heracleon, John is the "forerunner," who says of himself:

> I am not worthy that for my sake he should come down from the Greatness and should assume flesh as his sandal, concerning which I am not able to give any explanation or description, nor to unloose the arrangement of it.

The sandals that he puts on symbolize the world. The fact that he places himself beneath the Logos shows that the Creator is subordinate, which horrifies Origen and highlights one of the characteristic discrepancies between Gnosis and orthodoxy. For Origen, it is "the Father who has sent Him, the God of the Living, as Jesus himself attests, [...] who is the Lord of heaven and earth, because he created them; for only he is good [Matthew 19:17] and greater than the one he sent [John 14:28]."

Officially, Christianity is monotheistic, but barely able to conceal certain dualistic tendencies. Basically, Gnosis is also monotheistic, but in addition to the unrecognizable Father it recognizes a second, subordinate Creator-God. Alchemy has a *deus terrenus* or *terrestris* (earthly god), just as we find it in the *Corpus Hermeticum* (X 10). Laurentius Ventura[4] mentions the vision of Ezechiel, "the spirit of the living creatures was in the wheels" (1:20), and adds: "And for this reason some call this (mysterium) the 'the earthly god.'" This alchemist cites the maxim of Lilium and Lilius in a chapter entitled "May our stone exist as one and contain several substances." On the one hand, the miraculous stone of alchemy is loathed (*vilis*) and deemed inferior, whereas on the other it represents an image of God in matter, the "filius sapientiae," "a light above all other lights," the panacea (universal remedy), and the "corpus glorificationis" (the resurrected body).

---

[4] *Theatrum Chemicum*, vol. 2, p. 229.

The Hermetist is more explicit: he maintains that everything comes into being through contrariness (*Septem sermones ad mortuous* V 12 ff.) and therefore asks:

"Who is this material god, then?"
"The cosmos, which is beautiful but not good." (CH X 10)

This painful experience of the world shaped the figure of the demiurge. And there is an even more important reason for the negative image of the demiurge in Gnosticism: the image of the redeemer. Redemption results necessarily from the imperfection of the Creation and the suffering caused thereby. Demiurge and redeemer stand diametrically opposed.

Fragment 10, on John 1:29, makes a clear distinction with regard to the redeemer: when John sees Jesus approach, he declares: "Here is the Lamb of God." This refers only to the body of Jesus, which is about to be crucified, because it is inferior. Adding the words, "who takes away the sin of the world," John points to the essential part that alone is capable of redemption. We shall leave aside the docetism characteristic of many Gnostic systems,[5] and which arises from this distinction, and merely observe that redemption is a spiritual act. While it has not occurred historically once and for all, it exercises a lasting effect as the spiritual Christ.

Fragment 11, on John 2:12, says: "After this he went down to Capernaum." According to Heracleon, Capernaum means "these farthest-out parts of the world, the material realm into which he descended." In fragment 40, on John 4:46–53, which is the story of the king's officer in Capernaum whose son was sick, Heracleon interprets this place as being "in the lower part of the Middle (i.e., of animate substance), which lies near the sea, that is, which is linked with matter."

---

[5] Voorgang, *Die Passion Jesu*.

His interpretation of the king's officer leads him to discuss the nature of the demiurge in closer detail. According to fragment 11, redemption consists in the redeemer leaving his father's bosom and descending into the alien, material world, symbolized as Capernaum.

Psychologically, this means that a spiritual aspect had not incarnated itself until that time and led to a conflict between the earthly realities or the material world, and the ideal world of the spirit, the latter being experienced as suffering. In such a state exists a painful discrepancy between what is expected of the world and its harsh reality. Individuals experience this problem almost always in young adulthood, which represents the mentality of the eternal youth, which often manifests itself in dreams about flying.[6] In the spiritual condition of the collective of that time, this corresponded to an idealistic expectation about the world. According to Jung (CW 5 §175, 165, 523, etc.), all Near Eastern deities that die and rise from the dead (e.g., Osiris, Tammuz, Attis, Adonis, Christ, and Mithras) belong to one and the same type—the son of the Great Mother—who was destined to rise in the midday heat and descend again in the cold, dark night. Since time immemorial, this figure has been associated with expectations of renewal and the world beyond. The comparison with these gods of vegetation, who perish in the autumn and awaken to new life in Spring, suggests that they represent a youthful attitude, which must die and transform itself. The fact that Gnosticism qualifies the material world as dark, hostile, and even as evil indicates the resistance to complete incarnation. This is evident in Neoplatonic philosophy, from which Gnosticism borrowed many ideas. Plotinus places the One and the Good above everything else, just as Gnosticism elevates the unrecognizable Father, who emanates the *nous*, just as the Logos does for Heracleon. The Father, the Logos, is responsible for the subject-object dualism in human thinking. He produces the soul, which bridges

---

[6] von Franz, *Der ewige Jüngling*. Published in English as *Puer aeternus: A Psychological Study*, Sigo Press, Santa Monica, 2nd ed., 1981.

the extrasensory (transcendental) and the sensory aspects of Creation, which the alchemists call *anima media natura*. Existence figures on a scale between the earthly and the One, whose light gradually wanes, until it eventually ends in the darkness of matter.[7]

Again in psychological terms, the same occurs in the process of becoming conscious: the unconscious state represents the prenatal totality of the One in Plotinus or the pleroma in Gnosticism. From it emerges the beam of consciousness in a kind of *kenosis* (self-emptying); passing through eternal refractions, this light eventually develops into the material world. When this is referred to as the outermost darkness of matter, this indicates the spectrum of consciousness, which ranges from ultraviolet (spirit) to infrared (matter) (Jung, CW 8 §385 and 417). The origin is posited in the spiritual, in the unrecognizable Father, or the One, which is clearly transcendental; it ends in matter, whose actual essence is equally inaccessible to human consciousness. In-between lies incarnation, i.e., the process of becoming conscious or individuation (Jung, CW §825).

In Gnosticism looms the mindset that discovers the individual and its consciousness. Thus, a new worldview emerges on the one hand, just as suffering does on the other. We recognize consciousness only when we have advanced beyond that state. The Gnostics therefore sought to transcend the earlier, hylic state, in which humans are still caught up in *participation mystique* with the collective and the world.[8] So long as people knew nothing else, they felt no need for redemption. At the turning of the ages, which coincided synchronistically with the new aeon (Jung, *Aion*; CW 9/II), collective consciousness changed. As mentioned, this called into action the gods, who died at a young age as symbols of a transformation of the dominant collective consciousness.

In fragment 12, on John 2:13, Heracleon offers two interpretations of Passover: the lamb is slaughtered, which signals the

---

[7] Praechter, *Die Philosophie des Altertums*, pp. 596ff.
[8] von Franz, *Spiegelungen der Seele*.

suffering of the Lord and his passion; but it is also eaten, which leads to redemption, or in Heracleon's words "on being consumed, [it] provided rest as well. When sacrificed, it signified the passion of the Savior in this world; when consumed, the rest that is in the marriage." And yet it is not enough for the Lord to take suffering upon himself; we must all carry our own cross, which involves "eating the world." For it is only then, as fragment 13 interprets John 2:13, that He can ascend to Jerusalem, i.e., from material reality to the psychic region.

I. The Right Attitude

A new idea occurs in the same fragment: Heracleon understands John 2:14–17, where the money-changers are driven out of the temple, as meaning that the *pronaos* (porch) is impure, i.e., it is a place where all kinds of people with a trading mentality lurk, as expressed in the often-cited sacrificial formula *do ut des* ("I give so that you may give"). Widespread nowadays, this attitude is interested solely in the benefit before it makes any effort itself; it asks, "what good will this do me, and how will I profit most." For the opus, in this case gaining knowledge of Christ, this attitude is detrimental and must be driven out, because only the high priest may access the innermost part of the holy place (*hieron*) (Hebrews 9:7). Those who have cleansed their temple of the dirt of the world belong to the pneumatics, who are capable of attaining salvation. Thus, the psychics still have the wrong attitude to the divine and the numinous and will not recognize the self unless they adopt the right attitude.

Heracleon's 13th fragment occupies a major role in the discussion of the Valentinian teaching of predestination. Are the three categories of humans—hylics, psychics, pneumatics—already distinct in the Creation or does their separation occur later? Psychologically, both views seem correct: hereditary disposition and origin determine human attitude to a considerable extent, and yet our mindset depends on how we employ our disposition. But if we make the greatest effort possible, only an act of grace (a "calling" or "awakening" in Gnostic terms) can open our eyes. Heracleon interprets the whip with which Jesus drives out the money-changers as "the power and energy of the Holy Spirit which blows away the wicked." Here, indeed, he makes a crucial observation: *metanoia* (change of mind) is the essential condition for performing the work. All of us are entangled in the collective attitude of our times, in the materialist and extraverted attitude that only tolerates those realities perceptible to the senses and existing in the outside world. This attitude is unable to recognize the invisible reality of the spiritual world. The soul either means nothing to this attitude or is identified with consciousness. Psychologically, the pneumatics are those who gained an understanding of the "reality of the soul." Symbolically, the money-changers are trapped in the collective *zeitgeist* and general unconsciousness.

In the *Book of Cratès*, a ninth century alchemical text in Arabic, an angel instructs the author:

> Know, Cratès Es-Semaoui (Heavenly One), that not one single philosopher has not done everything in his might to reveal the truth. The difficulty that the philosophers have encountered in illuminating these matters for the ignorant ones has led them to proxility. They have said what ought to be done, and what not. The ignorants treated these books as a matter of fun; they derided and rejected them as evil, disheartening, saddening, and laughable, as far as the knowledge of the truth is concerned. How, I replied, would one not be disheartened by these books and volumes, in which one finds words that seem to say the same and whose difference lies solely in their application? One is troubled by not knowing how they should be understood or which lesson one needs them to impart.—My son, he replied, I will tell you where these errors and these worries come from. All people

necessarily belong to one of two categories: the first believes that the spirit is oriented entirely toward wisdom, the pursuit of science, the teaching of the laws of nature, their affinities, advantages, and inconveniences. Those who belong to this category are preoccupied with possessing and searching for books, to devoting mind, body, and soul to spreading the notions contained therein. When they discover something clear and precise, they thank God; if they come across an obscure point, they dedicate all their efforts to gaining an exact idea through their studies, to thereby reach a goal, which they propound and act upon by consequence.

The second category consists of those who think only of their stomach, who fret neither about the world nor about themselves, nor about the future; for these people, books only increase their ignorance and blindness; inevitably, their spirit is cumbersome and becomes so increasingly.[9]

The *Book of Cratès* (Quiratis al-Hakim) is a pseudepigraph transmitted by the Arabic tradition whose lexicon and content follows Greek alchemical texts.[10] It may well have emerged at the same time as the Nag Hammadi scriptures and also distinguishes between the pneumatics and the worldly.

The difference between the Gnostics and the alchemists is that the former project their work into the pleromatic world, the latter into the material one. The alchemists are more articulate, making it easier for us to understand them today.

An early modern alchemist, Theobald de Hoghelande, notes in the first part of his *De Alchimiae Difficultatibus* ("On the Difficulties of Alchemy") that Geber and Senior (ibn Umail) maintain that "this

---

[9] Berthelot, *La Chimie au Moyen Age*, vol. III, pp. 51–52—trans.
[10] Sezgin, *Geschichte des arabische Schriftums*, vol. IV, pp. 55–56.

science is nothing but a perfect divine inspiration and a secret of the glorious God who gives it to and takes it from whomever he chooses." He also cites the the Arabic alchemist Alphidius: "If you are devout, your wisdom will be perfect; if you are not, this disposition will remain hidden in your innermost," before citing Geber again: "You, however, must exert the greatest endeavor and the perseverance of infinite meditation, with which you shall find and without not." Thomas Aquinas' *Aurora consurgens* also cites Alphidius' fifth parable: "Know, that thou canst not have this science, unless thou shalt purify thy mind before God, that is, wipe away all corruption from thy heart."[11] The *Musaeum Hermeticum* (1625), a collection of alchemical treatises, contains a treatise entitled *Gloria Mundi* (or *Paradysi Tabula*), which claims to be a "true description of the science that God gave to Adam, Noah, Abraham, and Solomon as the sum of divine gifts, which all sages employed at all times and deemed to be the treasure of the entire world." The author of this treatise is unknown. Commenting on the attitude to the work, he writes:

> (God alone confers the secret.) But if God conveys his grace upon someone, and if that person understands this, this will strike the world as impossible; and those who love it [the secret] will be despised and deemed scoundrels: just as the learned and the doctores and others cannot find it, because they have never beheld the thing (*rem istam*), although it lies before their eyes; they distrust it, although it contains such power. And nobody can instruct them as long as they follow their nature and intellect: they are therefore unable to find it, despite all their wisdom, since it surpasses their comprehension, because it is a work of God and nature and is attained through nature. They will therefore remain inexperienced.[12]

---

[11] von Franz, *Aurora Consurgens*, p. 107.
[12] *Musaeum Hermeticum reformatum et amplificatum*, p. 212—trans.

This illustrates just how far the right, merciful attitude is removed from the "normal" one; indeed, it is so far removed that even the most learned men (*doctissimi viri*) are unable to understand it as long they only follow their nature and intellect. Typically, their intellect stands in their way, because the irrationality of God's and nature's works—i.e., the unconscious—surpasses their comprehension. Not only the Gnostic and the alchemist must possess the right attitude, but this attitude is also required to understand Gnosticism and alchemy.

The legendary Basilius Valentinus writes in his *Practica de Lapide Sapientum*:

> Only very few gain possession of this kingdom, although many are involved in making our stone. The Creator has not given true knowledge and its possession to all, but only to some few, who hate lies and embrace the truth and who devote themselves to the art with sighing hearts and who seek it with care, but most of all those who love God without any hypocrisy and therefore pray.[13]

This emphasizes the search for the truth. If humans, by the grace of God, detect the betrayal of the world and do not become resigned, they will embrace (*amplecti*) the truth and, helped by art, unhypocritically love God. But only very few will do so, because God has not distributed this gift widely.

Thomas Norton's *Ordinal of Alchemy* states:

> A wonderful science, secrete philosophie / A singulart grace and gyfte of almyghtie / which neuir was fownde bi labour of man, / But it bi teching or revelacion bigan. / It was neuir for money sold ne boght / Bi any man which for it hath sowght, / But govyn

---

[13] *Ibid.*, p. 382—trans.

to an able man bi grace / wrought with grete cost with longer leiser and space./ It helpith a man when he hath nede, / It voideth vaynglorie hope and also drede, / It voidith ambyciousnes extorcion and excesse, / It fensith adversite pat she do not oppresse. / He that thereof hath his fulle entente / Forsaking extremytees with mesure [is] content.[14]

This once again underscores the importance of grace, which grows from the experience that one long endeavors to resolve a problem until it suddenly lies before us, self-evidently and unquestioningly, as if it had fallen from the heavens. We realize that we have not worked out the solution ourselves; instead we have received it. We wonder if we would have received it without all our previous exertions. This question is unanswerable, because the solution sometimes appears out of the blue, unsearched for. Mostly, however—and this is the basic pragmatic principle—it arises only after feverish efforts. In actual fact, it is quite feasible that each creative "in-cursion" springs not from human endeavor, because "creative" means "something that we have never been conscious of before." Thus, although consciousness may exert itself as much as it likes, it will nevertheless impossibly find a content beyond itself. "In-cursion" expresses this aptly, i.e., something from outside the scope of consciousness invades it, from heaven or God. Gnosticism and alchemy therefore believed that the work is performed with divine inspiration. The human being is merely the implement in this process, which must, however, be cleansed from the dirt of the world if it is going to serve as a vessel of inspiration. Human need and hardship are capable of initiating this process, but as long as life runs its usual course, no "necessity" exists. Gnosticism and Christianity emerged from a spiritual crisis, which I have discussed earlier.

---

[14] John Reidy, ed., p. 10.

In 1619, Johann Ambrosius Siebmacher, a fairly unknown alchemist, published a treatise entitled "The Waterstone of the Wise," whose Latin translation ("Hydrolithus Sophicus seu Aquarium Saptientum") was included in the *Musaeum Hermeticum* (1625). Siebmacher chose Psalm 25:12, "Who are they that fear the Lord? He will teach them the way that they should choose" as the motto for the first part of his treatise, where he asserts:

> Therefore, if any man desire to reach this great and unspeakable Mystery, he must remember that it is obtained not by the might of man, but by the grace of God, and that not our will or desire, but only the mercy of the Most High, can bestow it upon us. For this reason you must first of all cleanse your heart, lift it to Him alone, and ask of Him this gift in true, earnest, and undoubting prayer. He alone can give and bestow it.
>
> Then fall upon thy knees, and with a humble and contrite heart render to Him the praise, honour, and glory due for the hearing of thy prayer, and ask Him again and again to continue to thee His grace, and to grant that, after attaining to full and perfect knowledge of this profound Mystery, thou mayest be enabled to use it to the glory and honour of His most Holy Name, and for the good of thy suffering fellow men.
>
> Now Nature may truly be described as being one, true, simple, and perfect in her own essence, and as being animated by an invisible spirit. If therefore you would know her, you, too, should be true, single-hearted, patient, constant, pious, forbearing, and, in short, a new and regenerate man. If you know yourself to be so constituted and your nature adapted to Nature, you will have an intuitive insight into her working, such as it would otherwise be impossible to obtain.

> Therefore, let your mind and thoughts be turned away from all things earthly, and, as it were, created anew, and consecrated to God alone. For you should observe that these three, body, soul, and spirit, must work together in harmony if you are to bring your study of this Art to a prosperous issue, for unless the mind and heart of a man be governed by the same law which develops the whole work, such an one must indubitably err in the Art.
>
> Yet our artist can do nothing but sow, plant, and water: God must give the increase.[15]

In the second part of this treatise, he writes:

> "With this spirit," says a certain philosopher, "you should not meddle until you first have a full and exact knowledge of it. For God is marvellous in His works, and He is not mocked. I could give some instances of men who set about this matter with great levity and were heavily punished by meeting (some of them) with fatal accidents in their laboratories. For this work is no light thing, as many suppose, perhaps, because the Sages have called it child's play. Those to whom God has revealed His secrets may indeed find the experiment simple and easy. But do thou carefully beware of exposing thyself to great danger by unseasonable carelessness. Rather begin thy work with reverent fear and awe and with earnest prayer, and then thou wilt lie in little danger."

This passage explains that the *artifex* (craftsman) must have a religious attitude, because he is dealing with a hidden spirit. Failing proper preparation, he may become entangled with this spirit and suffer harm. Psychically fragile people are especially attracted to the secret sciences. Instead of realizing that this attraction is related to their own problems,

---

[15] http://www.levity.com/alchemy/hydrolit.html, trans. Adam McLean.

they pounce on bits and pieces with superficial knowledge and end up in total chaos. C.G. Jung mentions a Paracelsist who followed his master's words so faithfully that he lost his mind, because he did not take the man's muddled thoughts with the necessary grain of salt (CW 12 §490). An 18th-century alchemical manuscript owned by Jung breaks off mid-thought, apparently for the same reason (*Ms. Figurarum aegyptiorum secretum*). Many people instinctively sense the impending threat of the hidden spirit and escape it by not immersing themselves more deeply in Gnosticism, alchemy, or depth psychology. As the above passage shows, these *doctissimi viri* (learned men) are unable to attain genuine understanding.

Let us return to Thomas Norton's *Ordinal of Alchemy*:

> Also no man code yet this science reche / But if god sende him a master hym to teche, / For it is so worshipfulle and so selcowth, / That it most nede be taght fro mouth to mouth; / Also he shalle, be he nevir so lothe, / Receyve it with moste sacred dredfulle othe, / That as we refuse grete dignite and fame, / So he must nedely to refuse the same; /... To teche this secrete to his own child, / For nyhenes of bloode ne consanguynte / Be not acceptide to this dygnynte; /... If oon evil man hadd herof alle his wille, Alle christian pees he myght hastly spille, / And with his pride he myght set a-downe / Rightful kingis and princis of renowne; / whereof the sentence, perile and Iupardie / upon the techer restith dredfullie.[16]

This passage adds a new idea, namely, that the teaching passes from master to disciple by word of mouth. Blood relatives are not the right students. The Gnostics probably formed circles, perhaps like the

---

[16] Reidy, ed., p. 11f.

Poimandres Community, where learning is transferred to members. Secretiveness is what binds the members of a community together (I explained the importance of the secret earlier on). "By becoming conscious, the individual is threatened more and more with isolation," writes Jung in the "Philosophical Tree," and adds:

> ...which is nevertheless the *sine qua non* of conscious differentiation. The greater this threat, the more it is compensated by the production of collective and archetypal symbols which are common to all men. (CW 13 §395)

Origen interprets Heracleon's 14th fragment, on John 2:17, which cites Psalm 69:10 ("It is zeal for your house that has consumed me"), as meaning that the powers were driven out by the savior and destroyed. He then adds verse 22, "They gave me poison for food, and for my thirst they gave me vinegar to drink." In Gnosticism, the powers (*dynamis*) are a technical term for the archons, those powers of fate that the Gnostic must overcome. They brought Christ to his passion, i.e., they are those psychic constellations that cause human suffering and spoil life. Human beings must carry their cross because of these powers, in order to eventually surmount them.

Origen makes another important point when he observes that the Holy Scripture does not speak about God or Christ in everyday language. In actual fact, the unconscious employs a curiously stilted language to express the numinous. This explains why the recorded testimonies of all religions are written in antiquated, occasionally even in incomprehensible languages. In this respect, religious statements differ from philosophical ones, which need to be as logical and as consistent as possible. Many scholars of Gnosticism are bothered by the contradictions in the Nag Hammadi treatises. But precisely these inconsistencies bear witness to the fact that these products have genuinely emerged from the unconscious. Many scholars believe that an original mythological core can be distinguished from layers that were revised at a later stage. This might be true in some cases, just as it might result from the fluctuating depths of the unconscious evident in modern people.

Fragment 16, on John 2:20, says that it took Solomon 46 years to build the temple. Heracleon interprets the number 6 as referring to matter, while 40 = 4 x 10 is "the number 40 [...] the tetrad that can be united with none other." It is the unity formed by the pre-existing principles in the Valentinian system, and with the number that the Pythagoreans have revered as the root of all things (1+2+3+4=10).[17] It is quite conceivable that this number symbolism meant little to Origen. It suggests that for the Gnostic everything becomes a parable for eternal truths, whereas the extravert continues to adhere to the external object.

II. Gnosis: The Water of Life

The next fragments are the most important, because they reveal the difference between the Gnostic's attitude and that of the members of the established church toward Jesus' encounter with the Samaritan woman at Jacob's well (John 4:6–26). While the disciples had gone to the town to buy food, Jesus, tired from the journey, rested at the well. A woman from Samaria came to draw water from the well, and Jesus asks her to give him a drink. The woman is very surprised that a Jew should request such a favor from a Samaritan woman. In reply, he says, "If you knew the gift of God, and who it is that is saying to you, 'Give me a drink,' you would have asked him, and he would have given you living water" (10). The woman questions Jesus about these strange words, and asks him whether he is "greater than our ancestor Jacob" (12). He replies: "Everyone who drinks of this water will be thirsty again, but those who drink of the water that I will give them will never be thirsty.

---

[17] Foerster, *Gnosis*, vol. 1, pp. 162ff.—trans.

The water that I will give will become in them a spring of water gushing up to eternal life" (13–14). Hearing these words, the woman asked for this water.

In fragment 17, on John 4:12–15, Heracleon explains that the water from Jacob's well, from which the woman has drunk so far, is "Insipid, temporary, and unsatisfying [...] for it was worldly. The proof of it being worldly is the fact that the cattle of Jacob drank from it (i.e. the well)." What is considered "insipid, temporary, and unsatisfying" was partial knowledge (1 Corinthians 13:12), in which she had lived until then. But when "the complete" comes, the previous partial knowledge will be overcome (1 Corinthians 13:10). Origen refuses to accept that Heracleon might mean the overcoming of the Old Testament. This concerns *metanoia*, the change of mind, which represents a "new way of seeing."

The water of the savior, says Heracleon, comes "from his spirit and his power," just as it does when Jesus drives out the money-changers from the temple (fragment 14). The words "shall never thirst again," Heracleon continues, mean that

> his life is eternal and never perishes as does the first (life) which the well provides, but rather is lasting. For the Grace and gift of our Savior cannot be taken away, and is not consumed or destroyed in the one who partakes of it. The first life is perishable.

Those who partake of this "gushing source" (John 4:14) will themselves become a refreshing source for their fellow humans.

Heracleon praises the Samaritan woman for accepting Jesus' words without hesitation. She was completely overwhelmed by the Logos and from then on she hated this place, because its water was difficult to capture and not nourishing. This interpretation is feasible, because those who have attained a better truth never return to the old one: *Water that gushes up to give eternal life* (John 4:14).

Gnosticism and alchemy again converge in water symbolism. In alchemy, water has a thousand names; it is called *acqua nostra* or *philosophica* to distinguish it from common water (drawn from Jacob's well). In the meaning of the water given by Jesus it is the *acqua permanens, aeterna, vitae, perpetua, mystica, spiritualis, coelestis* (celestial), *divina* (divine), *impalpabilis* (intangible), *munda* (pure), *marina* (marine), and so on.

Earlier on, I cited the *Gloria Mundi* ("Glory of the World") from the *Musaeum Hermeticum*. Its "Explanation" states:

> Our Stone is such that it cannot adequately be described in writing. For it is a stone, and becomes water through evaporation; yet it is no stone, and it by a chemical process it receives a watery form it is at first like any other liquid water, being a thin fluid; yet its nature is not like that of any other water upon earth. There is only one spring in all the world from which this water may be obtained. That spring is in Judaea, and is called, the Spring of the Saviour [Joel 3:18],[18] or of beatitude. By the grace of God its situation was revealed to the Sages. It issues in a secret place, and its waters flow over all the world. It is familiar to all, yet none knows the principle, reason, or way to find the spring, or discover the way to Judaea. But whoever does not know the right spring will never attain to a knowledge of our Art. For this reason, that Sage might well exclaim, "O water of a harsh and bitter taste!" For, in truth, the spring is difficult to find; but he who knows it may reach it easily, without any expense, labour, or trouble. The water is, of its own nature, harsh and bitter, so that no one can partake of it; and, because it is of little use to the

---

[18] Vulgata: Joel 3:8: *fons de domo Domini egredietur et inrigabit torrentem spinarum...*

majority of mankind the Sage doth also exclaim, "O water, that art lightly esteemed by the vulgar, who do not perceive thy great virtues, in thee lie, as it were, hid the four elements. Thou hast power to dissolve, and conserve, and join nature, such as is possessed by no other thing upon earth." If you would know the properties and appearance of this Stone, know that its appearance is aqueous, and that the water is first changed into a stone, then the stone into water, and the water at length into the Medicine.[19]

This passage is richer than what can be said about it here, just as the Stone of the Wise itself eludes description, because it is literally everything. A significant contrast seems to exist between stone and water. The alchemical process consists of the famous *solve et coagula* principle ("dissolve and coagulate"): thus, the stone represents the solid phase and water the dissolved phase of the same process. For the alchemists repeatedly emphasize that their stone is "lapis, non lapis" (a stone but not a stone). It is sublimated by the vapors (*vapores*), which already indicates the psychological process. Whenever anyone believes that they hold the Stone of the Wise in their hands, it evaporates, and one realizes that what one has discovered about oneself is not the answer to everything.

Water, as the indispensable source of life, is a well known symbol of the unconscious, from which also spring the energy of life and consciousness. Consequently, no water in the world resembles this water, no water like that from Jacob's well. Everyone knows this water, because we all dream, but no one knows its true source. Only the philosophers, i.e., the genuine alchemists, find the hidden source with great effort and by God's grace. Their chemical labors are accompanied

---

[19] https://archive.org/details/TextsFromTheMusaeumHermeticum

by meditations, in which the imagination swirls around the work with all unconscious contents, which thus become conscious.

C.G. Jung discusses another reason why so few find this source when he comments on this passage in *Mysterium Coniunctionis*. He explains:

> This is an obvious allusion to the arcane nature and moral significance of the water, and it is also evident that it is not the water of grace or the water of the doctrine but that it springs from the *lumen naturae*. Otherwise the author would not have emphasized that Judaea was in a "secret place," for if the Church's teachings were meant no one would need to find them in a secret place, since they are accessible to everyone. There can be no doubt that this is the *aqua permanens* or *aqua pontica*, the primal water which contains the four elements. The psychological equivalent of the chaotic water of the beginning is the unconscious, which the old writers could grasp only in projected form.... (CW 14 §341–342)

Turning to alchemy, he adds:

> The good tidings announced by alchemy are that, as once a fountain sprang up in Judaea, so now there is a secret Judaea the way to which is not easily found, and a hidden spring whose waters seem so worthless and so bitter that they are deemed of no use at all. We know from numerous hints that man's inner life is the "secret place" where the *aqua solvens et coagulans*, the *medicina catholica* or panacea, the spark of the light of nature, are to be found. Our text shows us how much the alchemists put their art on the level of divine revelation and regarded it as at least an essential complement to the work of redemption. True, only a few of them were the elect who formed the golden chain

linking earth to heaven, but still they were the fathers of natural science today. They were the unwitting instigators of the schism between faith and knowledge, and it was they who made the world conscious that the revelation was neither complete nor final [...]. (344)

He then elaborates further on alchemy:

> Alchemy announced a source of knowledge, parallel if not equivalent to revelation, which yields a "bitter" water by no means acceptable to our human judgment. It is harsh and bitter or like vinegar, for it is a bitter thing to accept the darkness and blackness of the *umbra solis* and to pass through this valley of the shadow. It is bitter indeed to discover behind one's lofty ideals narrow, fanatical convictions, all the more cherished for that, and behind one's heroic pretensions nothing but crude egotism, infantile greed, and complacency. This painful corrective is an unavoidable stage in every psychotherapeutic process. (346)

And he concludes:

> In spite of their undoubtedly "heretical methods" the alchemists showed by their positive attitude to the Church that they were cleverer than certain modern apostles of enlightenment. Also—very much in contrast to the rationalistic tendencies of today—they displayed, despite its "tortuousness," a remarkable understanding of the imagery upon which the Christian cosmos is built. This world of images, in its historical form, is irretrievably lost to modern man. (347)

Elsewhere, he writes:

"Mater Alchimia" could serve as the name of a whole epoch. Beginning, roughly, with Christianity, it gave birth in the sixteenth and seventeenth centuries to the age of science, only to perish, unrecognized and misunderstood, and sink from sight in the stream of the centuries as an age that had been outlived. But, just as every mother was once a daughter, so too was alchemy. It owes its real beginnings to the Gnostic systems, which Hippolytus rightly regarded as philosophic, and which, with the help of Greek philosophy and the mythologies of the Near and Middle East, together with Christian dogmatics and Jewish cabalism, made extremely interesting attempts, from the modern point of view, to synthetize a unitary vision of the world in which the physical and the mystical[20] aspects played equal parts. Had this attempt succeeded, we would not be witnessing today the curious spectacle of two parallel world-views neither of which knows, or wishes to know, anything about the other [...]

These attempts, however, inevitably came to grief for lack of any adequate knowledge of natural processes. Thus, in the course of the eighteenth century, there arose that notorious rift between faith and knowledge. Faith lacked experience and science missed out the soul. Instead, science believed fervently in absolute objectivity and assiduously overlooked the fundamental difficulty that the real vehicle and begetter of all knowledge is the psyche, the very thing that scientists knew the least about for the longest time." (CW 9ii §267–268)

Heracleon's 17th fragment emphasizes that crucial moment when the Samaritan woman recognizes the savior as the one who conveys the light of nature in the form of divine water. This knowledge is a sudden,

---

[20] Translator's note: Jung's original version reads "in denen die *physika* eine den *mystika* ebenbürtige Rolle spielten." Dr. Ribi points out that *mystika* alludes to the title of a treatise by the Greek alchemist Pseudo-Democritus.

merciful illumination, which utterly transforms the woman. "Now for the Gnostics—and this is their real secret—the psyche existed as a source of knowledge just as much as it did for the alchemists," observes Jung in *Aion*, and continues:

> Aside from the psychology of the unconscious, contemporary science and philosophy know only of what is outside, while faith knows only of the inside, and then only in the Christian form imparted to it by the passage of the centuries, beginning with St. Paul and the gospel of St. John. Faith, quite as much as science with its traditional objectivity, is absolute, which is why faith and knowledge can no more agree than Christians can with one another.
>
> Our Christian doctrine is a highly differentiated symbol that expresses the transcendent psychic—the God-image and its properties, to speak with Dorn. The Creed is a "symbolum." This comprises practically everything of importance that can be ascertained about the manifestations of the psyche in the field of inner experience, but it does not include Nature, at least not in any recognizable form. Consequently, at every period of Christianity there have been subsidiary currents or undercurrents that have sought to investigate the empirical aspect of Nature not only from the outside but also from the inside. (CW 9ii §269-270)

Therefore, water is as significant in Gnostic symbolism as it is in alchemy. Here, alchemy's *acqua divina* or *permanens* is the light-water, which, for instance, appears in the *Apocryphon of John* (BG 26,15–27,6):

> (It is) the one who knows Itself alone in the light-water that surrounds It, which is the spring of living water, the light which is full of purity. The spring of the Spirit flowed from the living

water of the light and it abundantly supplied all the aeons and the worlds. In every way It perceived Its own image, seeing It in the pure light-water which surrounds It. (III 7,2–10; II 4,19–29)

Similarly, Ermolao Barbarus, the great Italian Renaissance humanist and archbishop of Aquila, reportedly wrote the following lines about water in the corollary to his commentaries on Dioscorides:

> There is also the heavenly or rather the divine water of the alchemists, which was known to both Democritus and Hermes Trismegistus, who at times called it divine water, at others Scythic juice, at even others pneuma, that is, spirit, which descends from the nature of the ether and the quintessence of things.[21]

In alchemy, the spirit is frequently related to water or the root moisture (*humidum radicale*). As Jung writes, this "fact that may be explained simply by the empirical nature of the oldest form of 'chemistry,' namely the art of cooking." He comments:

> The steam arising from boiling water conveys the first vivid impression of "metasomatosis," the transformation of the corporeal into the incorporeal, into spirit or pneuma. The relation of spirit to water resides in the fact that the spirit is hidden in the water, like a fish. (CW 13 §101)

Considering the relation of the creative spirit to water, the alchemist Christophorus Steebus entertained some interesting ideas, as cited by Jung in the next paragraph:

---

[21] Cited in Michael Maier, *Symbola Aureae Mensae*—trans.

> The brooding of the Holy Spirit upon the waters above the firmament brought forth a power which permeates all things in the most subtle way, warms them, and, in conjunction with the light, generates in the mineral kingdom of the lower world the mercurial serpent, in the plant kingdom the blessed greenness, and in the animal kingdom the formative power; so that the supracelestial spirit of the waters, united with the light, may fitly be called the soul of the world. (CW 13 §102)

In a codex found at Nag Hammadi, the Trimorphic Protennoia speaks about herself in an aretology:

> I am the Invisible One within the All. It is I who councel those who are hidden, since I know the All that exists in it. I am numberless beyond everyone. I am immeasurable, ineffable, yet whenever I [wish, I shall] reveal myself of my own accord....
>
> I [descend to the] midst of the underworld and I shone [down upon the] darkness. It is I who poured forth the [water]. It is I who am hidden within [radiant] waters. I am the one who gradually put forth the All by my Thought. It is I who am laden with the voice. It is through me that Gnosis comes forth.[22] (NHC XIII, 35,24–30; 36,4–10)

While the similarity between this Gnostic text and alchemical ones is obvious, it goes much further than the above passage reveals: the trimorphic Protennoia, who at times appears as female, at others as male, is not merely a kind of *anima mundi* (world-soul), but indeed comes very close to alchemy's spirit Mercurius (Jung, CW 13 §239ff.). This is a versatile spirit, a distinctly arcane substance. Due to its liquid

---

[22] Turner, *Trimorphic Protennoia*; Hedrick, ed. *Nag Hammadi Codices* XI, XII, XIII; XIII, pp. 403–405.

state and evaporability, it is also known as water, even as *"aqua vitae"* (water of life), *"aqua alba"* (white water), *"aqua sicca"* (dry water), *"aqua non madefaciens manus"* (water that does not moisten the hands), or as *hydor theon* (divine water), a term common in Greek alchemy. One need not decide whether it is a spirit (spiritus), even one residing in matter, or a soul (anima). The alchemists understood the "soul" as that which exists between spirit and matter (*anima media natura*, i.e., the soul as an intermediate nature, the soul as medium). Thus, it is ethereal, like a breath-soul or a "subtle body." It is the invigorating force or the life principle. This aspect is strongly emphasized in the Gnostic Protennoia. Mercurius is one yet two, indeed ambivalent, a unity yet a trinity. Jung points out its pre-Christian character and then cites the following passage from Zosimus' *Concerning the Art*:

> The unity of the composition [produces] the indivisible triad, and thus an undivided triad composed of separate elements creates the cosmos,[23] through the forethought [πρόνοια] of the First Author, the cause and demiurge of creation; wherefore he is called Trismegistos, having beheld triadically that which is created and that which creates. (CW 13 §270, esp. footnote 2)

Thus Mercurius, like Hermes, is *tricephalus* (three-headed). Here, Jung emphasizes the fact that many gods of the underworld (e.g., Typhon, Hecate) were *trisomatos* (three-bodied). "Mercurius," he writes,

> ...is the Logos become world. The description [in the Aurelia occulta][24] may point to his basic identity with the collective unconscious, for as I tried to show in my essay "On the Nature of the Psyche," the image of the starry heaven seems to be a visualization of the peculiar nature of the unconscious.

---

[23] Given these similarities, one wonders whether there were also dependencies.
[24] *Theatrum Chemicum* IV (1659), p. 615.

> One peculiarity of Mercurius which undoubtedly relates him to the Godhead and to the primitive creator god is his ability to beget himself. (CW 13 §271–272)

Our discussion of Heracleon's first fragment did not consider his subtle distinction. Writing about John 1:3, "All things came into being through him [i.e., the Word, the Logos], and without him not one thing came into being," he remarks that the Logos merely gives the impulse for the creation of the world without, however, entering it. It leaves the work of creation to a demiurge, who logically enough stands under the Logos. Through the mediation of the Logos, the demiurge creates the All.

Origen considers such psychological subtlety incomprehensible. It seemingly contradicts the alchemists' notion of "Mercurius as the Logos become world." One needs to consider, however, that the latter idea represents a later, more mature mindset; also worth recalling in particular is that the alchemists projected their world-creating spirit into matter. In Heracleon and the Gnostics in general, the world-creating spirit does not wholly enter its creation, but remains partly outside time and space, and is hence eternal. This explains the denigrating attitude of Gnosticism toward the material world. In this respect, the Gnostics differ fundamentally from the alchemists, who, as is well known, were natural scientists and fascinated by matter.

When Heracleon emphasizes that the Logos does not enter creation, he professes a radical realism, whose reality is the world of the aeons. But the established church, and Origen as one of its most astute representatives (Jung, CW 6 §8), adopt a nominalist stance. The conflict over which reality is valid has lost none of its force since antiquity, if one considers how each depth-psychological approach is rejected as psychologistic. The Church fears that such a perspective will make its sacrosanct truths vanish into thin air. But no psychic content evaporates because of a depth-psychological explanation, not even illusions and hallucinations, because even pathological manifestations of the soul are still psychic contents. The fear of a "nothing-but" explanation stems from a fundamental underestimation of the psyche. In the end, we are unable to decide whether the realistic or the nominalist standpoint is true. Hence, Jung emphasizes that all we can say about any kind of truth is the mediating "esse in anima" (being-in-soul) (CW 6 §67).[25]

Heracleon's realism becomes even more apparent in the second fragment, when he refers to John 1:4 ("What has come into being in him was life") not to the Logos, but to the pneumatics. They experience life in the primordial image of the Logos, rather than as a reflection of matter as do the hylics.

Before fragment 2, Origen comments on John 1:5, "the life was the light of the people. The light shines in the darkness, and the darkness did not overcome it." The darkness is the *agnosia*, the unconscious state, like that of the Samaritan woman before she recognized Jesus. This state is not final, but—and here Origen cites Paul's Letter to the Ephesians 5:8 ("For once you were darkness, but now in the Lord you are light. Live as children of Light")—it can transform into light. This transformation, whether it occurs suddenly, as in the case of the woman from Samaria, or gradually, as is more common, corresponds to *acquiring consciousness*, which for the most part is expressed by *symbols of light*. Hence, the Logos initiates the process of becoming conscious, which means the emergence of the world. Each of us has this possibility, but the pneumatic possesses it to an even higher degree. Originally we are all darkness, from which, given the right impetus, the light of the savior can come into being. This is the *central idea of Gnosticism*.

In the *Trimorphic Protennoia*, she says of herself, as cited above, that "I descended to the midst of the underworld, and I shone down

---

[25] Ribi, *Die feindlichen Brüder*, p. 66.

upon the darkness" (NHC XIII, 1). Irritatingly, according to John 1:5, darkness did not accept light, as this resulted in their eternal conflict, such as in Manichaeism. Only after Christ descended to the underworld after his death were its shackles broken (see the *Gospel of Bartholomew* CPV 10f.) and a certain union of the opposites achieved. Yet even this has escaped Protestantism, whereas the Protennoia's Gnosticism has symbolically achieved a union, which later led her to proudly declare that she "had brought forth Gnosis" (36,10).

The opposite of Gnosis, the unredeemed, unenlightened state in which humanity languishes, is *agnosia* or *agnoia*, the self-inflicted uncertainty or unconsciousness. The central concern of Gnosticism is the deliverance from this unfortunate state of being arrested in matter. Here is a relevant passage from the Gnostic *Gospel of Mary*:

> And Desire said, 'I did not see you go down, yet now I see you go up. So why do you lie, since you belong to me?'
>
> The soul answered, 'I saw you. You did not see me, nor did you know me. You mistook the garment I wore for my true self. And you did not recognize me.'
>
> After it had said these things, it left, rejoicing greatly. (NHC V, 2–5 and IV; Papyrus Berolinsis 8502, 1 and 4)

In Gnosticism, clothing is a well known symbol for the body, which the soul, as it were, attracts during incarnation and leaves behind after its death. This part of matter would like to entangle the soul in vice, but from it the pneumatic's soul is freed, so that the powers can no longer harm it. Psychologically, this is particularly interesting: the Gnostic knows these vices, and he need not eschew them, because his core remains unaffected. This is an utterly different concept of sin than that of the established church. While the Gnostic knows that he cannot escape the planetary forces, these do not penetrate his soul. The Gnostic need not be perfect; on the contrary, he can approve of the most terrible evil without, however, condoning it, and in spite of it remain unbowed. He knows that these powers are stronger than him, but they cannot possess him.[26]

The soul then encounters ignorance:

> Again, it came to the third power, which is called 'Ignorance.' [It] examined the soul closely, saying, "Where are you going? You are bound by wickedness. Indeed, you are bound! Do not judge."
>
> And the soul said, "Why do you judge me, since I have not passed judgment? I have been bound, but I have not bound anything. They did not recognize me, but I have recognized that the universe is to be dissolved, both the things of earth and those of heaven."
>
> When the soul had brought the third power to naught, it went upward." (BG 1; 15,10–16,3)

To be governed by a bad disposition means to be possessed. Succumbing to obsession makes one unconscious and unfree. Overcoming unconsciousness means attaining greater freedom. *Freedom only exists where there is consciousness.* This explains why, ultimately, unconsciousness is a painful state. Considering that humanity has spent millions of years in spiritual darkness, the appearance of the light of the Logos in the primordial darkness is *redemption*. The Gnostics are the actual discoverers of the redeeming function of consciousness. Therefore, the soul, after it has overcome the fourth power, the seven powers of wrath, says:

---

[26] *The Search for Roots*, p. 118.

> What binds me has been slain, and what surrounds me has been destroyed, and my desire has been brought to an end, and ignorance has died. In a [world], I was set loose [17] from a world and in a type, from a type that is above, and from the chain of forgetfulness, which exists in time. From this hour on, for the time of the due season of the age, I will receive rest in silence. (BG 1, 16,16–17,7)

Repose (*anapausis*), as observed, is the final condition, the redeemed state of the Gnostic.[27] This is a conscious state of freedom from unconscious ties. It is achieved by the pneumatic seeing the archetypal behind every worldly image and thereby dissolving his projections onto this world. Although he still lives in this earthly world, he has overcome it, which affords him equanimity and repose. He lives beyond time, as it were, because he lives in eternal images.

In the *First Apocalypse of James* (NH V, 3) the Lord gives James secret instructions about suffering, about the death of the Lord, and about the ascent of the soul after death. Here, James the Righteous is the brother of the Lord. He is taught that he will recognize the various evil powers only if he discards blind reason, the shackling flesh surrounding him. Only then will he "no longer be James; rather you are the One Who Is" (NH V, 3; 27,1–10). James fears the armed powers, but the Lord instructs him that these are directed as much against him as against James. James then tells the Rabbi:

> You have come with knowledge,
> that you might rebuke their forgetfulness.
> You have come with recollection,
> that you might rebuke their ignorance.
>
> But I was concerned because of you.

---

[27] Ménard, "Le repos," pp. 71–81.

> For you descended into a great ignorance,
> but you have not been defiled by anything in it.
> For you descended into a great mindlessness,
> and your recollection remained.
>
> You walked in mud,
> and your garments were not soiled,
> and you have not been buried in their filth,
> and you have not been caught. (28,7–20)

The Lord is obviously a role model for the Gnostic, who either reads or hears this apocalypse. What happens to the Lord also happens to the perfect Gnostic. He remembers the unrecognizable Father, whom he brings onto earth for all those who suffer from forgetfulness. In this sense, he is the redeemer and brings Gnosis. The dark powers stand opposed to knowledge and attempt to make the human being perish in their mire. Like the Lord, the Gnostic must wage a constant battle against the powers of darkness (Ephesians 6:12). To do so, he must awaken from his oblivion.

In the Valentinian *Tripartite Tractate* (NH I,5), ignorance about the All is referred to as death: "The vice of soul is ignorance," says the *Corpus Hermeticum*:

> For the soul, when it is blind and discerns none of the things that are nor their nature nor the good, is shaken by the bodily passions, and the wretched thing becomes—in ignorance of itself—a slave to vile and monstrous bodies, bearing the body like a burden, not ruling but being ruled. (CH X 8)

Logically for the Gnostic, *agnosia*, the deliberate persistence in unconsciousness, is the greatest evil. About those who remain in this state, the text says:

Where are you heading in your drunkenness, you people? Have you swallowed the doctrine of ignorance undiluted, vomiting it up already because you cannot hold it? Stop and sober yourselves up! Look up with the eyes of the heart—if not all of you, at least those of you who have the power. The vice of ignorance floods the whole earth and utterly destroys the soul shut up in the body, preventing it from anchoring in the havens of deliverance. Surely you will not sink in this great flood? Those of you who can will take the ebb and gain the haven of deliverance and anchor there. Then, seek a guide to take you by the hand and lead you to the portals of knowledge. There shines the light cleansed of darkness. There no one is drunk. All are sober and gaze with the heart toward one who wishes to be seen, who is neither heard nor spoken of, who is seen not with the eyes but with mind and heart. But first you must rip off the tunic that you wear, the garment of ignorance, the foundation of vice, the bonds of corruption, the dark cage, the living death, the sentient corpse, the portable tomb, the resident thief, the one who hates through what he loves and envies through what he hates. (CH VII 1)

This text, which could just as well have been written for our time, illustrates even more plainly the negative aspects of agnosia. The evil and destruction in our world are caused mostly not by intentional malice, but by stupidity, short-sightedness, thoughtlessness, superficiality, lack of self control, indifference, and so on, i.e., by weaknesses in which the unconscious is dominant. While the unconscious is the seedbed of evil, it is not evil per se. It assumes this quality if it is ignored. If excluded from daily life, it rears its head, unpleasantly, and manifests itself in nightmares. Instead of promoting life as usual, it perversely changes into a figure hostile to life. Hence, the Hermetic text describes this state as living death, as a sentient corpse, as a grave that one carries around with oneself, and as a thief in one's own house who plunders it unnoticed and deprives us of our best intentions. Whoever understands this will do everything in their power to put an end to this state.

According to Irenaeus, the established church is aware of human misery and the salvation from this condition, although in quite a different sense:

> This, therefore, was the [object of the] long-suffering of God, that man, passing through all things, and acquiring the knowledge of moral discipline, then attaining to the resurrection from the dead, and learning by experience what is the source of his deliverance, may always live in a state of gratitude to the Lord, having obtained from Him the gift of incorruptibility, that he might love Him the more; for "he to whom more is forgiven, loveth more."[28] [Luke 7:42–43] (*Against Heresies* III 20,2)

As this passage reveals, the established church regards God as the great educator, who inflicts all sorts of hardship on human beings so they he may save them from their woes and receive their gratitude. This fits the notion of God as an authoritative Father, who must educate the disobedient. Gnosis, however, sees the human being as an adult, responsible creature.

The established church, represented here by Irenaeus, one of the church fathers, God employs evil as an educational tool. This requires God to stand above evil at all times, and to mete it out according to His will. This plan, however, could also fail if evil becomes autonomous:

---

[28] I have slightly adapted the original Latin: *Haec ergo fuit magnanimtas Dei, ut per omnia pertransiens homo et mortis agnitionem percipiens, dehinc veniens ad resurrectionem quae est a mortuius et experimento discens unde liberatus est, semper gratus exsistat domino, munus incorruptelae consecetus ab eo, ut plus diligeret eum, cui enim plus demittitur plus diligit.*

> For if man, who had been created by God that he might live, after losing life, through being injured by the serpent that had corrupted him, should not any more return to life, but should be utterly [and for ever] abandoned to death, God would [in that case] have been conquered, and the wickedness of the serpent would have prevailed over the will of God. (*Against Heresies* III, 23,1)

This leads Irenaeus to quite logically conclude:

> It is good to obey God, and to believe in Him, and to keep His commandment, and this is the life of man; as not to obey God is evil, and this is his death. Since God, therefore, gave [to man] such mental power (*magnanimitatem*) man knew both the good of obedience and the evil of disobedience, that the eye of the mind, receiving experience of both, may with judgment make choice of the better things; and that he may never become indolent or neglectful of God's command. (*Against Heresies* IV 39,1)

Paul the Apostle considered at length the validity of the law after the coming of Christ. John 1:17 asserts: "The law indeed was given through Moses, grace and truth came through Jesus Christ." On the other hand, Matthew 5:19 says: "Therefore, whoever breaks one of the least of these commandments, and teaches others to do the same, will be called least in the kingdom of heaven; but whoever does them and teaches them will be great in the kingdom of heaven." In early Christianity, there seemed to exist a dilemma about whether the law was annulled by Christ or not. In his Letter to the Romans, Paul writes:

> While we were living in the flesh, our sinful passions, aroused by the law, were at work in our members to bear fruit for death. But

now we are discharged from the law, dead to that which held us captive, so that we are slaves not under the old written code but in the new life of the Spirit. (Romans 7:5–6)

The hylics are those "in the flesh," those who need the law. But as Paul realized, most subtly, the law also arouses the passions within us. Overcoming the law does not mean lawlessness, but the moral responsibility of the spirit. The established church evidently hesitated to take this step. The Gnostics led the way in this respect. Such a step requires the overcoming of agnosia. Those who are not connected with their inside need the written code. Those, however, who recognize their own moral authority as a *vox Dei* (voice of God), are freed from the letter of the law that kills (2 Corinthians 3:6), and embrace the living spirit.

III. The Gnostic Notion of Sin

Sin occupies a far less prominent role in Gnosticism than in orthodoxy, as the previous section may have helped establish. Only in a legalistic religion does the question of good and evil hinge on the violation of the law. In a movement that places greatest emphasis on the attainment of consciousness the question of sin becomes secondary. As we have seen, the Gnostics consider persisting in unconsciousness a sin, in fact the cardinal sin, or a sin committed against the Holy Spirit (Mark 3:29).

Nevertheless, the Gnostic is not permitted to do as he pleases, even though he is not subject to the law. The Gnostics grew radically serious about turning from the law of the Old Testament to overcoming the law through love and consciousness. The Gnostics were so radical, in fact, that they even saw the demiurge of the Old Testament as the law-giver and as hostile to newness. Scholars of Gnosticism have been locked in endless discussions about why the Old Testament God, in the guise of the demiurge (i.e., Yaldabaoth) or

Samael (i.e., the blind man), has played such an inglorious role in Gnosticism. Gilles Quispel believes that this suggests that Gnosticism originated in heterodox Jewish or Jewish-Christian circles in Alexandria.[29]

A much simpler and more verifiable explanation is that *Gnosis overcomes legalistic religion*. According to a psychological law, what is overcome is demonized, as the example of the ancient gods in early Christiantity shows. Demonization simulates fear and acts as a barrier against regression. When the process of becoming conscious reaches a new stage, it risks being lost again. Therefore, newly gained consciousness erects a barrier. Gnosticism's demonization of the demiurge is symptomatic of a progression in consciousness. Orthodox Christianity sought to balance the Old and the New Testaments, and thereby remained largely trapped in legalism.[30] Anti-Semitism—and this shows that it is not merely an academic question—has its roots in the Christian's unsurmounted Judaism. Likewise, the Jew possesses a Christian shadow in the shape of the "eternal Jew" (Ahasveros), who crucified the Christ within himself. Because the contrast between the Old and the New Testaments was not brought into consciousness, the conflict occurred outside, as the brutal suppression of Gnosticism throughout the centuries or as Aryan racial fanaticism. While this conflict is historical, it can be resolved only by the individual becoming conscious. As in individual development, in the collective the level of law represents a more youthful mentality, and that of becoming conscious a more adult one. These mindsets exclude one another, so that a compromise, as aspired to by the established church, is impossible.[31] Gnosticism sympathetically accepted many Old

---

[29] "The Origins of the Christian Demiurge," *Gnostic Studies*, vol. 1, p. 218.

[30] See C.G. Jung's discussion of the Jewish shadow lurking within European Christians in his *Seminar on Dream Analysis*.

[31] I have discussed Jung's biographical confrontation with this problem in *The Search for Roots*, p. 110.

Testament truths, so that there is no question of any hostility toward Judaism. Gnosticism merely rejected the Old Testament God as a surmounted dominant. Psychologically, the notion of God represents an overarching conscious-unconscious idea, which directs the life of the individual and that of an entire people. This idea is highly conservative, but it changes over the centuries. Thus, here, once again, we come across a question that has remained unanswered in the history of Christianity.

This brings us back to Heracleon and the woman from Samaria. In fragment 18, on John 4:16, "Jesus said to her, 'Go, call your husband, and come back.'" Origen believes that Heracleon is here saying:

> "If you wish to receive this water, go call your husband." The husband of the Samaritan woman mentioned by Jesus is her Fullness, so that, on coming with him to the Savior, she may obtain from him power and union and the mingling with her Fullness. For he was not speaking to her about her earthly husband and telling her to call him, for he knew quite well that she had no lawful husband...The Savior said to her, "Call your husband and come hither," and meant by this her partner from the Fullness... In the spiritual sense she did not know her husband; in the simple sense she was ashamed to say that she had an adulterer, not a husband... (The words) "You have rightly said that you do not have a husband" (John 4:17) mean that in the world the Samaritan woman had no husband, for her husband was in the Aeon (i.e., Fullness). (In John 4:18: "You have had five husbands and the one you have now is not your husband.") The six men indicate the whole of the material evil in which she was involved and with which consorted, when she lived irrationally in debauchery, and was insulted, rejected and abandoned by them (the men).

Heracleon once again foregrounds the central Gnostic myth: on the objective level (Jung, CW 8 §510) on the one hand, the Samaritan woman is the psychic, whose encounter with the savior transforms her into a pneumatic, as fragment 17 shows; on the subjective level, on the other hand, she is the soul lost in the world and yet saved. The most beautiful version of this myth, as I have explained, is the *Exegesis on the Soul*.[32] (NH II,6)

The female figure described in the Gnostic text represents, as the reader may easily establish, what Jung calls the anima. Because the man is often unaware of the anima, she seems to come from the afterworld. She is indeed identical with the prenatal totality from which consciousness separates itself. As a rule, she is not recognized as an inner reality until the second half of life, until when she tends to confront the man as the woman who shapes his destiny. In the first half of life, this reality is projected largely onto the external world, where she confronts him as the man's image of *the* woman. In this Gnostic myth, this is expressed as the harlotry of the soul: she appears in highly diverse external images. In a broader sense, she represents everything that fascinated a man in life, be it his occupation, his pastime, a person, an idea, an object, in short everything that the Indian calls the Maya. "Maya is Existence," writes Heinrich Zimmer,

> both the world of which we are aware, and ourselves who are contained in the growing and dissolving environment, growing and dissolving in our turn. At the same time, Maya is the supreme power that generates and animates the display: the dynamic aspect of the universal Substance. Thus it is at once, effect (the cosmic flux), and cause (the creative power). In the latter regard it is known as Shakti, "Cosmic Energy."[33] If misunderstood, this term may lead one to conclude that the

---

[32] See Ribi, *Bericht über das 2. Gnosis Seminar*; see also Chapter 8.
[33] Zimmer, *Myths and Symbols in Indian Art and Civilization*, p. 25.

outer world and the ego lack all reality, that they are unsubstantial, incorporeal.[34]

The woman losing herself to the world in the Gnostic myth reveals that her illusions are that reality which appears to us. When we "cling" to an object or person, we notice just how much we have succumbed to this illusion. We can detach ourselves only through the difficult withdrawal of the projection.

The Gnostic abhors this loss of self to the world, because he thereby loses himself and his relationship to his Self. Solely in this greatest misery, in his suffering from the world, does he recall the his celestial home and regret his entanglement with the world. He then turns to his syzygos, that part of himself which he has left behind, to be wedded to his true Self in a holy marriage. The "world" does not have the best reputation in the Bible either. In the temptation narrative, the (mighty) devil shows Jesus all the kingdoms of the world and promises them to him if he worships him (Matthew 4:9). The devil is the *princeps huius mundi* (John 14:30). Whoever becomes involved with the world, becomes its victim. Jesus has overcome the world (John 16:33) and thus the Gnostic should also overcome it. His kingdom is therefore not of this world (John 18:36). Out of love, however, God has sent his only son into the world to save it (John 3:17). And yet human beings love darkness more than light (John 3:19). Just as Jesus descended from heaven and then reascended (John 3:13), in the myth the soul descended from the house of the Father into the world, where it is violated, before it rises up to the Father again.

The First Epistle of John states:

> Do not love the world or the things in the world. The love of the Father is not in those who love the world; for all that is in the

---

[34] Ibid., *Philosophie und Religion Indiens*, p. 30f.—trans.

world—the desire of the flesh, the desire of the eyes, the pride in riches—comes not from the Father but from the world. And the world and its desires are passing away, but those who do the will of God live forever. (2:15–17)

Nevertheless, the Gnostics are said to be heretics, whereas in fact the opposite is true: they are good Christians, although with a different concept of the Holy Scripture than the church fathers. The Gnostics took certain statements in the Scripture far more seriously than the established church, which ever since Constantine (306–337) had become embroiled with the rulers of the world. "They are from the world; therefore what they say is from the world, and the world listens to them," writes John in his first letter (4:5). John's words in the next verse could be interpreted as follows: the Gnostics "are from God. Whoever knows God listens to us, and whoever is not from God does not listen to us" (4:6). It is probably no coincidence that the Gnostics, most of all Heracleon, appreciated the Gospel of John, because it is written in the same vein. Based on psychological evidence, Jung assumed that the author of the letters and the apocalypse were identical, which various scholars, including Professor Quispel, have confirmed. The letters are optimistic, whereas the apocalypse is pessimistic and their unconscious compensation.

Jung comments:

> His [i.e., John's] conscious attitude is orthodox, but he has evil forebodings [...] John is a bit too sure, and therefore he runs the risk of a dissociation. Under these circumstances a counter-position is bound to grow up in the unconscious, which can then irrupt into consciousness in the form of a revelation. (CW 11 §698)

In many respects, the established church followed John's optimism, whereas the Gnostics took a rather compensatory, pessimistic approach, most of all regarding the dangers posed by the world for the well-being of the soul. Albeit with certain variations, the following lines have come down to us from the synoptic Gospels: "For what will it profit them if they gain the whole world but forfeit their life?" (Matthew 16:26; Mark 8:26; Luke 9:25).

Crucially, in the Gnostic myth to turn away from this world means to turn toward the invisible world. As for the Indian, for the Gnostic this is the "true" world, which will survive the body's death and means its redemption, which consists in the restoration of the prenatal totality, not, however, through a return to the Father, but through the union with the brother sent by the Father. In alchemy, the *coniunctio* occurs through incest, as we read in the *Visio Arislei*:

> Lord, although you are King, you govern poorly, for you unite the male with the male, although you know that the male cannot beget. The new arises from the conjunction of male and female, when nature is wed to nature, male with female, and what belongs to one thing becomes it, when the appropriate finds the righteous. He [the King] says: I have a son and daughter, and therefore I am the King of the subordinate, who have nothing of the kind: I have given birth to my son and daughter in my brain. I [the alchemist] say: Bring us your son Thabritius. After he had heard this, I demanded that he also bring his [Thabritius'] sister Beya. The King asks: Why do you want Beya? I reply: Because there is no procreation without her; although she is her brother's sister, she is still a woman: She improves him, because she is made of the same substance as he was. And so Beya was brought, a pure virgin (puella candida), delicate, and sweet. About the union of Thabritius and Beya, the King says that never had a groom ever taken home such a bride. And I say: This did Adam command his

daughters and you, O King, will be happy, for you will acquire many kings and queens, several grandsons and granddaughters. Your son Thabritius and his sister Beya will enrich you and when they have died, they will live again.[35]

In the first instance, the comparison of a sacrosanct Gnostic myth with a profane alchemical vision may seem strange. But this need not surprise us, because all products of the collective unconscious are numinous. Hence, they may also be compared with time-honored biblical passages without, however, detracting anything from their value. The Holy Scripture does not attain its numinosity only through the belief that it represents the revealed word of God, but by touching upon the universally human in the collective unconscious. But, then, so do Gnosticism and alchemy.

Let us return to the brother-sister incest, which is beautifully illustrated in Michael Maier's *Atalanta fugiens*. [Figure 4] The incest archetype is one of the most important psychic events, or how else, as Jung writes in *Mysterium Coniunctionis*:

> Could they [i.e., the alchemists] have come upon that strange myth of the country of the King of the Sea, where only like pairs with like and the land is unfruitful? It was obviously a realm of innocent friendship, a kind of paradise or golden age, to which the "Philosophers," the representatives of the physical, felt obliged to put an end with their good advice. But what happened was not by any means a natural union of the sexes; on the contrary it was a "royal" incest....

He continues, moreover:

---

[35] *Artis Aurifae* (1593), vol, 1, p. 147—trans.

A subtle feature of the "Visio Arislei" is that the very one who is meditating a pairing of the sexes is king of the land of innocence. Thus the *rex marinus* says: "Truly I have a son and a daughter, and therefore I am king over my subjects, because they possess nothing of these things. Yet I have borne a son and a daughter in my brain." Hence the king is a potential traitor to the paradisal state of innocence because he can generate "in his head," and he is king precisely because he is capable of this sin against the previous state of innocence. Since he can be different from them he is more than any of his subjects and therefore rightly their king [...]

Here again we see the contrast between alchemy and the prevailing Christian ideal of attempting to restore the original state of innocence by monasticism and, later, by the celibacy of the priesthood. The conflict between worldliness and spirituality, latent in the love-myth of Mother and Son, was elevated by Christianity to the mystic marriage of sponsus (Christ) and sponsa (Church), whereas the alchemists transposed it to the physical plane as the coniunctio of Sol and Luna. The Christian solution of the conflict is purely pneumatic, the physical relations of the sexes being turned into an allegory or—quite illegitimately—into a sin that perpetuates and even intensifies the original one in the Garden. Alchemy, on the other hand, exalted the most heinous transgression of the law, namely incest, into a symbol of the union of opposites, hoping in this way to bring back the golden age. For both trends the solution lay in extrapolating the union of sexes into another medium: the one projected it into the spirit, the other into matter. But neither of them located the problem in the place where it arose—the soul of man." (CW 14 §105–106)

EMBLEMA IV. *De secretis Naturæ.* 25

Conjunge fratrem cum sorore & propina illis poculum amoris:

EPIGRAMMA IV.

Non hominum foret in mundo nunc tanta propago,
    Si fratri conjunx non data prima soror.
Ergo lubens conjunge duos ab utroque parente
    Progenitos, ut sint fœmina másque toro.
Præbibe nectareo Philothesia pocla liquore
    Utrisque, & fœtus spem generabit amor.
                                             D   Lex

Figure 4. Michael Maier, *Atalanta Fugiens*, 1618

This suggests that the myth of the *Exegesis on the Soul* (II,6) stands still firmly on the pneumatic side, in that the brother-sister incest serves to restore the overall state and the rejection of the world. But this restoration takes place on a new level, in that the brother of the "lost soul" is sent down to earth as her savior, and with whom she unites not in her father's house but in the bridal chamber. The Samaritan woman in fragment 17 recognizes Jesus as that power of the Logos that allows her to unite with her real husband.

The *coniunctio* is a widespread motif in Gnosticism as the *protanthropos*, the firstborn of the highest deity and the *deuteros theos*, who either falls into or is enticed into matter. In the "Poimandres," the Father,

> Who is life and light, gave birth to a man like himself whom he loved as his own child. The man was most fair: he had the father's image; and god, who was really in love with his own form, bestowed on him all his craftworks. (CH I, 12)

And then,

> The man broke through the vault and stooped to look through the cosmic framework, thus displaying to lower nature the fair form of god. Nature smiled for love when she saw him whose fairness brings no surfeit ⟨and⟩ who holds in himself all the energy of the governors and the form of god, for in the water she saw the shape of the man's fairest form and upon the earth its shadow. When the man saw in the water the form like himself as it was in nature, he loved it and wished to inhabit it; wish and action came in the same moment, and he inhabited the unreasoning form. Nature took hold of her beloved, hugged him all about and embraced him, for they were lovers. (14)

While they repel each other in consciousness, secretly the opposites attract each other. The myth of "Poimandres," a Hermetic text dating from the time of Zosimus, represents the incarnation of the son of God as an anthropos. Looking back over two thousand years, we can barely imagine what this knowledge actually meant for the Gnostics. One insight is certain, however, as manifold evidence from the texts shows: unlike the established church, the Gnostics equated male and female.[36] Assuming that the leading Gnostics were male, as were the church fathers, they certainly adopted a positive attitude toward their female aspect. This finds visible expression in their irrational tendency whereas feeling is often rudimentary in their texts. By contrast, their positive attitude toward the feminine manifests itself in an almost infinite trust in inspiration. While this was cultivated in the established church at the time of the church fathers, it was later completely stifled.

A remarkable version of this myth occurs in the "Hymn of the Pearl" in the *Acts of Thomas*:

The Hymn of the Pearl

When I was a little child,
and dwelling in my kingdom, in my father's house,
and was content with the wealth and the luxuries
of my nourishers from the East, our home,
my parents equipped me (and) sent me forth:

And of the wealth of our treasury
they took abundantly, (and) tied up for me a load
large and (yet) light, which I myself could carry,

gold of Beth-Ellaya,
and silver of Gazak the great,

---

[36] King, *Images of the Feminine in Gnosticism.*

and rubies of India,
and agates from Beth-Kashan,

and they furnished me with the adamant,
which can crush iron.

And they took off from me the glittering robe,
which in their affection they made for me,

and the purple toga,
which was measured (and) woven to my stature.

And they made a compact with me,
and wrote it in my heart, that it might not be forgotten:

"If thou goest down into Egypt,
and bringest the one pearl,

which is in the midst of the sea
around the loud-breathing serpent,

thou shalt put on thy glittering robe
and thy toga, with which (thou art) contented,

and with thy brother, who is next to us in authority,
thou shalt be heir in our kingdom."

I quitted the East (and) went down,
there being two guardians,

for the way was dangerous and difficult,
and I was very young to travel it.

I passed through the borders of Maishan,
the meeting-place of the merchants of the East,

and I reached the land of Babel,
and I entered the walls of Sarbug.

I went down into Egypt,
and my companions parted from me.

I went straight to the serpent,
I dwelt in his abode,

(waiting) till he should slumber and sleep,
and I could take my pearl from him.

And when I was single and alone
(and) became strange to my family,

one of my race, a free-born man,
and Oriental, I saw there,

a youth fair and loveable,
the son of oil-sellers;

and he came and attached himself to me,
and I made him my intimate friend,

an associate with whom I shared my merchandise.
I warned him against the Egyptians,

and against consorting with the unclean;

And I dressed in their dress,
that they might not hold me in abhorrence,

because I was come from abroad in order to take the pearl,
and arouse the serpent against me.

But in some way other or another
they found out that I was not their countryman,

and they dealt with me treacherously,
and gave their food to eat.

I forgot that I was a son of kings,
and I served their king;

and I forgot the pearl,
for which my parents had sent me,

and because of the burden of their oppressions
I lay in a deep sleep.

But all these things that befell me
my parents perceived, and were grieved for me;

and proclamation was made in our kingdom,
that every one should come to our gate [kingdom],

kings and princes of Parthia,
and all the nobles of the East.

And they wove a plan on my behalf,
that I might not be left in Egypt;

and they wrote to me a letter,
and every noble signed his name to it:

"From thy father, the king of kings,
and thy mother, the mistress of the East,

and from thy brother, our second (in authority),
to thee our son, who art in Egypt, greeting!

Call to mind that thou art a son of kings!
See the slavery, whom thou servest!

Remember the pearl,
for which thou wert sent to Egypt!

Think of thy robe,
and remember thy splendid toga,

which thou shalt wear and (with which) thou shalt be adorned,
when thy name hath been read out in the list of the valiant,

and thy brother, our viceroy,
thou shalt be in our kingdom."

My letter is a letter,
which the king sealed with his own right hand,

(to keep it) from the wicked ones, the children of Babel,
and from the savage demons of Sarbug.

It flew in the likeness of an eagle,
the king of all birds;

it flew and alighted beside me,
and became all speech.

At its voice and the sound of its rustling,
I started and arose from my sleep.

I took it up and kissed it,
and I began (and) read it;

and according to what was traced on my heart
were the words of my letter.

I remembered that I was a son of royal parents,
and my noble birth asserted itself.

I remembered the pearl,
for which I had been sent to Egypt,

and I began to charm him,
the terrible loud breathing serpent.

I hushed him asleep and lulled him into slumber,
for my father's name I named over him,

and the name of our second (in power),
and of my mother, the queen of the East.

And I snatched away the pearl,

and turned to go back to my father's house.

And their filthy and unclean dress I stripped off,
and left it in their country;

and I took my way straight to come
to the light of our home in the East.

And my letter, my awakener,
I found before me on the road;

and as with its voice it had awakened me,
(so) too with its light it was leading me.

It, that dwelt in the palace,
gave light before me with its form,

and with its voice and its guidance
it also encouraged me to speed,

and with its love it drew me on.

I went forth (and) passed by Sarbug;
I left Babel on my left hand;

and I came to the great Maisan,
to the haven of merchants,

which sitteth on the shore of the sea.

And my bright robe, which I had stripped off,
and the toga that was wrapped with it,

from Rantha and Reken
my parents had sent thither

by the hand of their treasures,
who in their truth could be trusted therewith.

And because I remembered not its fashion—
for in my childhood I had left it in my father's house—

on a sudden, when I received it,
the garment seemed to me to become like a mirror of myself.

I saw it all in all,
and I too received all in it,

for we were two in distinction
and yet again one in one likeness.

And the treasurers too,
who brought it to me, I saw in like manner

to be two (and yet) one likeness,
for one sign of the king was written on them (both),

of the hands of him who restored to me through them
my trust and my wealth,

my decorated robe, which
was adorned with glorious colors,

with gold and beryls
and rubies and agates

and sardonyxes, varied in color.
And it was skillfully worked in its home on high,

and with diamond clasps
were all its seams fastened;

and the image of the king of kings
was embroidered and depicted in full all over it,

and like the stone of the sapphire too
its hues were varied.

And I saw also that all over it
the instincts of knowledge [gnosis] were working.[37]

---

[37] Wright, *Apocryphal Acts of the Apostles*, pp. 238ff.

The Gnostic character of the hymn is easily recognizable. The *Acts of Thomas* originated in Jewish-Christian Syria, where Thomas Judas Didymis, the supposed twin brother of the Lord, played a major role. Thomas is invoked by the *Gospel of Thomas* (NH II 2), by the *Book of Thomas* (NH II 7), and by the St. Thomas Christians in India.

Regarding interpretation, the Peratae,[38] a group of Gnostic astrologers, consider Egypt, where the king's son is sent, as the body, the Egyptians as the unknowing, and the Red Sea as the waters of perdition that sent the Egyptians to their deaths in their chariots (Exodus 14f.). The unknowing, to whom the king's son likens himself, are those who have forgotten their royal descent and have succumbed to the world. He preaches his wise counsel to others, instead of applying it to himself. In that country reside the dreadful old serpent, the sea-dragon, the devil and Satan (Revelation 12:9, 20:2), who—no one knows how—possesses the precious pearl. When he found it, a merchant sold all his belongings (Matthew 13:45–46), because it is the kingdom of heaven. This helps us understand why the royal father sent his son on such a hazardous journey: his adversary had inexplicably acquired his greatest treasure, which must be recovered at all costs.

The myth of the "Hymn of the Pearl" explains why in the *Exegesis on the Soul* (NH II 6) the soul was forced to leave its father's house. In this abhorrent world, the treasure is difficult to obtain and must be wrested from the dragon. The motif of the battle with the dragon is universal. The "Father" stands for moral law and represents the spirit. The dragon represents the basic drives and instincts, as the story of paradise (Genesis 3) had revealed. He is more cunning than all field animals (Genesis 3:5). He knows that transgressing what the father prohibits opens people's eyes and makes them knowledgeable (Genesis 3:5). Therefore, the pearl probably means Gnosis

---

[38] Hippolytus, *Ref.* V 16,4; Foerster, *Gnosis* I, p. 369.

(knowledge), because observing commands and proscriptions prevents humans from becoming conscious. For the king's son is said to have accomplished the Father's commands (verses 113, 100).

Essentially, Gnosis means becoming conscious, which makes it so interesting for us today. The core conflict that Gnosis grappled with was that between spirit and soul, father and daughter, brother and sister. Thus, the Gnostic's redemption seeks to unite the opposites in the bridal chamber for good reason. Yet the union of opposites is often projected to a time beyond death. When in the "Hymn of the Pearl" the king's son is said to have left his soiled, impure robe in Egypt (verses 111, 62), for the Gnostic this means his material body, which he takes off after dying to put on his glittering robe.

Another text deserves mention here to further illustrate this myth: the *Hypostasis of the Archons* (NH II 4):

> The great apostle—referring to the "authorities of the darkness"—told us that "our contest is not against flesh and blood; rather, the authorities of the universe and the spirits of wickedness" [Ephesians 6:12]. I have sent this (to you) because you inquire about the reality of the authorities.
>
> Their chief is blind; because of his power and his ignorance and his arrogance he said, with his power, "It is I who am God; there is none apart from me" [Isaiah 45:5]. When he said this, he sinned against the entirety. And this speech got up to incorruptibility; then there was a voice that came forth from incorruptibility, saying, "You are mistaken, Samael"—which is, "god of the blind."
>
> His thoughts became blind. And, having expelled his power—that is, the blasphemy he had spoken—he pursued it down to chaos and the abyss, his mother, at the instigation of Pistis Sophia. And she established each of his offspring in conformity with its power—after the pattern of the realms that are above, for

by starting from the invisible world the visible world was invented.

As incorruptibility looked down into the region of the waters, her image appeared in the waters; and the authorities of the darkness became enamored of her. But they could not lay hold of that image, which had appeared to them in the waters, because of their weakness—since beings that merely possess a soul cannot lay hold of those that possess a spirit—for they were from below, while it was from above [John 3:31]. This is the reason why "incorruptibility looked down into the region (etc.)": so that, by the father's will, she might bring the entirety into union with the light. (86,21–87,23)

The citation from Paul's Letter to the Ephesians might be seen as a motto for the entire Gnostic movement: namely, the conflict between the world of the pure spirit and that of material reality. The latter is ruled by blindness and ignorance. This, in turn, is the introverted standpoint, for which the outside world is full of demons and dangers.

IV. *Cognitio sui ipsius*: Gnosis as True Self-Knowledge

For the Gnostic, the material world and its fate-determining powers are the unconscious; their leader is Samael, the god of the blind. He also appears in the *Apocryphon of John* (II 11,15), where the ruler of the powers bears three names: Yaldabaoth (i.e., the Son of Chaos), Sakles (i.e., the demented Creator-God), and Samael. These three names also occur in the above-cited *Trimorphic Protennoia* (XIII, 39,26–31). When he exclaims, "I am the Lord, and there is no other" (Isaiah 45:5), he turns out to be Yahweh and the Creator-God. As observed, this fact leads Gilles Quispel to conclude that Gnosis emerged among heterodox Jewish circles in Alexandria, which is, of course, pure speculation.[39] In

---

[39] "The Origins of the Christian Demiurge," *Gnostic Studies* I, pp. 213–230.

fact, this simply suggests that Gnosis was a reaction to obsolete Judaism in the New Testament. For those who have just overcome Yahwistic religion, Yahweh becomes an inflated Creator-God. This, however, is not the essence of the story, but the contrast with immortality. Samael is simply an inferior god. For how could the highest god have willed such an imperfect creation, which is governed by ignorance, darkness, and malice? So he is no more than a blind, incapable dabbler after all! This is how matters look to the introvert, who measures the empirical world against his inner *mundus archetypus*, and in Gnostic thought, against the aeons of the pleroma. Here, only a psychological perspective leads to genuine understanding: the Creator of the world is consciousness, which is a derivative of the self and often forgets its origin and considers itself the highest god, which prompts Isaiah's exclamation (45:5). Augustine described this most subtly in *De Genesis Ad Litteram* and in *Civitas Dei (City of God)*.[40] According to Augustine, the first day of creation begins with the *cognitio sui ipsius* (the knowledge of the self). Its aim is the knowledge of the All, i.e., the self, and not of the ego. Thus, it strives to objectify its own existence. This is the *cognitio matutina* (morning knowledge). Gradually, this ages and loses itself among the plethora of the world. Eventually, it reaches human beings, who ask themselves who, of all beings, recognizes this. Toward evening, *scientia creatoris* (the consciousness of the creator) gradually becomes *scientia hominis* (human consciousness), which regards itself as the center from which and toward which all knowledge proceeds (Jung, CW 13 §301). *Scientia creatoris* is the revealed light of morning, the coming into being of consciousness out of the primordial darkness of the unconscious. *Cognitio vespertina* (evening knowledge) is the fading light of human consciousness which no longer knows its origin.

---

[40] Ribi, "Morgen und Abenderkenntnis."

The exclamation in Isaiah 45:5 and its claim occur frequently in Gnosticism, consistently in terms of evening knowledge. Not only does this match Gnosticism's outlook, which revered morning knowledge, but also its contempt for the Old Testament's outdated view of God, according to which Yahweh at times behaves like a jealous old lady and at others like an unruly despot who treats human beings as the mood takes him. Can those who aspired to a new image of God be blamed for erasing these aspects of the old conception? Already Irenaeus cites what the Barbelo-Gnostics said about the demiurge (*Against Heresies*, I 29,4) and reports the teachings of the Ophites and the Sethians (30,6). He cites the teaching of Saturninus verbatim:

> ...he [i.e., Saturninus] maintained that the God of the Jews was one of the angels; and, on this account, because all the powers wished to annihilate his father, Christ came to destroy the God of the Jews, but to save such as believe in him; that is, those who possess the spark of his life.[41] (24,2)

This plainly reveals that the Gnostics considered the Jewish god to be an *obsolete view of God* that was superseded by Christ. While Yahweh is still recognized as the Creator of the world, he is no longer the bearer of the life force (*scintilla vitae*).

In *Answer to Job*, Jung describes the transformation of the concept of God from the Old to the New Testament and the associated necessity of God becoming human. Jung writes:

> ...the "just" God could not go on committing injustices, and the "Omniscient" could not behave any longer like a clueless and thoughtless human being. Self-reflection becomes an imperative necessity, and for this Wisdom is needed. Yahweh has to remember his absolute knowledge; for, if Job gains knowledge of

---

[41] See also Hippolytus, *Ref.* VII 28,5.

God, then God must also learn to know himself. It just could not be that Yahweh's dual nature should become public property and remain hidden from himself alone. Whoever knows God has an effect on him. The failure of the attempt to corrupt Job has changed Yahweh's nature. (CW 11 §617)

The drama of Job's fate raised the question of good and evil, which the Gnostics took up because the established church left it unanswered with some few exceptions. The contrast between the images of God announces itself already in the Apocalypse of John, in the guise of the dragon who pursues the woman, and in John's letters as the anti-Christ (1 John 2:18, 22; 4:3). The Gnostics saw the demiurge as a kind of adversary to the highest god, who had created the world and people without their permission and who had even boasted about his achievement. They experienced the moral problem far more acutely than the established church did.

One passage in the above-cited *Hypostasis of the Archons* (NH II 4) reads:

> A veil exists between the world above and the realms that are below; and shadow came into being beneath the veil; and that shadow became matter; and that shadow was projected apart. And what she had created became a product in the matter, like an aborted fetus. And it assumed a plastic form molded out of shadow, and became an arrogant beast resembling a lion. It was androgynous, as I have already said, because it was from matter that it derived.
>
> Opening his eyes, he saw a vast quantity of matter without limit; and he became arrogant, saying, "It is I who am God, and there is none other apart from me." When he said this, he sinned against the entirety. And a voice came forth from above the realm of absolute power, saying, "You are mistaken, Samael." (94, 9–25)

In the *Apocryphon of John*, the demiurge places the rulers over the heavens and the abyss and shares his fire with them,

> for he is ignorant darkness.
>
> And when the light had mixed with the darkness, it caused the darkness to shine. And when the darkness had mixed with the light, it darkened the light and it became neither light nor dark, but it became dim.
>
> Now the archon who is weak has three names. The first name is Yaltabaoth, the second is Saklas, and the third is Samael. And he is impious in his arrogance which is in him. For he said, "I am God and there is no other God beside me," for he is ignorant of his strength, the place from which he had come. (NH II 11;10–22)

With this dark Creator-God, something became possible that was impossible with the benign Christian Father-God. While the Logos illuminates the darkness, it does not become less dark (John 1:5). In the Valentinian *Apocryphon of John*, however, light is darkened, while darkness is illuminated. Given that material creation is dark and unconscious, we may suspect that the divine light brought forth a hazy consciousness in the creature.

In the Old Testament, Satan was still a son of God in the heavenly court (Job 1:6), a fact which dampens the splendor. In the New Testament, by contrast, Jesus is the "light of the world," and whoever follows him "will never walk in darkness, but will have the light of life" (John 8:12). Here, light no longer has anything in common with darkness (2 Corinthians 6:14). "God is light and in him there is no darkness at all" (1 John 1:5).

This development of the spirit in Gnosticism already anticipates a *deus absconditus* in matter; that god will subsequently play a major role in alchemy. At least something from the world of light has fallen into, and is able to illuminate, dark matter. In Manichaeism, it is a question of gathering the seeds of light in matter. These are probably various luminosities, which go on to play a significant role in alchemy. As Jung has shown, these luminosities represent conscious-like states of unconscious contents (CW 8 §388). They are a *lumen naturae* or an all-pervasive world soul. If darkness were impenetrable, no knowledge of it would be possible. The Gnostics enthusiastically turned to these seeds of light to penetrate the darkness with consciousness.

It is crucial in which myth we live. It directs our words and actions. As a rule, this myth is unconscious. The Gnostics attempted to formulate it. Whoever believes that the world soul fell from heaven onto earth, and whoever believes that his or her task is to redeem that soul, not only has a meaningful mission in life, but also has a certain attitude toward life. Those who believe that the redeemer is a non-earthly female figure, that merely serves the Holy Spirit as a vessel, will have a different attitude toward the feminine. Unable to decide which of these attitudes is correct, we need to ask which promotes life and its development better. In my view, it is the one that presents us with a task. Christianity, it seems to me, shifts this task onto the redeemer, leaving humans with nothing else than to believe that they have been redeemed. The question is simply how many people really felt redeemed? For the Gnostics, the task remains unresolved, and they seek resolution with the help of the (inner) redeemer. For Christians, the task is merely to become perfect like their redeemer and, by leading a devout life, not to ruin his work of redemption. Gnostics must save the fallen soul or the seeds of light in matter through their own lives, which are necessary for the cosmic process. Each one takes part in cosmic events, which are directed toward an eschatological objective.

This also explains why the Gnostics took a greater interest in Mary Magdelene than in the mother of Jesus: she is represented as an earthly woman who has a dark side. It was Mary who anointed the feet of Jesus, who had come to Bethany to celebrate Passover, and who dried his feet with her hair (John 12:3; Matthew 26:7; Mark 14:3). Only

John gives her name as Mary, the sister of Martha and the resurrected Lazarus. Luke 7:37 simply asserts that a sinner, meaning a prostitute, had entered the Pharisee's house where Jesus was eating. In the other narratives, the Pharisee is called Simon, as he is here, so that Mary Magdalene was beyond any doubt the sinner. This prefigures Simon Magus' fallen soul, above all since in the Gospel of Luke Jesus teaches the Pharisee that whoever has committed many sins will also be forgiven much (7:47–48).[42]

In my view, the doctrines of Carpocrates can be better understood in this light. Irenaeus says:

> They deem it necessary, therefore, that by means of transmigration from body to body, souls should have experience of every kind of life as well as every kind of action (unless, indeed, by a single incarnation, one may be able to prevent any need for others)... [so that] as their writings express it, their souls, having made trial of every kind of life, may, at their departure, not be wanting in any particular. It is necessary to insist upon this, lest, on account of some one thing being still wanting to their deliverance, they should be compelled once more to become incarnate.[43] (*Against Heresies* I 25,4)

Discussing this subject, C.G. Jung says that the soul can ransom itself from its imprisonment in the demiurge's somatic world only by fulfilling *all* the demands of life. The existence chosen resembles a hostile brother, whose conditions must first be met (CW 11 §133). In another context, Jung writes:

---

[42] The fact that modern historical-critical biblical research doubts these identities in no way diminishes the power that they have exercised over people and art for almost two thousand years.
[43] See also *The Search for Roots*, p. 114.

> The word "human" sounds very beautiful, but properly understood it does not mean anything particularly beautiful, or virtuous, or intelligent, but just a low average. This is the step which Zarathustra could not take, the step to the "Ugliest Man," who is real man. Our resistance to taking this step, and our fear of it, show how great is the attraction and seductive power of our own depths. To cut oneself off from them is no solution; it is a mere sham, an essential misunderstanding of their meaning and value. For where is a height without depth, and how can there be light that throws no shadow? There is no good that is not opposed by evil.... What is down below *is not just an excuse for more pleasure, but something we fear* because it demands to play its part in the life of the more conscious and more complete man. (CW 10 §271; emphasis added)

Elsewhere he asserts:

> ...the aim of the mystical peregrination is to understand all parts of the world, to achieve the greatest possible extension of consciousness.... Not a turning away from its empirical "so-ness," but the fullest possible experience of the ego as reflected in the "ten thousand things"—that is the goal of the peregrination. This follows logically from the psychological recognition that God cannot be experienced at all unless this futile and ridiculous ego offers a modest vessel in which to catch the effluence of the Most High and name it with his name. (CW 14/I §284)

Presumably, Mary was also important for the Gnostics on account of the two attitudes evident in the story of Mary and Martha (Luke 10:38–42): Martha is devoted to work, Mary to the spirit. In the end, the established church, with its worldly reality, committed itself to Martha, and Gnosticism to Mary.

The *Gospel of Mary* reports an interesting circumstance: Peter demands that Mary tell the apostles what the redeemer has told her alone:

> She said, "I saw the Lord in a vision and I said to him, 'Lord, I saw you today in a vision.'
>
> "He answered me, 'Blessed are you for not wavering at seeing me. For where the mind is, there is the treasure.'
>
> "I said to him, 'So now, Lord, does a person who sees a vision see it <with> the soul <or> with the spirit?'
>
> "The Savior answered, 'A person does not see with the soul or with the spirit. Rather, the mind, which exists between these two, sees the vision, and that is [what]....'" (BG 10, 10–23)

This scene contrasts with the description in the "Gospel According to John," where Mary believed that the resurrected Jesus was merely the gardener, until he addresses her by name, and she recognizes him as the Rabbouni (20:14–18). In the so-called "Greater Questions of Mary," handed down by Epiphanius in the *Panarion*, it says:

> For in the so-called "Greater Questions of Mary"—there are also "Lesser" ones forged by them—they claim that he reveals it to her after taking her aside on the mountain, praying, producing a woman from his side, beginning to have sex with her, and then partaking of his emission, if you please, to show that "Thus we must do, that we may live."
>
> And when Mary was alarmed and fell to the ground, he raised her up and said to her, "O thou of little faith, wherefore didst thou doubt?" (26 8,2–3)

Epiphanius goes on to report that these Gnostics invoked John 3:12, "If I have told you about earthly things and you do not believe, how can you believe if I tell you about heavenly things?" Mary, evidently, did not understand these words either, but instead took them literally when she fainted. She failed to understand that Jesus meant to show her a symbolic truth. This secret too seems to have eluded Epiphanius and certain libertine Gnostic circles. Jung writes, "This symbolism may well have been based, originally, on some visionary experience," and then adds:

> such as happens not uncommonly today during psychological treatment. For the medical psychologist there is nothing very lurid about it. The context itself points the way to the right interpretation. The image expresses a psychologem that can hardly be formulated in rational terms and has, therefore, to make use of a concrete symbol, just as a dream must when a more or less "abstract" thought comes up during the *abaissement du niveau mental* that occurs in sleep. These "shocking" surprises, of which there is certainly no lack in dreams, should always be taken "as-if," even though they clothe themselves in sensual imagery that stops at no scurrility and no obscenity. They are unconcerned with offensiveness, because they do not really mean it. It is as if they were stammering in their efforts to express the elusive meaning that grips the dreamer's attention.

> The context of the vision (John 3:12) makes it clear that the image should be taken not concretistically but symbolically; for Christ speaks not of earthly things but of a heavenly or spiritual mystery—a "mystery" not because he is hiding something or making a secret of it (indeed, nothing could be more blatant than the naked obscenity of the vision!) but because its meaning is still hidden from consciousness. The modern method of dream-

analysis and interpretation follows this heuristic rule. If we apply it to the vision, we arrive at the following result:

1. The MOUNTAIN means ascent, particularly the mystical, spiritual ascent to the heights, to the place of revelation where the spirit is present. This motif is so well known that there is no need to document it.

2. The central significance of the CHRIST-FIGURE for that epoch has been abundantly proved. In Christian Gnosticism it was a visualization of God as the Archanthropos (Original Man = Adam), and therefore the epitome of man as such: "Man and the Son of Man." Christ is the inner man who is reached by the path of self-knowledge, "the kingdom of heaven within you." [...] The quaternity of Christ, which must be borne in mind in this vision, is exemplified by the cross symbol, the rex gloriae, and Christ as the year.

3. The production of the WOMAN from his side suggests that he is interpreted as the second Adam. Bringing forth a woman means that he is playing the role of the Creator-God in Genesis. Just as Adam, before the creation of Eve, was supposed by various traditions to be male/female, so Christ here demonstrates his androgyny in a drastic way. The Original Man is usually hermaphroditic; in Vedic tradition too he produces his own feminine half and unites with her. In Christian allegory the woman sprung from Christ's side signifies the Church as the Bride of the Lamb.

The splitting of the Original Man into husband and wife expresses an act of nascent consciousness; it gives birth to a pair of opposites, thereby making consciousness possible. For the beholder of the miracle, Mary, the vision was the spontaneous visualization or projection of an unconscious process in herself. Experience shows that unconscious processes are compensatory to a definite conscious situation. The splitting in the vision would therefore suggest that it is compensating a conscious condition of unity. This unity probably refers in the first place to the figure of the Anthropos, the incarnate God [...] The antique revelation depicts the birth of Eve from Adam on the spiritual level of the second Adam (Christ), from whose side the feminine pneuma, or second Eve, i.e., the soul, appears as Christ's daughter; she is [...] the woman who "embraces the man" (Jeremiah 31:22) and anoints the Lord's feet....

4. But to turn back to the first vision: the bringing forth of the woman is followed by COPULATION [...] The alchemists likewise speak of an Adam who always carries his Eve around with him. Their *coniunctio* is an incestuous act, performed not by father and daughter but, in accordance with the changed times, by brother and sister or mother and son [...] That is why no visible creature arises from the taking in of seed; it means a nourishing of life, "that we may live." And because, as the text itself shows, the vision should be understood on the "heavenly" or spiritual plane, the pouring out (ἀπόρροια) refers to a λόγος σπερματικός, which in the language of the gospels means a living water "springing up into eternal life." The whole vision reminds one very much of the related alchemical symbolisms. (CW 9ii §315ff.)

The Samaritan woman in Heracleon's 18th fragment may have had a similar vision when the savior told her to call her husband, although he knew that she was unmarried. Thus, Heracleon transposes everyday events onto the spiritual level. It is fitting, therefore, that the woman receives the water from Jesus only on this condition. Epiphanius relates another peculiar story in "The Birth of Mary":

They say that Zacharias was killed in the temple [Luke 11:51; Matthew 23:35] because he had seen a vision, and when he wanted to reveal the vision his mouth was stopped from fright. For at the hour of incense, while he was burning it, he saw a man standing there, they say, with the form of an ass [Luke 1:11–13]. And when he had come out and wanted to say "Woe to you, whom are you worshiping?" the person he had seen inside in the temple stopped his mouth so that he could not speak. But when his mouth was opened so that he could speak [Luke 1:20; 1:64], then he revealed it to them and they killed him. And that, they say, is how Zacharias died. This, they say, is why the priest was ordered to wear bells [Exodus 28:33–35] by the lawgiver himself. Whenever he [i.e., the priest] went in to officiate, the object of his worship would hear them jangle and hide, so that no one would spy the imaginary face of his form. (*Panarion* 26,12,1)

There is a Gnostic cameo that depicts a female donkey suckling her foals; above this scene stands the figure of Cancer and the following circumscription: *Dominus noster Jesus Christus Dei Filius*. Christ is known to have ridden into Jerusalem on a young donkey (John 12:14), which refers to Zacharias: "Rejoice greatly, O daughter Zion! Shout aloud, O daughter Jerusalem! Lo, your king comes to you; triumphant and victorious is he, humble and riding on a donkey, on a colt, the foal of a donkey" (9:9). The donkey belongs to the "second sun," Saturn, which is the star of Israel, and with whom Yahweh is therefore identified. In 1856, Raphael Garucci discovered a so-called mock-crucifix on Rome's Palatine Hill; this 2nd or 3rd century graffito depicts a human figure with a donkey's head hanging on a cross. Before the crucified man stands a figure with a hand raised in adoration. Also visible is a Greek inscription, which translates as "Alexamenos prays to his god." Already Tertullian (*Apologeticum*, 16.14) was vexed that an image of God was exhibited in Carthage that depicted the Lord with donkey's ears and bore the following inscription: "The God of the Christians Onokoites."[44] Whether a donkey cult existed, and what role it played, is the subject of fierce controversy.[45]

Despite the uncertainty surrounding transmission, one fact remains clear: Zacharias beheld God's posterior, animal-demonic aspect. Instead of placing his finger on his mouth and remaining silent like Job (Job 39:34–35; 42:5), the priest tried to recount what he had seen, although his speechlessness should have made him know better. Like everything else, the magnificent image of God has a terrible rear end, about which one cannot speak. Perhaps the Egyptian Mary intuited thus, and was therefore elected to receive the revelation, because "she has shown great love" (Luke 7:47). Fragment 18 of Heracleon's commentary then continues with the following explanation:

> The six men indicate the whole of the material evil in which she was involved and with which she consorted, when she lived irrationally in debauchery, and was insulted, rejected and abandoned by them (the men).

This is the well-known motif of the fallen soul, which recurs here in almost the same words as in the *Exegesis on the Soul* (NHC II 6).

Fragment 19 invokes John 4:19–20, "The woman said to him, 'Sir, I see that you are a prophet.' Our ancestors worshipped on this mountain, but *you* say that the place where people must worship is Jerusalem." Heracleon comments,

> The Samaritan woman acknowledged what was said to her by him. For it is characteristic of a prophet to know all things... She behaved in a way suited to her nature, for she neither denied nor

---

[44] The meaning of the word "Onokoites" is unclear.
[45] Opelt, "Esel," *Reallexikon für Antike und Christentum* VI, col. 564–595.

explicitly acknowledged her shame. She was convinced that he was a prophet and, by her question, she revealed at the same time the reason for which she had committed immorality. Because of ignorance of God and of the worship agreeable to God, she had also neglected all the things that were essential for her life, whereas what is necessary in life was always otherwise available to her.

Once again, the Samaritan woman, the prototypical pneumatic, has no difficulty in admitting her lapses, i.e., her shadow psychologically speaking. Her shortcomings arise from agnosia, which can be dispelled only after the confrontation with the Lord. This is the typical Gnostic view, which Origen finds impossible to fathom. This again reveals how fundamentally the Gnostic view differed from that of the established church, which explains why they could neither understand each other nor achieve reconciliation.

In fragment 20, Heracleon explains:

> The mountain represents the Devil, or his world, since the Devil was one part of the whole of matter, but the world is the total mountain of evil, a deserted dwelling place of beasts, to which all who lived before the law and all Gentiles render worship. But Jerusalem represents the creation or the Creator whom the Jews worship... The mountain is the creation which the Gentiles worship, but Jerusalem is the creator whom the Jews serve. You then who are spiritual should worship neither the creation nor the Craftsman, but the Father of Truth. And he (Jesus) accepts her (the Samaritan woman) as one of the already faithful, and to be counted with those who worship in truth.

In light of the previous remarks, this passage is straightforward. Again, the Gnostics distance themselves from the Jews and from the pagans, because only the appearance of the Son of God makes true knowledge possible. Thus, the concept of God in the Old Testament is outdated and degrades the Lord to a demiurge. I can detect no hostility toward Judaism in this concept. Once again, escapism becomes apparent. All material things are the work of the devil. And thus, only the pneumatics, who worship the Father of the Truth, are redeemed.

In fragment 22, Heracleon explains that "to worship in truth" means to worship "the one who is in the Aeon (i.e., the Savior), and those who have come with him." This remark refers to John 4:22: "You worship what you do not know [says the Lord]; we worship what we know, for salvation is from the Jews." Heracleon adds:

> The words "salvation is of the Jews" are said because he was born in Judea, but not among them and because from that race salvation and the Word came forth into the world. As far as the spiritual sense is concerned, salvation came from the Jews because they are images of those who are in the Fullness... (In John 4:23, it continues, "But the hour is coming, and now is, when the true worshipers will worship the Father in spirit and truth, for such the Father seeks to worship him.") For the previous worshippers worshipped in flesh and in error him who is not the Father... They worshipped the creation and not the true creator (cf. Romans 1:25), who is Christ, since "all things came into being through him, and apart from him nothing came into being." (John 1:3)

If any aversion toward the Jews existed among the Gnostics, surely it would be evident in such a passage. Like the sinful woman of Samaria, however, the Jews did not yet possess the right knowledge. And like the psychics of the established church, they still prayed to the flesh and in error. But when it says, "salvation is from the Jews," this needs to be understood symbolically as an image of those who are within the pleroma.

In fragment 23, on John 4:23, "But the hour is coming, and is now here, when the true worshippers will worship the Father in spirit and truth, for the Father seeks such as these to worship him," Heracleon explains:

> Lost in the deep matter of error is that which is akin to the Father, which is sought after in order that the Father may be worshipped by those who are akin to him.

This passage strikes me as pivotal, not only because it foreshadows alchemy, which searches for the sunken God in matter, but also because the Gnostic must seek the divine aspect of his nature that has gone astray in the world. For the Gnostic is able to recognize and correctly worship the unrecognizable only with that part of himself which is related to the Father. Earlier, I referred to the *extractio animae*. The previous passage takes matters one step further, to the extraction of the divine spark in the human being from its projection into the world. Again, Origen is unable to comprehend this thought; he says that he would have understood Heracleon if he had at least spoken of the lost sheep (Luke 15:11–32). Here, however, more than the rescuing of the lost soul is at stake: namely, the making of humankind in the image of God (Genesis 1:26). Considering the human likeness to God, Tertullian observes:

> O these fools, who from things human form conjectures about things divine, and because in mankind passions of this sort are taken to be of a corruptive character, suppose that in God also they are of the same quality. (*Adversus Marcionem* II 16,6)

In *Contra Celsum*, Origen specifies this idea:

> ...we hold that far beyond all bodies is the soul, and especially the reasonable soul; for it is the soul, and not the body, which bears the likeness of the Creator. For, according to us, God is not corporeal. (VIII 49)

Through this passage shines the hostility toward the body that was already widespread among the early Christians. Origen, however, swiftly plays down the human likeness to God asserted in Genesis 1:26:

> I need to consider that the Lord and Savior is "the image of the invisible God" [Colossians 1:15] and realize that my soul is made "in the Creator's image," so that it is an image of the Image. My soul is not directly an image of God; it was created as the image of an Image that already existed.[46]

This is the typical Christian view, in which the Creator towers above his creature, who is no more than a pale reflection, "an image of an Image." Origen repeats this idea in his *Homilies on Genesis*:

> Therefore, "God made man, according to the image of God he made him." We must see what that image of God is and inquire diligently in the likeness of what image man is made. For the text did not say that "God made man according to the image or likeness," but "according to the image of God he made him." Therefore, what other image of God is there according to the likeness of whose image man is made, except our Savior who is "the firstborn of every creature."[47] (Colossians 1:15)

---

[46] Origen, *Homilies on Luke*, VIII, 2.
[47] Ibid., *Homilies on Genesis*, I, 13.

But he does at least conclude that:

> But it is our inner man, invisible, incorporeal, incorruptible, and immortal which is made "according to the image of God." For it is in such qualities as these that the image of God is more correctly understood.[48]

I shall discuss the human likeness to God more extensively elsewhere[49] and therefore confine myself to some passing remarks here. Nevertheless, I hope to have established that the Gnostic must seek the piece of his God-likeness erroneously lost in matter to free himself from this world. This helps us to understand fragment 24, on John 4:24: "God is spirit, and those who worship him must worship in spirit and truth." Commenting on "God is spirit" (pneuma), Heracleon declares: "Undefiled, pure, and invisible is his divine nature."

I suspect that this passage was crucial for Heracleon, although Origen barely comments on it. Perhaps God's spiritual nature is so self-evident for the Gnostics that no further commentary is needed. In the *Apocryphon of John*, the self-revealing monad declares: "I am the Father, I am the Mother, I am the Son. I am the undefiled and incorruptible one" (NHC II 2, 13–15). Furthermore, "Father of everything, the invisible One who is above everything, who exists as incorruption" (2,27–30).

On John 4:24, "and those who worship him must worship in spirit and truth," Heracleon states:

> Those who worship him must worship in spirit and truth. Worthily of the one who is worshipped, in a spiritual, not a fleshly fashion. For those who have the same nature as the Father are themselves spirit, and they worship in truth, not in error, as

---
[48] Ibid., I, 13.
[49] *Anthropos*.

the Apostle teaches when he calls this kind of piety "a rational service." (Romans 12:2)

The pneumatic himself has become a spirit and worships correctly if he does so spiritually. This seems yet a further indication that the sacraments of the Gnostics were probably all spiritual. Origen, however, does not seem to have understood this either when he complains that the Samaritan woman prostituted herself. He does not understand that this is still the state of deficiency (*Hysterema*) of the image lost by mistake. Only when that image has been liberated does correct worship become possible.

John 4:25–26: "The woman said to him, 'I know that Messiah is coming' (who is called Christ). 'When he comes, he will proclaim all things to us.' Jesus said to her, 'I am he, the one who is speaking to you.'" Because the Father is unrecognizable, and because the Son possesses the same nature as the Father, the Gnostic receives knowledge (gnosis) from the Son. This is the function of the Gnostic redeemer, upon whom the Samaritan woman pins her hopes. Heracleon's fragment 26 says:

> (According to John 4:26, Jesus said to her,) "I who speak to you am he." Since the Samaritan woman was convinced that Christ, when he came, would announce everything to her, he said 'Know that I who speak with you am he whom you expect.' And when he acknowledged that he, the expected one, had come, "his disciples came" (John 4:27), for on their account he had come to Samaria.

One wonders whether the pneumatic could already understand Christ as an inner voice, as her *syzygos*, who from that point would explain everything to her. Fragment 31 might point in this direction:

The will of the Father is that human beings should know the Father and be saved. This is the work of the Savior, on account of which he was sent to Samaria, that is, into the world.

This text also eluded Origen. But if we are familiar with certain key Gnostic words, we will understand that this was the aim toward which the process strives.

Conclusion

Those readers who have borne with me to this stage have traversed a wide expanse in the intellectual and spiritual history of late antiquity. Regarding Hellenism, they will have had to revise several key aspects of their general humanistic education. The gods on Olympus were not only dethroned; they also changed the way in which they manifested themselves. They approached human life in unforeseeable ways, becoming heroes with decidedly human traits and stories, in which human beings saw their daily trials and tribulations. Indeed, as heroes the gods did not succumb to the earthly powers of fate, but overcame them by dying a martyr's death, thereby becoming immortal. Thus, the Olympian god sets an example to the one who would redeem the faithful. This is the common denominator of all Hellenistic mysteries of redemption, including Christianity.

By the end of the classical period, antiquity had brought forth a large repository of ideas and knowledge. From this reservoir, the new currents drew on their resources to create new systems. Despite containing highly familiar aspects, these creations are all distinctly original, because they originate in the unconscious. And, as I have emphasized time and again, these creations are not conscious deliberations.

Out of this spiritual heritage, the collective unconscious forged new ideas of redemption to compensate for the unbearable state of collective consciousness. The consciousness of ancient humans had evolved. The individual, of which there were very few in the classical age, now extended to ever wider strata of the population. To be sure, enhancement of the individual arose from the mysteries of redemption, which formulated the mystery of human existence. This collision of classical Greek culture with an alien Oriental culture produced new mystery cults with a hitherto unknown character. Christianity is probably a late blossom on this tree of mysteries. It synthesizes many related currents and thus best unites the different strands. This probably explains its historic victory over all similar manifestations. As a psychologist, I am unable to see a particular kind of divinity as the crucial, distinguishing feature of Christianity, because parallel religions were just as profound and serious. I believe it is important for modern individuals to recognize these various currents in order to better differentiate the outstanding nature of Christianity.

This leads to a fundamental question: what is revelation? Given the existence of similar religious phenomena, the Christian revelation can no longer claim to be unique. Revelation is a general religious phenomenon, evident at all times and among all peoples. Whereas the soul of the believer can content itself with the uniqueness of the Christian revelation, this is often impossible for the modern person. Today, therefore, we must find other criteria that do justice to the status of Christianity, which has shaped Western civilization for the past two thousand years. The necessity to find other criteria arises from comparing Christian revelation with similar phenomena in Hellenism.

Common to all these phenomena is the God-Man, a god in human form, whom I called heroic at the beginning of this book. Psychologically, the hero corresponds to a primordial image in the human psyche, the archetype of the *anthropos*. This idea is prefigured in the biblical creation narrative, where God made humans in his own image (Genesis 1:26). But if the human being is an image of God, it follows that not only God possesses a human shape, but also that human beings carry within themselves something divine, a divine core. This core has sunken into the dark material world, where it is searched for and meant to be redeemed. This is the salvific deed of the Hellenistic redeemer. As a God-Man, he represents this kernel himself and, through his life, exemplifies how it may be delivered from its manifold entanglements with matter. He takes upon himself the work and suffering, in which his disciples are meant to follow him, in exemplary fashion. Following this example, human beings work on their own redemption far more intensely than before. Just as the anthropos has set an example of finding a way through all the sufferings of the world, so his followers will also achieve redemption.

Thus individual life was enhanced to an unprecedented degree and lifted out of the drab uniformity of the masses. This was the moment when the *individual* was born. Today, we take the individual for granted, and yet the communist relapse into mass psychology teaches us that the individual leads a threatened existence. Originally, humans lived in an archaic identity with their surroundings, from which they struggled to become individuals in a lengthy process of acquiring consciousness. Becoming conscious is indispensable for the emergence of the individual. Gnosis made this process its chief concern. Expressing itself theologically, it practices a psychology of the unconscious. Gnosis means knowledge, which is not gained intellectually, but holistically.

What we now call the process of becoming individual (*individuation*, in Jungian terms) was Gnosis in Hellenism, a process aimed not at the ego but at knowing God. Both the old Gnostics and the modern person are conscious of their ability to gain knowledge on their own. They realize that this is possible only with divine assistance. Therefore Gnosis is not, as is often mistakenly assumed, self-redemption. To be sure, the redeemer has a different function in Gnosis: he awakens human beings and guides them in the right direction. Hermes has a similar function in Hermeticism, as does Mercurius in alchemy. They represent the first approaches to self-becoming and to the redemption of the divine spark in the human being. Due to a curious synchronicity, these spiritual currents converged in the same span of time. Thus, a new level of consciousness was reached at the turning of the ages. The factors initiating this development were the external, untenable circumstances and the fundamental uncertainty that took hold of human beings at the time. They felt trapped in universal fate (*Heimarmene*), by factors alien to consciousness, which nevertheless determined their existence. They therefore strove to liberate themselves from these overbearing powers. This could not, however, be achieved by sheer determination. Irrational powers were required.

Circumambient nature and matter became more and more sinister. These forces bound humans to an unforeseeable, arbitrary world from which they sought to escape. Tyche (the goddess of fortune) seemed increasingly blind. Thus, humans tried to overcome the powers of darkness through becoming conscious, because these powers—agnosia or agnoia (unconsciousness)—were essentially opposed to consciousness. After two thousand years of Christianity, collective consciousness has moved away from that phase, so that it would be highly opportune now to recognize the creative aspect of the unconscious as well. Precisely the human being's divine kernel is a positive unconscious factor that could help to set antiquated notions aright. I hope that the reader of this book realizes that depth psychology, rather than detracting in any way from religious phenomena, leads to deeper understanding of these human experiences.

In the second half of life, the human being is in constant search for the sacred spring of life. And if the churches are growing increasingly empty in our times, this indicates that modern theology is no longer able to animate modern life. The sacred lies before us, and yet barely anyone sees it. Perhaps analytical psychology will help individuals access the sacred inherent in the soul. For ultimately all religious practice originates in the soul. I have attempted to recall Hellenistic religions to a place in the human psyche because similar manifestations of the psyche can also be observed in the modern person. Thus, all forms and expressions of contemporary life could—literally—become divine service. This would help our life to regain what it has lost: *meaning*.

For Hellenistic people, nature and the world became increasingly inimical. This enmity explains Gnosticism's contempt for the world, which is also evident in Christianity. It means a radical turning away from the outside world while simultaneously turning inward. The outer world had to be blanked out to such a degree that the inner world would become more prominent. From this emphasis stems the ascetic trait pervading all Hellenistic religions. This reversal of the stream of life back toward the source was associated with a tremendous awakening of the unconscious world, which became evident, among other things, in the Gnostic's vivid imagination, which swirled around revelations conveyed in ancient texts and illuminated the abysses of the unconscious. I steadfastly refute the notion that the Gnostics were heretics. They did not reject the revelations in the least, but often took them literally. For psychological reasons, which I have set out in the first volume, I believe that a pistis-like notion of the Christ event and a Gnostic concept developed side by side. Only when the concretistic notion had sufficiently gained the upper hand did it turn against its counterpart, branding it heretical. Today, some people also feel closer to the "Gnostic" notion. Many are no longer content simply to accept matters in good faith, but instead wish to understand how these ancient truths are related to their present life. Gnosticism, a precursor of depth psychology, helps them. All shades of philosophy, from Hermeticism and Gnosticism to the mystery religions, are attempts to satisfy various human needs. When a State Church hardens into orthodoxy (i.e., incorrigible doctrine), it merely breeds even greater sectarian mutations. People will not let themselves be squeezed into a restrictive schema, even if current theology acquires a differentiated dogmatics. After all, we are not seeking a confined system, but a way of accessing primary experience, which has become a very distant prospect.

The religious problem of the modern person cannot be resolved by adopting exotic cults. The foreign is still fresh and promises new experiences while the conventional has become hackneyed and banal.

We should not graft foreign slips onto dead branches. Instead, we need to return to the roots, where the life-force is still fresh. Such is the intention of this book. This understanding, however, requires some historical knowledge, which I have tried to convey in the previous chapters. Some readers may be disappointed that this book does not provide a ready-made recipe or clear-cut instructions that might be applied directly in daily life. This, however, would be nothing but patronizing and lead readers back to the very situation from which they wish to break out. I must, and would like to, leave the intelligent reader to discover that particular application which is unique to his or her life by enlisting the aid of their personal unconscious. Hellenism was a first flowering of the creative unconscious. We can learn a great deal from the faith that Hellenistic people placed in the unconscious and its creativity during a difficult period in human history. The more difficult the external circumstances, the more helpful the impulses we receive from the unconscious. This truth might become even more important in future.

Christianity is still caught up far too much in the opposition between good and evil. Having barely attempted to take on the nature of this pair of opposites, it could learn from the approaches of the Gnostics, because we recognize our own darkness only when set against a contrasting background. The redeemer figures of the mystery religions could more exactly describe what redemption means. I have asked many of my patients who are average Christians whether they feel redeemed by Christ's sacrificial death, and their answers have been consistently negative. Does redemption mean that my life is problem-free or does it imply an eschatological hope for a blissful life after death? Modern people would like their fate to turn in the here and now; they lack the patience to wait for the promise of the world beyond. We can no longer claim that the Bible alone offers convincing answers to the questions of human life. We must instead place these questions within the larger spiritual context of a time in which other helpful answers were given.

One important insight about the Hellenistic age is that the Father-God had transformed into a Son of God. All divine hierarchies in classical antiquity culminate in a Father of the gods. In Hellenism, the Son rises to prominence as an intermediary between God and humans. This expresses a transformation of collective consciousness. Associated with the Father of the gods is a certain human devotion toward the gods. The shift to God assuming the guise of a Son corresponds to the elevation of human self-worth; the human being now becomes God's equal partner (for instance, Job). Today a new stage in the God-human relationship would actually be timely, but at present no more than the first indications of a transformation of the concept of God are gradually emerging.

All pleas for peaceful co-existence and against racism are futile as long as the value of the human being is not reflected and enhanced. This, however, cannot be achieved intellectually, but demands an all-encompassing inner transformation. Obstructing this development are the massification and stereotyping of human beings by the media and politics. Overpopulation is another factor that impedes the perception of the individual as an individual, instead turning individuals into numerical entities in statistical charts. Only gaining insight into the secret of human existence, then or now, can remedy this situation. At the center of all spiritual currents during Hellenism stood the *mystery*. The mystery is not artificial, but the essential mystery of life. This is expressed vividly in numerous secret Gnostic revelations and in the stories of discovery in secret Hermetic books. When we speak of the unconscious in negative terms these days, that points both to a sense of embarrassment and to the unnamable mystery.

Good and evil are human categories that spring from our moral sense. In nature, and in the unconscious, the only generators of psychic energy (libido) are pairs of opposites. They condition each other, and without them human existence is inconceivable. Thus, redemption cannot consist in eliminating this fundamental contrariness of life. This would amount to a regressive desire for a lost paradise. Redemption, instead, consists in a union of opposites, whose achievement involves psychic work. It is associated with adopting a fundamentally altered stance toward life, one that regards all the difficulties encountered on the journey through life as a meaningful task worth tackling. When we do so, we soon notice that scarcely ever are we able to resolve our difficulties alone, unless helped from within by a dream, an impulse, an idea, or a cathartic insight. This is the function that Gnosticism assigns to the redeemer. He is not expected to remove all difficulties, but his illuminating power is transformative.

Every person finds himself or herself in darkness to begin with, and thus contributes to the darkness in the world. The more conscious we become, the more we carry the light of consciousness into the world. In their work, the Hermetists have Hermes, and the alchemists Mercurius, as their inner guide. This corresponds to the guiding function of the Self in the manifestations of the unconscious. Feeling that one is being guided in one's difficult work not only presupposes a religious stance, but also constitutes a religious experience.

Contemporary theologians have increasingly been moving away from this experience, because they are looking in the wrong direction. It would never have occurred to the Gnostic to search for the ur-text Q of the gospels or to conduct historical-critical research on the text. Both methods express a certain malaise in the face of the naive stories in the gospels. These methods are wholly inadequate to religious texts. They make the sacred word evaporate into thin air, which is exactly what theology suspects depth psychology of doing. The malaise exists not in the text itself, but in its unvaryingly simple-minded interpretation. Studying Gnostic texts could teach today's theologians a new kind of interpretation, a new method of hermeneutics. But, of course, they refuse to take Gnosticism seriously and at best find parallels to the gospels in Gnostic writings.

We have yet to realize that the gospels are modes of receiving the Christian message, a form of reaction by the unconscious to the life of Christ. Since most traditional scholars of Gnosticism were theologians, they had no vantage point beyond their orthodox discipline. Hence, Gnosticism is still misunderstood, despite the world-shaking discovery at Nag Hammadi, and even though a considerable amount of study has been devoted to these texts. One easily forgets that religious texts compensate for a collective consciousness existing at any given time, and instead treats them as conscious statements. Therein lies a fundamental error in most theological efforts. Gnosticism does not open itself to this traditional form of hermeneutics.

Hellenism revived an approach of the Pre-Socratic philosophers of nature that was concerned with the question of *primal matter*. Some found this in water, others in fire, and yet others in infinity or in being. Alchemy studied this question in great depth and employed chemical language to explore the mystery of the psyche. Contrary to the mystery religions, and to Gnosticism and Hermeticism, from which it borrowed extensively, alchemy considered above and below as equals. The alchemical process strives to bring down the upper forces and unite them with those below. Alchemy brought forth a complete doctrine of redemption, which probably explains its longevity. It searched for the god in matter, and sought its liberation. Because alchemy's concept of redemption is impersonal, it remains quite difficult to understand; yet it never conflicted with Christianity, and remained a parallel if secondary cultural current for many hundreds of years.

Whereas all other spiritual movements in Hellenism believed that matter shackled the spirit or even that it was evil, alchemy turned its attention precisely toward this complex idea. Some strands within Gnosticism regarded the Creation as unfinished, in need of elaboration, or even as partly chaotic. That elaboration was seen, moreover, as a task facing the human being. In alchemy, redemption concerns Creation as a whole, it is not simply an objective pursued by human effort. It is astonishing how fully Greek alchemy recognized these problems and how creatively these same themes were taken up by Arabic alchemy and thence transmitted to the Latin Middle Ages.

Hermeticism is the bridge reaching from Gnosticism to alchemy. Its principal concern is the *extractio animae* (the extraction of the soul) from matter. These movements did not consider matter dead. The fact that matter exerts such a profound fascination on us, or that we cling to certain material objects, shows that something spiritual lives in matter that fascinates us, and that needs to be extracted and rescued. In effect, modern natural science, as the outgrowth of alchemy, is still spellbound by matter, enraptured by its mystery, and captivated by materialism.

This happens to the natural scientists because, unlike the ancient alchemists, they never wonder what exactly enchants them about matter. Perhaps it is believed to contain the mystery that once existed on Mount Olympus. But once Olympus was de-deified, the mystery hid in matter. If one is unaware of what fascinates one, one remains spellbound. Our everyday materialistic attitude is symptomatic of this fact. And yet this obsession cannot be dispelled by rational means. Thus, it is foreseeable that we will remain in the clutches of our fascination with matter for quite some time before finally achieving the elusive synthesis of spirit and matter.

Bibliography

1. Texts

Nag Hammadi Codices

Evangelium Veritatis, Malinine, M., Puech, H.-Ch., Quispel, G. (editio princeps). Studies from the C.G. Jung Institute VI; Rascher, Zurich, 1956.

Supplementum Evangelium Veritatis, Codex Jung F. XVII-XVIII (pp. 33–36). Malinine, M., Puech, H.-Ch., Quispel, G., Till, W; Rascher, Zurich and Stuttgart, 1961.

Nag Hammadi Codex I (The Jung Codex) 2 vols. Attridge, H. W., ed.; Brill, Leiden, 1985.

L'Evangile de Vérité. Menard, J.-E. Nag Hammadi Studies II; Brill, Leiden, 1972.

Epistula Iacobi Apocrypha, (NHC I 4) Codex Jung F. I-VIII (p. 116). Malinine, M., Puech H.-Ch., Quispel, G., Till, W, Kasser, R., Wilson R. McL.; Rascher, Zurich and Stuttgart, 1968.

Tractatus Tripartitus, (NHC I 5) Pars I de Supernis. Codex Jung F. XXVI-LII (pp. 51–104). Kasser, P., Malinine, M., Puech, H.-Ch., Quispel, G., Zandee, J., Vycichl, W, Wilson, R. McL.; Francke, Bern, 1973. Part II: De Creatione Hominis. Codex Jung F. LII–LXX, pp. 104–140. Part III: De Generibus Tribus; Bern, 1975.

Nag Hammadi Codex II 2–7 together with XIII, 2, Brit. Lib. Or. 4926, and Oxy; P. 1, 654, 655. Layton, B., ed. 2 vols. Nag Hammadi Studies XX; Brill, Leiden, New York, Copenhagen, Cologne, 1989.

Barc, B., Hypostase des Archontes (NH II 4). Bibliotheque Copte de Nag Hammadi. (BCNH) Section: "Textes" 5 Les Presses de l'Universite Laval, 1980.

Nag Hammadi Codices V, 2-5 and VI with Papyrus Berolinensis 8502,1 and 4. Parrot, D. M.; Brill, Leiden, 1979.

Pearson, B. A., ed., Giversen, S., contributor. IX 2: The Thought of Norea, pp 87f. Nag Hammadi Studies XV; Brill, Leiden, 1981.

Hedrick, Ch. W, ed. Nag Hammadi Studies XXVIII; Brill, Leiden, New York, Copenhagen, Cologne, 1990.

Tardieu, M., Sources Gnostiques et Manicheennes 1; Les Editions du Cerf, Paris, 1984.

Krause, M., ed., in: Die Gnosis, Vol. II, Part 1; Artemis, Zurich and Stuttgart, 1971.

Robinson, J. M., ed.; The Nag Hammadi Library; Brill, Leiden, New York, Copenhagen, Cologne, 1977, 1988.

Hermetic Texts

Hermetica. The Greek Corpus Hermeticum and the Latin Asclepius in a New English translation, with notes and introduction; Copenhaver, B. P., Cambridge University Press, 1992.

Hermetica. The Ancient Greek and Latin Writings which Contain Religious or Philosophic Teachings Ascribed to Hermes Trismegistus. Scott, W., ed., Ferguson, A. S., Addenda, 4 vols. Reprint: Shambala, Boston, 1985.

Corpus Hermeticum. Hermes Trismegiste. Nock, A. D., and Festugiere, A.-J., 4 vols; Les Belles Lettres, Paris, 1945-54.

Patristic Sources

Die Gnosis, Vol. I: Zeugnisse der Kirchenvater. Foerster, W. ed. and trans.; Artemis, Zurich and Stuttgart, 1969.

Irenaeus: Against Heresies. Unger, J. Dominic, ed. and trans.,: Paulist Press, New York, N.Y./Mahwah, J.J.

Clement of Alexandria. Stromateis. The Gnostic Library Society (http://gnosis.org/library/strom1.htm).

Hippolytus: Refutatio omnium haeresium. The Refutation of All Heresies. Trans. Rev. J.H. MacMahon.

Epiphanius of Salamis: The Panarion. Book I (Sections 1–46) Williams, F, trans. Nag Hammadi Studies XXXV; Leiden, New York, Copenhagen, Cologne, 1987. Books II and III (Sections 47-80, De Fide) Williams, F., trans. Nag Hammadi and Manichaean Studies XXXVI; Brill, Leiden, New York, Cologne, 1994.

Justinus: Saint Justin. Apologies. Wartelle, A., trans., Etudes Augustiniennes; Paris, 1987.

Alchemical Texts

Affifi, A.E.: The Influence of Hermetic Literature on Moslem Thought. Bulletin of the School of Oriental and African Studies. London, 1951. Reprinted 1975, pp. 840–855.

Artis Auriferae quam Chemiam vocant, First ed.: Basileae apud Petrum Pernam, 1572. Second ed.: Basileae, C. Waldkirch, 1593 (2 vols.) Third ed.: Basileae, C. Waldkirch, 1610 (3 vols.)

Collection des Anciens Alchimistes Grecs. 3 vols. Berthelot, M., and Ruelle, Ch.-Em., ed. Reimpression de l'edition 1888; Zeller, Osnabrock 1967.

Congeries Paracelesicae chemiae de transmutationibus metallorum. Gerard Dorn. Theatrum Chemicum I, 491.

Dorneus, Gerardus: Physica Trismegisti. Theatrum Chemicum I, 380 f. 1659. De practica operis spagirici ad medicinam vitae longae parandam.

Fabre, Pierre-Jean: Alchmyista Christiana. Toulouse, 1632.

Franz, Marie-Louise von: Muhammad ibn Umail's Hall Ar-Ramuz ("Clearing of Enigmas"). Historical Introduction and Psychological Comment. Egg, 1999.

Fück, J.W. The Arabic Literature on Alchemy according to an-Nadim (a.d. 987). A translation of the Tenth Discourse of "The Book of the

Catalogue" (al-Fihrist) with Introduction and Commentary. Ambix 4, pp. 86–144 (1951).

Les Alchimistes Grecs. Papyrus de Leyde, Papyrus de Stockholm, Recettes. Vol. 1 R. Halleux, trans. Collection des Universites de France, Bude, G.; Les Belles Lettres, Paris, 1981.

Les Alchimistes Grecs. Zosimos de Panopolis, Mémoires authentiques, Vol. IV, Part 1. Mertens, M., Les Belles Lettres, Paris, 1995.

Lindsay, Jack: Les Origines de l'Alchimie dans l'Egypte Gréco-Romaine. Le Rocher, Monaco, 1970.

Maier, Michael: Atalanta Fugiens, hoc est Emblemata Nova De Secretis Naturae Chymica. Bärenreiter-Verlag, Kassel, 1964. Facsimile reprint of the Oppenheimer Originalausgabe of 1618 containing 52 engraved illustrations by Matthaeus d. Ae.

Maier, Michael: Symbola Aurea Mensae Duodecim Nationum. Akademische Druck- und Verlagsanstalt, Graz, 1972. Photomechanical Reproduction. Typis Antonij Hummijm impenfis Lucae Iennis, 1617.

Musaeum Hermeticum Reformatum et Amplificatum; Francofurti, 1677. The Hermetic Museum. Waite, Arthur Edmund (1893). https://archive.org/details/TheHermeticMuseum

Reidy, John, ed. Thomas Norton: Ordinal of Alchemy. The Early English Text Society. Oxford University Press, Oxford, 1975.

Rhenanus Johannes: Harmoniae imperscrutabilis Chymico-Philosophicae sive Philosophorum Antiquorum Consentientium Decades duae apud Com. Eifridum; Francofurti, 1625.

Ruska, J.: Tabula Smaragdina. Ein Beitrag zur Geschichte der Hermetischen Literatur; Winter, Heidelberg, 1926.

Ruska, J.: Turba Philosophorum; Springer, Berlin, 1931.

Ruspoli, St.: 'Arabi, Mohyiddin Ibn: L'alchemie du bonheur parfait. Berg International éditeurs, Paris, 1981.

Sezgin, Fuat: Geschichte des Arabischen Schrifttums. Vol. III. Ed. J. Brill, Leiden, 1970.

Siebmacher, Joh. Ambrosius. The Waterstone of the Wise. http://www.levity.com/alchemy/hydrolit.html

Theatrum Chemicum, praecipuos selectorum auctorum tractatus de chemiae et lapidis philosophici. Argentorati, E.; Zetzner, 1659–1661. Reprint, Bottega d'Erasmo, Torino, 1981.

Turab, Ali M., H.E. Stapleton and H. Husain: Three Arabic Treatises on Alchemy (10th Century CE–) by Muhammad ibn Umail. Mem. Asiatic Society Bengalen XII, pp. 1–213, 1933.

2. List of Sources

Adler, Alfred. Über den nervösen Charakter. Grundzüge einer vergleichenden Individualpsychologie und Psychotherapie. J. E. Bergmann, Wiesbaden, 1919.

Cornelius Agrippa, Of Occult Philosophy, Book II, chapter LVII.

Heinrich Cornelius Agrippa von Nettesheim: De occulta philosophia, libri tres. V. Perrone Compagni, ed. Studies in the History of Christian Thought, vol. XLVIII; Brill, Leiden, New York, Cologne, 1992.

Aland, Barbara: Gnosis und Kirchenväter. Festschrift für Hans Jonas. Vandenhoeck und Ruprecht, Göttingen, 1978. Erwählungstheologie und Menschenklassenlehre, pp. 158–215.

Ancilla to the Pre-Socratic Philosophers. A Complete Translation of the Fragments in Diels, Fragmente der Vorsokratiker, trans. by Kathleen Freeman (Cambridge: Harvard University Press), p. 28.

Andreae, Joh. Val.: Fama Fraternitatis (1614), Confessio Fraternitatis (1615), Chymische Hochzeit: Christiani Rosencreutz. Anno 1459 (1616). R. Van Dulmen, ed. Calwer, Stuttgart, ³1981.

Andresen, C.: Die Kirchen der alten Christenheit. Die Religionen der Menschheit, vol. 29, 1/2. Schroder, Ch. M., ed.; Kohlhammer, Stuttgart, Berlin, Cologne, Mainz, 1971.

Angelus Silesius: Cherubinischer Wandersmann. Rhody, T., ed.; Pattloch, Aschaffenburg, 1947.

Appollonius von Tyana. Weisser, Ursula: Das "Buch über das Geheimnis der Schöpfung" von Pseudo-Appollonius. Ars Medica. Texte und Untersuchungen zur Quellenkunde der Alten Medizin. III. Abt. Arabische Medizin. Bd. 2. De Gruyter, Berlin, New York, 1980.

Armstrong, A.H, ed.: The Cambridge History of Later Greek and Early Medieval Philosophy. Cambridge University Press, London, New York, Port Chester, Melbourne, Sydney. Reprinted with corrections 1970, 1991. 1967.

Aristotle, Metaphysics. Translated by Hugh Tredennick. Loeb Classical Library; Cambridge MA: Harvard University Press, 1935. Bardenhewer, O.: Geschichte der Altkirchlichen Literatur. 5 vols. Facsimile reprint of the second edition, 1913; Wissenschaftl. Buchgesell., Freiburg i. Br. and Darmstadt, 1962.

Benz, E.: Ecclesia spiritualis. Kirchenidee und Geschichtstheologie der Franziskanischen Reformation; Wissenschaftl. Buchgesell., Darmstadt, 1969.

Bergmann, H.: Martin Buber and Mysticism, in The Philosophy of Martin Buber, Library of Living Philosophers, vol. 12, Schillp, P. A., and Friedman, M., eds. Cambridge Univ. Press, London.

Bergmeier, R.: "Konigslosigkeit" als nachvalentinisches Heilspradikat; Novum Testamentum 24, Leiden, 1982, pp. 316-339.

Betz, H. D.: The Greek Magical Papyri in Translation, Including the Demotic Spells, Vol. 1, The Texts; Chicago, University of Chicago Press, 1985.

Bezold, C.: Die Schatzhöhle, aus dem Syrischen Me'arrath Gazzç; cited C.G. Jung, CW 14/II. §220.

Bonnet, H.: Reallexikon der Aegyptischen Religionsgeschichte; Gruyter, Berlin, New York, 1971.

Booth, K.N.: "Deficiency": A Gnostic Technical Term. Text und Untersuchungen zur Geschichte der Altchristlichen Literatur, Bd. 117. Akademie Verlag, Berlin, 1979.

Bousset, Wilhelm: Die Himmelsreise der Seele. Archiv für Religionswissenschaft. IV 155f.

Bousset, Wilhelm: Hauptprobleme der Gnosis (Forschungen zur Religion und Literatur des Alten und Neuen Testaments 10); Vandenhoek und Ruprecht, Gottingen, 1907.

Broek, R. van den, and Vermaseren, M. J.: Studies in Gnosticism and Hellenistic Religions, prestented to Gilles Quispel on the Occasion of his 65th Birthday. Etudes Preliminaires aux Religions Orientales dans l'Empire Romain, Vol. 91; Brill, Leiden, 1981.

Charlesworth, James H., ed. The Old Testament Pseudepigrapha. Apocalytic Literature & Testaments, vol. 1. Doubleday, New York, London, Toronto, Sydney, Auckland, 1983.

Clement of Alexandria: The Excerpta ex Theodoto of C. A. Casey, R. P., ed.; Studies and Documents. London, 1934.

Clement of Alexandria, Stromateis. Clément d'Alexandrie, Les Stromates, Stromate V, Introduction, texte critique et index, Le Boulluec, A., ed., Voulet, P., trans.; Sources Chrétiennes.

Codrington, The Melanesians (Oxford: Oxford University Press, 1891), p. 118; quoted by Jung CW 8, §123.

Copenhaver, B. P.: Hermetica, 1994. German: J. Holzhausen, Das Corpus Hermeticum Deutsch, 1997.

Deussen, Paul: Sechzig Upanishads des Veda; Wisschenschaftl. Buchges., Darmstadt, 1963.

Dillon, John: The Descent of the Soul in Middle Platonic and Gnostic Theory, in: Bentley Layton, ed., The Rediscovery of Gnosticism. Leiden, 1980, pp. 357–364.

Droysen, Johann Gustav: Geschichte des Hellenismus. Wissenschaftliche Buchgesellschaft, Darmstadt, 1998, 3 vols.

Egli, Hans: Das Schlangensymbol. Walter, Olten und Freiburg im Breisgau, 1982.

Eliade, Mircea: Die Religionen und das Heilige. Otto Müller, Salzburg, 1954.

Ellenberger, H. E.: The Discovery of the Unconscious. Basic Books, New York, 1970.

Euripides. The Complete Greek Drama, edited by Whitney J. Oates and Eugene O'Neill, Jr. in two volumes. 2. Helen, translated by E. P. Coleridge. New York. Random House, 1938.

Fauth, W.: Helios Megistos: Religions in the Graeco-Roman World, vol. 125. Brill, Leiden, New York, Cologne,1995.

Festugière, La Révélation d'Hermes Trismégiste, vol. 1, L'Astrologie et les Sciences Occultes. Collection d'Etudes Anciennes. Série Grecque No. 75. Les Belles Lettres, Paris, 1989–1990.

Fowden, G.: The Egyptian Hermes. A Historical Approach to the Late Pagan Mind; Princeton University Press, Princeton, 1993; [1]1986.

Franz, Marie-Louise von: Alchemical Active Imagination; Spring Publications Inc., University of Dallas, Texas; 1979.

Franz, Marie-Louise von: Archetypische Dimensionen der Seele; Daimon, Einsiedeln, 1994.

Franz, Marie-Louise von: Aurora Consurgens: A Document Attributed to Thomas Aquinas on the Problem of Opposites in Alchemy: A Companion Work to C.G. Jung's Mysterium Coniunctionis (Studies in Jungian Psychology); Inner City Books, Toronto, 2000.

Franz, Marie-Louise von: C.G. Jung. His Myth in Our Time, trans. William H. Kennedy; C.G. Jung Foundation, New York, 1975.

Franz, Marie-Louise von: Number and Time. Reflections Leading towards a Unification of Psychology and Physics, Andrea Dykes, trans.; Rider and Co., London, 1974.

Franz, Marie-Louise von: Projection and Re-Collection in Jungian Psychology, Reflections of the Soul, W. H. Kennedy, trans.; Open Court, Chicago, 1980.

Franz, Marie-Louise von: Spiegelungen der Seele, Projektion und innere Sammlung in der Psychologie C.G. Jungs; Kösel Verlag, Munich, 21988.

Franz, Marie-Louise von: On Dreams and Death: A Jungian Interpretation. Open Court, 1999.

Ganzenmuller, W: Alchemie und Religion im Mittelalter; Deutsches Archiv für Geschichte des MA 5; 1942, pp. 329-346.

Granet, Marcel: Das chinesische Denken. Porkert, M., ed.; Piper, Munich, 1963.

Heraclitus: The Cosmic Fragments, G. S. Kirk, ed.; Cambridge University Press, Cambridge, 1954.

Hermetica Oxoniensia (HO) III 1: Les hommes ont établi la loi par opinion.... délaissant la justice véritable et l'âme... 3. C'est pourquoi le ciel est pur de telles lois. J. Paramelle and J. Mahé, Extraits Hermétiques.

Histoire des Religions. 3 vols. Encyclopedie de la Pleiade. Puech, H.-Ch., ed. vol. 2: La Gnose, pp. 364f. Doresse, J.: L'Hermetisme Egyptianisant; Paris, 1972, pp. 430f.

Hoeller, S.: The Gnostic Jung and the Seven Sermons to the Dead; Theosophical Publishing House, Wheaton, IL 1982.

Holmyard, E. J.: Abu' l-Qasim al-Iraqi, Isis 8, 1926, pp. 403–426.

Horace, The Complete Works of Horace, Charles E. Passage, trans., Frederick Ungar Publishing Co., New York, 1983.

James, M.R.: "The Acts of Peter," in: The Apocryphal New Testament: Translation and Notes. Oxford: Clarendon Press, 1924.

Julien, H., Yvonne Janssens et Jean-Marie Sevrin, eds. Gnosticism et Monde Héllenistique. Actes du Colloque de Louvain-la-Neuve (11–14 Mars). Publications de l'Institut Orientaliste de Louvain 27. Louvain-la-Neuve, 1982.

Jung, C.G.: Analytical Psychology, Notes of the Seminar Given in 1925, ed. W. McGuire, Bollingen Series XCIX; Princeton University Press, Princeton; 1989, pp. 40f.

Jung, C.G.: Bibliothek. Katalog; Kusnacht-Zurich, 1967.

Jung, C.G.: Collected Works, 2nd edition, 20 vols., Herbert Reed and others, ed.; Princeton University Press, Princeton, 1966-1992.

Jung, C.G.: Dream Analysis, ed. W. McGuire, Bollingen Series XCIX, Princeton University Press, Princeton, 1984.

Jung, C.G., and Marie-Louise von Franz, The Grail Legend; Princeton University Press, Princeton, 1998.

Jung, C.G.: Jung Speaking. McGuire, W. ed.; New Jersey, 1977.

Jung, C.G.: Letters, 2 volumes, G. Adler, ed.; Princeton University Press, Princeton; 1975–1977.

Jung, C.G.: Memories, Dreams, Reflections, recorded and edited by Aniela Jaffé, trans. by Richard and Clara Winston, Vintage, New York, 1989.

Jung, C.G.: Seminar: Modern Psychology. Notes on Lectures given at the Eidgenossische Technische Hochschule, Zurich. October 1933–July 1935; October 1938–March 1940. 2nd edition 1959; for private use only.

Jung, C.G.: The Seven Sermons to the Dead written by Basilides in Alexandria, the City where the East toucheth the West, in Dreams, Memories, Reflections, recorded and edited by Aniela Jaffé, trans. by Richard and Clara Winston; Vintage, New York, 1989.

Kautzsch, E., ed.; Tubingen, 1900. Reprint, Olms, Hildesheim, 1962. New Testament Apocrypha in German translation. 2 vols. Hennecke, E., and Schneemelcher, W., eds.; Mohr, Tubingen, ³1959 and 1964. Schneemelcher, W., ed.; Mohr, Tübingen, ⁵1987 and 1989.

Kerényi, K., The Religion of the Greeks and the Romans, trans. by Christopher Holme (New York: Dutton, 1962).

Koschorke, K., Nag Hammadi Studies 12 (Leiden, 1978), pp. 91–174.

Layton, Bentley: "The Soul as a dirty Garment," *Le Muséon* 91 (1978), pp. 155–169.

Lewy, Hans: Chaldean Oracles and Theurgy: Mysticism, Magic and Platonism in the Later Roman Empire. Nouvelle édition par Michel Tardieu. Paris: Etudes Augustiniennes, 1978.

Lucius Apuleius, The Golden Ass (Metamorphoses).

Marjanen, Antti. The Woman Jesus Loved. Nag Hammadi and Manichaean Studies XL. E. J. Brill, Leiden, New York, Cologne, 1996.

McGuire, William, ed. C.G. Jung Speaking: Interviews and Encounters. Thames and Hudson, London, 1978.

Ménard, Jacques Etienne: "Le Repos, Salut du Gnostique" Rev. Sci. Rel. 51, pp. 71–88. 1977.

Ménard, Jacques Etienne: L'Authentikos Logos. Bibliothèque Copte de Nag Hammadi. Section: "Textes" 2. Les presses de l'Université Laval, Québec, Canada, 1977.

Meyer, Marvin, ed.: The Nag Hammadi Scriptures: The Revised and Updated Translation of Sacred Gnostic Texts. Harper Collins, New York, 2008.

Needham, J.: Science and Civilisation in China; Cambridge University Press, Cambridge, 1962.

Nelken, J.: Analytische Beobachtungen uber Phantasien eines Schizophrenen, in: Jb. für psychoanalyt. und psychopathol. Forschung IV (1912), pp. 504-562.

Neumann, Erich: Tiefenpsychologie und neue Ethik. Geist und Psyche; Fischer Tb, Frankfurt a.M., 1984.

Origen: Commentary on the Gospel of Matthew.
    Origen: Contra Celsum (Against Celsus), ed. Alexander Robert,

1885. Origen. Homilies on Genesis and Exodus. Trans. Richard E. Heine. The Catholic University of America Press, Washington D.C., 1982

Origen: Homilies on Leviticus 1–16. Trans. Gary Wayne Barkley. The Catholic University of America Press, Washington D.C., 1990.

Origen: Homilies on Luke. Trans. Joseph T. Lienhard. The Catholic University of America Press, Washington D.C., 1996.

Origen: On First Principles. Trans. G.W. Butterworth. Harper and Row, New York, 1966.

Otto, Rudolf: The Idea of the Holy: An Inquiry into the Non-Rational Factor in the Idea of the Divine and Its Relation to the Rational, trans. by John W. Harvey Oxford University Press, London, 1952.

Ovid, Metamorphoses, Charles Martin, trans. W. W. Norton, New York, 2004.

Rosch, E., ed.; Wissenschaftl. Buchgesellschah, Darmstadt, 1983. Sammlung Tusculum. Authorized edition; Artemis Verlags, Munich.

Paramelle, J., and Mahé, J.-P.: Extraits Hermetiques inédits dans un Manuscrit d' Oxford. Revue des Etudes Grecques. Vol. 104, pp. 109-139; Paris, 1991.

Petty, Robert, ed.: Fragments of Numenius of Apamea. Prometheus Trust, 2012.

Pearson, B. A., ed., Nag Hammadi Codices IX and X, in The Coptic Gnostic Library, J. M. Robinson, ed. Brill, Leiden, 1981.

The Collected Dialogues of Plato, Hamilton, E., and Cairns, H, eds. Princeton University Press, Princeton, 1961.

Plato, The Republic. Translated by Chris Emlyn-Jones and William Preddy. Loeb Classical Library. Harvard University Press, 2013.

Plutarch: Über Isis und Osiris. Hopfner, Th., trans.; Prague, 1940. Reprint: Wissensch. Buchges., Darmstadt, 1967.

Pohlenz, Max. Stoa und Stoiker. Artemis, Zürich, 1950.

Pritchard, James B, ed.: Ancient Near Eastern Texts. Princeton University Press, New Jersey, 1955.

Quispel, G.: Jewish Gnosis and Mandaean Gnosticism. Some Reflections on the writing Brontè. Les Textes de Nag Hammadi. Colloque du Centre d'Histoire des Religions. Strasbourg 23-25 October 1974. Menard, J. E., ed. Nag Hammadi Studies VII, pp. 82–122; Brill, Leiden, 1975.

Quispel, G.: Hermes Trismegistus and the Origins of Gnosticism. Vigiliae Christianae 46, pp. 1–19 (1992).

Quispel, G.: De Hermetische Gnosis in de loop der eeuwen; Tirion, Baarn, 1992.

Quispel, G.: Hesse, Jung und die Gnosis. Die "Septem Sermones ad Mortuos" und Basilides, Gnostic Studies II, Nederlands Historisch-Archaeologisch Instituut te Istanbul, 1975, pp. 241–258.

Rahner, H.: Symbole der Kirche. Die Ekklesiologie der Vater; Otto Muller, Salzburg, 1964.

Rehm, B., and Strecker, G.: Die Pseudoklementinen. I Homilien; II Rekognitionen in Rufins Übersetzung. Die Griechischen Christlichen Schriftsteller der ersten Jahrhunderte; Akademie, Berlin, ²1994.

Reitzenstein, R.: Poimandres. Studien zur griechisch-agyptischen und frühchristlichen Literatur; Leipzig, 1904. Reprint: Darmstadt, 1966.

Rex, Friedemann: Zur Theorie der Naturprozesse in der Früharabischen Wissenschaft. Wiesbaden, Franz Steiner, 1975.

Ribi, Alfred: Anthropos. Der ewige Mensch. Das uralte und das neue Bild vom Menschen; P. Lang, Bern and New York, 2002.

Ribi, Alfred: Eros und Abendland: Geistesgeschichte der Beziehungsfunktion. Bern: Peter Lang, 2005.

Ribi, Alfred: Was tun mit unseren Komplexen; Kösel-Verlag, Munich, 1989.

Ribi, Alfred: Morgen und Abenderkenntnis bei Augustinus. Address at the Psychologischen Club Zürich, 1992.

Ribi, Alfred: Die Auffassung C.G. Jungs von der Schizophrenie. Schweizer Archiv für Neurologie und Psychiatrie; 144, 1993, Number 6, pp. 487-500.

Ribi, Alfred: Die Dämonen des Hieronymous Bosch: Versuch einer Deutung. Stiftung für Jungsche Psychologie, Küsnacht, 1990.

Ribi, Alfred: Die feindlichen Brüder. Extraversion-Introversion, zwei komplementäre Seiten eines einseitigen Weltbildes; Kundschafter, Wettingen, 1993.

Ribi, Alfred: Ein Leben im Dienst der Seele. Part II, Gesammelte Aufsätze und Vorträge; P. Lang, Bern, Berlin, Bruxelles, Frankfurt am Main, New York, Oxford, Vienna, 2007.

Ribi, Alfred: "Magia naturalis als Ursprung der Homöopathie," Nova Acta Paracelsica, Neue Folge 13, pp. 237–292.

Ribi, Alfred: "Morgenerkenntnis und Abenderkenntnis bei Aurelius Augustinus: Wo stehen wir heute?" Vortrag im Psychologischen Club Zürich vom 27. Juni 1992.

Ribi, Alfred: Wahrheit: Was ist das? Fragen anhand gnostischer und alchemister Texte. Karger, Basel, 1998.

Ribi, Alfred: Was tun mit unseren Komplexen? Über die Dämonen des modernen Menschen. Kösel, München, 1989.

Ribi, Alfred: Zeitenwende: Die geistigen Wurzeln unserer Zeit in Hellenismus, Hermetik, Gnosis und Alchemie; P. Lang, Bern and New York, 2001.

Ribi, Alfred: Zum schöpferischen Prozess bei C.G. Jung. Aus den Excerptbänden zur Alchemie, Analyt. Psychol., vol. 13; 1982, pp. 201–221.

Ribi, Alfred: The Search for Roots: C.G. Jung and the Tradition of Gnosis. Foreword by Lance S. Owens. Gnosis Archive Books, 2013.

Robinson, James M.: The Jung Codex. The Rise and Fall of a Monopoly. Religious Studies Review 3, 1977, p. 17.30.

Robinson, James M.: Preface. The Facsimile Edition of the Nag Hammadi Codices. Introduction; Brill, Leiden, 1984.

Robinson, James M. ed.: The Nag Hammadi Library; Brill, Leiden, New York, Copenhagen, Cologne, 31988.

Rohrich, L.: Lexikon der sprichwörtlichen Redensarten, 4 vols.; Herder, Freiburg, Basel, Wien, 1973.

Rottenwöhrer, Gerhard.: Der Katharismus. Band IV/1. Glaube und Theologie der Katharer. Bock-Herchen, Bad Honnef, 1993.

Rudolph, K., ed.: Gnosis und Gnostizismus. Wege der Forschung, Vol. 257; Wissenschaftliche Buchgesellschaft, Darmstadt, 1975.

Ruska, Julius: Tabula Smaragdina. Ein Beitrag zur Geschichte der Hermetischen Literatur, Heidelberg, 1926.

Ruska, Julius: Turba Philosophorum. Ein Beitrag zur Geschichte der Alchemie. Quellen und Studien zur Geschichte der Naturwissenschaften und der Medizin. Springer, Berlin, 1931.

Schiller, Friedrich: The Robbers and Wallenstein; Penguin Books, London, 1979.

Schenke, Hans-Martin: Der Gott "Mensch" in der Gnosis. Ein religionsgeschichtlicher Beitrag zur Diskussion über die paulinische Anschauung von der Kirche als Leib Christi; Vandenhoeck und Ruprecht, Gottingen, 1962.

Scholten, C.: Martyrium und Sophiamythos im Gnostizismus nach den Texten von Nag Hammadi. Jahrbuch für Antike und Christentum, Ergänzungsband 14. Münster, Aschendorff, 1987.

Segal, R. A.: The Gnostic Jung. Including "Seven Sermons of the Dead"; Routledge, London, 1992. Therein: Quispel, G.: Jung and Gnosis.

Seneca, Epistles 1–65. Loeb Classical Library. Translated by Richard M. Gunmere; Cambridge MA: Harvard University Press, 1917/2002.

Sevrin, Jean-Marie: Le dossier baptismal Séthien. Etudes sur la sacramentaire gnostique. BCNH 2; Universite Laval, Quebec, 1986.

Sevrin, Jean-Marie. Les noces spirituelles dans l'Évangile selon Philippe. Le Museon. Revue d'Études Orientales 87, Louvain, 1974, pp. 143-193.

Siggel, Alfred: Das Sendschreiben. Das Licht über das Verfahren des Hermes der Hermesse dem, der es begehrt. Der Islam 24, 1937, pp. 287–306.

Simplicius, On Aristotle's Physics, trans. J. O. Urmson. New York, Cornell University Press, 2002.

Studies in Gnosticism and Hellenistic Religions Presented to Gilles Quispel on the Occasion of his 65 Birthday, ed. R. van den Brock and M. J. Vermasern; Brill, Leiden, 1981.

Stroumsa, Gehaliahu A.G.: Another Seed: Studies in Gnostic Mythology. Nag Hammadi Studies, XXIV. Brill, Leiden, 1984.

Suzuki, D. T.: Die Grosse Befreiung. Einführung in den Zen-Buddhismus, with a foreword by C.G. Jung; Rascher, Zurich and Stuttgart, 1958.

Synesius of Cyrene. Essays and Hymns. Trans. Augustine Fitzgerald. Oxford University Press, London, 1930.

Tardieu, Michel: "Psychaios Spinter: Histoire d'une métaphore dans la tradition platonicienne jusqu'à Eckhart," in: Revue des Etudes Augustiniennes 21 (1975), pp. 225–255.

Thiel, von, ed.: Leben und Taten Alexanders von Makedonien. Der griechische Alexanderroman nach der Handschrift L. Texte zur Forschung 13; Wissenschaftl. Buchges., Darmstadt, 1983.

Trüb, H.: Individuation, Schuld und Entscheidung. Ober die Grenzen der Psychologie, in: Die Kulturelle Bedeutung der Komplexen Psychologie, Festschrift zum 60. Geburtstag von C.G. Jung, pp. 529–555.

Vereno, Ingolf: Studien zum ältesten alchemistischen Schriftum. Auf der Grundlage zweier erstmals editierter arabischer Hermetica, Klaus Schwarz, Berlin, 1992.

Vollenweider, Samuel: Neoplatonische und christliche Theologie bei Synesios von Kyrene. Inaugural Dissertation Theologische Fakultät Zürich. Forschungen zur Kirchen- und Dogmengeschichte 35. Vandenbroeck und Ruprecht, Göttingen, 1985.

Voorgang, Dietrich. Die Passion Jesu und Christi in der Gnosis. Europäische Hochschulschriften, Reihe XXIII Theologie, vol. 432.

Weisser, Ursula: Das "Buch über das Geheimnis der Schöpfung" von Pseudo-Appollonius von Tyana. Ars Medica. Texte und Untersuchungen zur Quellenkunde der Alten Medizin. III. Abt. Arabische Medizin. Bd. 2. De Gruyter, Berlin, New York, 1980.

Wickes, F. G.: The Inner World of Man; Henry Holt, New York, 1948.

Wilamowitz-Moellendorf, Ulrich von. Der Glaube der Hellenen. 2 Vols. Weidmann, Berlin, 1931–1932. 2nd ed., Darmstadt: Wissenschaftliche Buchgesellschaft 1955, reprinted 1959, 1984, 1994.

Williams, Michael Allen: The Immovable Race. A Gnostic Designation and the Theme of Stability in Late Antiquity. Nag Hammadi Studies XXIX; Brill, Leiden, 1985.

Wright, William. Apocryphal Acts of the Apostles. Williams and Norgate, London, 1871.

Yates, Francis A.: Giordano Bruno and the Hermetic Tradition. Routledge and Kegan Paul, The University of Chicago Press, 1964.

Zacharias, Gerhard: Satanskult und schwarze Messe. Limes, Wiesbaden, 1964.

Zandee, J.: The Teaching of Sylvanus. Nag Hammadi Codex VII,4: Text, Translation, Commentary. Leiden, 1991.

Zeller, Eduard: Die Philosophie der Griechen. Eine Untersuchung über Charakter, Gang und Hauptmomente. Ludwig Friedrich Fues, Tübingen, 1844.

Zimmer, Heinrich. Myths and Symbols in Indian Art and Civilization, ed. Joseph Campbell, Harper Torchbooks, New York, 1962.

Zimmer, Heinrich. Philosophie und Religion Indiens. Rhein Verlag, Zürich, 1961.

Printed in Great Britain
by Amazon